school
bullying

School Bullying: Insights and Perspectives examines the nature and extent of bullying in schools and gives a succinct and authoritative account of research into ways of reducing this problem. Here, for the first time in the UK, is a comprehensive evaluation of the success of different approaches such as:

- developing a whole-school policy;
- tackling bullying through classroom and curriculum materials;
- training lunchtime supervisors;
- improving the playground environment; and
- working directly with pupils involved in bullying situations.

The book and the companion volume *Tackling Bullying in Your School*, which gives detailed guidance on implementing these strategies, will be essential reading for all professionals wishing to reduce the problem of bullying in schools.

Peter K. Smith is Professor of Psychology at the University of Sheffield, has researched extensively on children's social development and play, and has published widely in this field.
Sonia Sharp is an Educational Psychologist for Barnsley LEA and has worked extensively with schools to develop successful anti-bullying policies.

ASSOCIATED TITLES FROM ROUTLEDGE

tackling bullying in your school
A PRACTICAL HANDBOOK
Sonia Sharp and Peter K. Smith

breaktime and the school
UNDERSTANDING AND CHANGING PLAYGROUND BEHAVIOUR
Peter Blatchford and Sonia Sharp

school
BULLYING

INSIGHTS
AND
PERSPECTIVES

edited by

PETER K. SMITH

and

SONIA SHARP

LONDON AND NEW YORK

First published 1994
by Routledge
11 New Fetter Lane, London EC4P 4EE

Simultaneously published in the USA and Canada
by Routledge
29 West 35th Street, New York, NY 10001

Reprinted 1995

Typeset by Florencetype Limited, Stoodleigh, Devon
Printed and bound in Great Britain by Clays Ltd,
St Ives PLC

British Library Cataloguing in Publication Data

A catalogue record for this book is available from
the British Library

*Library of Congress Cataloguing in Publication
Data*

A catalogue record for this book is available from
the Library of Congress

ISBN 0-415-10372-X (hbk)
ISBN 0-415-10373-8 (pbk)

contents

Illustrations

Figures

Tables

contributors

Michael J. Boulton is Lecturer in the Department of Psychology at the University of Keele, Keele, Staffs ST5 5BG.

Helen Cowie is Director of Counselling at Bretton Hall University College, Bretton, Wakefield, West Yorkshire.

Cath Higgins is Lecturer in Landscape Design at the Department of Landscape, University of Sheffield, Sheffield S10 2TN.

Ian Rivers is Lecturer in Psychology, School of Psychology, University of Luton, Park Square, Luton, Beds LU1 3JU.

Sonia Sharp is an Educational Psychologist at Barnsley Psychological Service, Education Department, Bernselai Close, Barnsley S70 2HS.

Peter K. Smith is Professor of Psychology at the Department of Psychology, University of Sheffield, Sheffield S10 2TN.

David Thompson is Senior Lecturer and Director of the MSc Educational Psychology course, Division of Education, University of Sheffield, Sheffield S10 2TN.

Irene Whitney is a Research Psychologist at the Greenwood Institute of Child Health, Westcotes House, Westcote Drive, Leicester LE3 0QU.

preface

It is likely that bullying has gone on in schools for as long as schools have existed. In recent years, systematic investigation has confirmed that it is a pervasive phenomenon. At the same time, many parents and teachers have become more determined that action must be taken to stop severe bullying. It is clear that bullying can blight the life of many pupils who experience it, while those pupils who get away with bullying others are learning values at odds with any proper preparation for citizenship. Schools have become increasingly aware that bullying is a problem to be addressed, and that doing so openly will get grateful recognition from parents and pupils.

In the last few years, many more resources have become available to help schools, teachers, governors and parents deal effectively with bullying situations, and assist pupils who get involved in them. But how useful are these different approaches? Do they work?

In this book, we survey investigations into bullying generally, but also document in some detail the researches carried out over the last four years in Sheffield. This work has been funded by the Economic and Social Research Council (Swindon), and by the Calouste Gulbenkian Foundation (UK branch, London); and, over the last three years, by the Department for Education (London). This funding has enabled a team of researchers based here to monitor and evaluate the success of different kinds of approaches and interventions used by schools. We hope that, together with the efforts of other researchers and writers on the topic, the information gathered will help schools significantly to reduce and contain bullying, and make the most severe cases of torment which some children and young people have endured a thing of the past.

This book tells how the research was done, what we found, and the implications for schools. The companion volume, S. Sharp and P. K. Smith (eds), *Tackling bullying in your school: A practical handbook for teachers* (Routledge, 1994), provides detailed guidance as to how to go about many of the procedures, interventions and strategies discussed and evaluated in this book.

The work described in this book has been greatly assisted by many people. Sarah Barron provided secretarial and administrative support, often beyond the call of duty, and we are very grateful for her support. Several honours undergraduate students at the University of Sheffield gathered data as part of their project work: Kathryn Childs, Pat Lucas, Hugh Mellor-Smith, Mary Anne Pitfield, Sayra Shah, Sudha Sharma, Julie Simms and Deborah Tonge. Three placement students from Northern Ireland, Kate Kelly, Siobhan Moran and Maeve Thornton, also helped us in monitoring the work of schools on the ESRC and DFE-funded projects. Siobhan Mooney and Nicola Kerr assisted in checking the bibliography and preparing the indexes.

In our collaboration with Sheffield LEA, the Schools Officer, Martin Gazzard, and the chief Educational Welfare Officer, Don Pennock, were of immense help and support. We also have greatly enjoyed working with so many staff, pupils, governors and parents of Sheffield schools. A large number of schools took part in our projects, and in the great majority of cases we have experienced help and appreciation of the work we were doing, even when difficulty or disruption was experienced. We hope that the research process will have helped these schools, and that the results of this and other research on bullying will be of assistance to schools across the country.

PETER K. SMITH
SONIA SHARP
Sheffield, December 1993

O·N·E

the problem of school bullying

PETER K. SMITH
SONIA SHARP

they were older than me, they took a dislike to me . . . various things happened . . . they would take my cardigan and kick it around as a foot-ball, and they would kick me out of the way and carry on . . . one boy pulled my hair so hard that some came out, he dropped it in front of me . . . I was pushed off the climbing-frame, I didn't realise I had concussion but that's what it was . . . I remember feeling very alone – no-one would help me . . . I dreaded going to school.

I'm quite insecure, even now . . . I won't believe that people like me.

Bullying in schools has long been a matter of concern. This concern is a very understandable one, since most adults will have had some experience of the problem, either as children themselves, or through their own children or their friends' children. In the above extract, a 28-year-old woman recalls some of the systematic bullying she experienced at school. Although now leading a normal life, she also mentions the long-lasting effects which she believes these experiences had for her.

What has emerged over the last few years is that schools can do a great deal to stop bullying, bringing new hope to the many children who experi-ence it. In this book we review the work on dealing with bullying in the UK. We document in some detail the relative success of a number of measures to reduce bullying. Some of this knowledge comes from a series of investi-gations in twenty-three schools which took part in a two-and-a-half year project based in Sheffield. This has been the largest monitored intervention project to date, in terms of number of pupils participating. It received funding from the Department for Education, the Economic and Social Research Council, and the Calouste Gulbenkian Foundation (UK). Also, other information from additional studies, both in Sheffield and elsewhere, has been drawn upon.

What is bullying?

Bullying can be described as the systematic abuse of power. There will always be power relationships in social groups, by virtue of strength or size or ability, force of personality, sheer numbers or recognised hierarchy. Power can be abused; the exact definition of what constitutes *abuse* will depend on the social and cultural context, but this is inescapable in examining human behaviour. If the abuse is systematic – repeated and deliberate – bullying seems a good name to describe it.

Bullying can occur in many contexts, including the workplace and the home; it is particularly likely to be a problem in social groups with clear power relationships and low supervision, such as the armed forces, prisons and also schools. While not denying the importance of other contexts for bullying, school bullying perhaps arouses particular revulsion because the problem is so general – it can affect anyone as a child – and because children do not have the rights or the awareness of rights that adults have. Adults do not usually put up with theft, extortion or bodily assault, and if it happens to them may rightly seek legal redress.

Studies of school bullying

In a way, it is surprising that so much bullying has been tolerated for so long in schools. In part, this may reflect the rather little systematic investigation of bullying which was available until recently. Of course, novels such as *Tom Brown's schooldays* had treated the topic; and we can surmise that just as much bullying went on in earlier decades as now. But almost no research had been published, certainly outside Norway and Sweden. There had been an article entitled 'Teasing and bullying' by Burk in the *Pedagogical Seminary* for 1897; and then a long gap. In the 1970s a few small articles appeared (e.g. Lowenstein, 1978a, b); and in 1978, Olweus published an English version of his book *Aggression in the schools: Bullies and whipping boys*. But school bullying remained a low-key issue in the UK well into the 1980s.

It is only in the last five years that bullying has appeared firmly on the educational agenda. During this recent period, two things have happened. First, it has become clear that bullying happens in most, if not all, schools in Britain; and probably to a greater extent than most teachers and parents realise, since so many children who are bullied keep quiet about it. It can be quite frequent, and can have severe and occasionally tragic consequences. Second, reasonable evidence has accumulated that schools can do a considerable amount to reduce bullying.

The background to the recent explosion of interest in the UK has been the two decades of work in Scandinavia on the topic, and news of the relatively successful intervention programme there. Following earlier writings for example by Heinemann (1973), the Scandinavian research has been pursued most vigorously by Olweus, first in Sweden and then, based at Bergen University, in Norway. Olweus' book (1978) described the basic nature of the problem and ways of assessing it through self-report questionnaires. Results of the Norwegian intervention campaign of 1983–85 (described later) started to come through in the late 1980s.

In the UK, public and media attention became particularly focused on the issue in 1989-90. In 1989 three books on the topic appeared: D. Tattum and D. Lane (eds), *Bullying in schools*; E. Roland and E. Munthe (eds), *Bullying: An international perspective*; and V. Besag, *Bullies and victims in schools*. The Elton Report (DES, 1989) on discipline in schools, although primarily on teacher–pupil relations and discipline, did mention problems of bullying in a few paragraphs. It stated (pp. 102–3) that 'recent studies of bullying in schools suggest that the problem is widespread and tends to be ignored by teachers . . . . Research suggests that bullying not only causes considerable suffering to individual pupils but also has a damaging effect on school atmosphere . . .'. It recommended that schools should encourage pupils to tell staff of serious cases of bullying, deal firmly with bullying behaviour, and take action based on clear rules and backed by appropriate sanctions and systems to protect and support victims.

No direct action on bullying was taken by the DFE in the immediate wake of the Elton Report. However the Gulbenkian Foundation set up an advisory working group on 'Bullying in schools' in 1989. This funded several initiatives. One was a thirty-two page booklet, *Bullying – a positive response*, by Delwyn Tattum and Graham Herbert (1990), available at a low cost. With the launch of this booklet it also supported a three-month extension of the Childline telephone service to a special Bullying Line which received some 40–200 calls a day; an analysis of these was later published (La Fontaine, 1991).

The Gulbenkian Foundation also supported our own survey work, to be described shortly (this led directly on to the DFE funding the Sheffield Anti-Bullying Project, an intervention project inspired by that in Norway). It also funded materials for Kidscape, presentations by the Neti-Neti Theatre Company, and the preparation of an annotated bibliography and resource guide on anti-bullying materials and strategies (Skinner, 1992). More recently, it has supported the preparation of *'We don't have bullies here!'*, a package of materials for schools by Besag (1992); *Cycle of violence*, video materials by Tattum, Tattum and Herbert (1993); and *Countering bullying*, a compilation of case studies by Tattum and Herbert (1993). These varied support activities have contributed greatly to not only keeping bullying 'on the agenda', but to providing sources of practical help for schools and teachers.

In 1991 two edited collections on bullying appeared, both looking at practical approaches to help teachers – *Practical approaches to bullying*, by Smith and Thompson (1991a), and *Bullying: A practical guide to coping for schools*, by Elliott (1991). Media interest in bullying peaked again in 1992, and the BBC *That's Life* programme pursued the topic vigorously following the suicide of an adolescent girl due in part to bullying at school. Questions were asked in Parliament about what action the government was taking on bullying. At this point, the Sheffield Project was midway through; while stating that the report of this project was awaited, the DFE decided in the interim to circulate the 'Scottish Pack' to all schools in England and Wales. This pack, *Action against bullying* (1992), prepared by Margaret Johnstone, Pamela Munn and Lynne Edwards of the Scottish Council for Research in Education, had been circulated to schools in Scotland some months previously.

An excellent review of research on bullying up to mid-1992 is provided by Farrington (1993). In 1993, the SCRE team produced a second pack, *Supporting schools against bullying*, with particular advice for parents and non-teaching staff (Mellor, 1993; Munn, 1993). Tattum produced an edited collection, *Understanding and managing bullying* (1993). Olweus published a fuller account of the Bergen study in *Bullying: What we know and what we can do* (1993b).

What we know about bullying

In general, much of what we know about bullying has arisen from two groups of studies: studies asking teachers their views on the nature and incidence of the bullying problems in schools; and direct studies of children who bully others and who are bullied, their personalities, background, attitudes and family influences.

The teacher opinion studies give a picture of bullying being a long-term problem, often extending over years, involving about 5–10 per cent of children as being bullied and about 5 per cent of children as bullying others. The bullying takes place in general interactions of children and young adults in what are generally caring and educating institutions, and can exist quite well whilst the rest of the organisation is fulfilling the tasks it is expected to. The bullying is generally hidden from the adult supervising community, and when it is noticed is quite difficult to stop, because of the reluctance of the peer groups to provide information and the reluctance of the bullied pupils to complain very loudly.

The studies of the individual personalities and attitudes of the pupils involved in bullying others gave a picture of the children who bully as quite outgoing and socially confident, showing very little anxiety or guilt, who very much conform to their own ideals as being dominant and powerful in their own peer group. Significantly, they also tend to see aggression as an acceptable and realistic way of expressing their social position, perceiving it as being supported by the attitudes of their family.

Bullied pupils, on the other hand, in many ways have the opposite characteristics: not feeling confident in peer interactions in general, having poor self-assertive skills, poor handling of the aggressive reactions in particular, and being much more likely to show anxiety in social interactions. Perry, Kusel and Perry (1988) specifically found that children's victimisation scores were uncorrelated with their own aggression scores. However, their victimisation scores positively correlated with peer rejection scores and negatively correlated with peer acceptance.

There has been some work suggesting that children who bully others, and are bullied, may fall into various subgroups. For example, Pikas (1989) distinguished between the 'classic' or ordinary victim, whose behaviour does not particularly cause the bullying, and the 'provocative' victim, who by being disruptive and behaving inappropriately can be seen as contributing to the bullying they receive. Stephenson and Smith (1989), on the basis of teacher descriptions, also described 'bully/victims', and 'anxious bullies' as well as ordinary 'bullies'.

Putting the teachers' views of the problem together with the studies of the individual pupils involved in bullying situations, it becomes clear that bullying exists as a part of the 'normal' interactions between children with particular backgrounds and personality characteristics. Furthermore, it is carefully controlled by the bullying pupil to exist inside those 'normal' patterns of interaction. This maintains both his or her own position and the psychological rewards of validating self-image over a period of time. It also keeps the process safe from the attention of the adult supervisors. During this process, the peer groups generally know of the existence of the bullying;

probably most of the children in the same age groups as the bullied pupils know of many of the specific incidents of bullying, do not like it, but lack the will, the leadership or the sense that a different style of social relationships is possible, to do much about it.

This analysis suggests that there are definite ways forward for the adults: to create a clear moral climate in school in which bullying is not tolerated, and in which the 'silent majority' of non-bullying pupils are enabled to help those bullied, and/or in which bullied pupils can seek help from adults without fear of ridicule or retribution.

The nature of bullying

School bullying can take a variety of forms; some are direct and physical – hitting, tripping up, taking belongings; some are direct and verbal – name-calling and taunting, perhaps about race or disability; and some are indirect – passing nasty stories or rumours about someone behind their back, or excluding someone from social groups.

There are typical gender differences in types of bullying, as in aggression generally. Often, these differences have been thought of as physical (more by boys) versus verbal (more by girls). But this generalisation appears to be over-simple. Research by Bjorkqvist, Lagerspetz and Kaukainen (1992) has recently clarified that sex differences in aggression are not so much physical/verbal, as direct/indirect; boys tend to use more direct methods, girls more indirect. This research in Finland has been replicated in the UK (Ahmad and Smith, 1994). Since direct bullying is easier and more obvious to observe, it is likely that girls' bullying has been underestimated in the past.

Racist bullying has been a particularly worrying feature in some schools (Kelly and Cohn, 1988); and in one well-known case racist bullying resulted in a child's death (Burnage Report, 1989). In two studies, children of Asian origin have been shown to experience more racist name-calling (though not other forms of bullying) than did White children of the same age and gender (Boulton, submitted; Moran, Smith, Thompson and Whitney, 1993).

 Survey work by Yates and Smith (1989) and Whitney and Smith (1993) in the UK has shown that about half the incidents of bullying are one-to-one; about half involve a larger group. The playground is the most likely place for bullying in school – it is the least well supervised, usually – but bullying can occur in classrooms, corridors and other locations. A particularly important if worrying finding is that about one-half of all pupils who will admit to having been bullied in a private, anonymous questionnaire, say that they have not told anyone about it, either at home or at school. All too often, the victims of bullying either are frightened to tell, or blame themselves and lack the confidence to tell.

Does bullying matter?

There is considerable evidence now that continued or severe bullying can contribute to long-term problems as well as immediate unhappiness. Children who are bullied at school risk continuing misery and loss of self-esteem, with possible long-term effects; while those who bully others are learning that they can get their own way by abusing power in their relationships with other people.

Boulton and Smith (1994) found that at middle school, victims of bullying tended to be lower on several measures of self-esteem. Olweus (1993a) has shown that boys who were victims at school between 13 and 16 years were, at age 23, more likely to show depressive tendencies and continued to have poor self-esteem. They were not especially likely to still be experiencing victimisation at this age, so these effects are probably long-lasting effects of the earlier bullying. Research into the effects of stress on learning indicate clearly that worried or upset children do not learn well, finding it hard to concentrate or solve problems effectively (Turkel and Eth, 1990). Sharp has recently investigated how children respond to and cope with bullying behaviour (Sharp and Thompson, 1992). From a total sample size of 723 secondary-aged pupils, of whom 40 per cent had been bullied during that academic year, she found that 20 per cent of pupils said they would truant to avoid being bullied; 29 per cent found it difficult to concentrate on their school work; 22 per cent felt physically ill after being bullied and 20 per cent had experienced sleeping difficulties as a result of the bullying.

There is also evidence, less direct, that continued low self-esteem or feelings of lack of self-worth make later close relationships of trust and intimacy more difficult, for example in close relationships with the opposite sex (Gilmartin, 1987). The worst possible outcome is that a severely bullied child takes their own life. There are several such cases each year in the UK. In these cases it seems that severe bullying has contributed to or precipitated the suicide, even if it is not necessarily the sole cause.

The children caught up in bullying others may also need help to change. Sometimes, children are involved with a gang of peers, bullying only as a result of peer pressure. But other children seem to take part in bullying more actively, sometimes it seems as an almost necessary part of their relationships. These children often seem to see the world as a very tough place, and are much more ready to interpret the actions of others as aggressive or provocative than are most children. Typically, they may excuse their bullying as justified by provocations by the victim; for example, Boulton and Underwood (1992) found that 44 per cent of bullies felt that victims were picked on because of provocation, whereas only 12 per cent of non-involved children thought this. Bullying children often show a need to appear tough and avoid being bullied themselves; typically, also, they may show little awareness of the feelings of the victim. Longitudinal research, again by Olweus (1991), has found that boys who persistently bullied others in adolescence were three to four times more likely to be involved in repeated anti-social behaviour and physical violence by their early twenties. Similar findings are reported in the UK by Lane (1989), while Farrington (1993) has reported links between generations, with fathers who were aggressive and bullying at school being more likely to have sons who were also bullying at school.

Origins of bullying behaviour

What leads some children to be victims of bullying and others to take part in bullying? It should first be said that almost anyone might occasionally get involved in bullying, or being bullied, at some time or another. But certain factors may *predispose* a child to persistent bullying, or being bullied, even if they do not make it inevitable – the 'risk factors'. It is clear that many such factors are involved. Some are individual characteristics such as temperament; Olweus (1980, 1991, 1993a, b) describes bullying children as having impulsive and aggressive temperament, and children who are bullied as having shy or weak temperament. Some children who get bullied may lack assertiveness skills. There is some debate about whether children who bully may lack social skills (P.K. Smith, 1991); some of them seem actually quite socially skilled in manipulating situations to their advantage. Generally, being different in some way (for example, ethnic group), or being vulnerable, are risk factors for being bullied. Also, as is clear from research reported in Chapter Nine, children with special educational needs, often with a physical disability or mild/moderate learning difficulties, are especially at risk of being bullied.

Another important set of factors relate to parents and the home environment. This is reasonably well documented, especially for high aggression. Research in the USA (Patterson, DeBaryshe and Ramsay, 1989) suggests that home factors predisposing to high aggression are: lack of warmth between parents or in the family; use of physical violence within the family; and lack of clear guidelines for behaviour and monitoring of children's activities.

Olweus (1980) has found similar links in the family background of children involved in bullying in his Norwegian studies.

So far as bullied children are concerned, Olweus (1993a) has found that over-protective parenting may be a risk factor; this is also suggested by the findings of Bowers, Smith and Binney (1992). Perhaps children in over-protected family environments do not develop the same skills of independence as their peers and are more vulnerable to exploitation by potential bullies.

Bowers, Smith and Binney (1992) and Smith, Bowers and Binney (1993) used several different assessment procedures to get children's perceptions of their families. They compared perceptions of bullies, victims, bully/victims and control children. Many bullies and bully/victims perceived their families as relatively lacking in affection, and having poor monitoring procedures, confirming the earlier research. However, this work also confirmed the need to distinguish provocative victims or bully/victims from both bullies and ordinary victims. Children involved only in bullying perceived the family more in terms of power relationships with siblings and other family members, whereas the bully/victims perceived difficulties with parental behaviour such as punitiveness and lack of involvement, and seemed to be more concerned with their own position in the family, sometimes defensively. It is possible that a more refined or detailed taxonomy of different kinds of bullying or victim behaviour will come from future research, which may well have implications for help or treatment directed at individual pupils or particular families.

What schools can do about bullying

Whatever individual differences and difficulties may exist between school pupils, they are in a shared school environment, and it is in this environment that a lot of bullying can occur. What can schools do about this? It has to be said that in the past some schools, perhaps many schools, have not done very much. But until recently, little was known about the nature of bullying and its consequences, and little was available in the way of resources to help teachers. In such a context, there was a temptation to ignore the problem or to deal with it on a piecemeal basis. But this situation is now changing rapidly.

Norway has led the way in helping schools deal with bullying. In late 1982 it happened that three children at different schools in Norway committed suicide, as a result of bullying, within a week or so. Naturally there was great public concern. The prior research by Olweus and others could demonstrate that these were *not* just isolated instances of bullying – in fact, Olweus had found that about one child in seven was involved in bully/victim problems, one way or another, during any school term. Together with the suicides, these research findings led to sufficient pressure that the Ministry for Education funded a Nationwide Campaign against Bullying in all 3,500 Norwegian schools.

This campaign was launched in late 1983. A survey on bullying was carried out in all schools; and a package of materials was provided for teachers, including a video for classroom discussion of the issue, and a folder of advice for parents. There was also considerable national discussion of the problem.

Two evaluations of this campaign were carried out in the mid-1980s. One of these was directed by Olweus in Bergen; he worked with forty-two schools, and particularly the age ranges 11 to 14 years. Using primarily anonymous self-report questionnaires, he assessed levels of bullying at three time points – just before the intervention started, one year later and two years later. He analysed his results in terms of age-equivalent comparisons – that is to say, he compared 11-year-olds in 1983 who had not experienced any intervention, with 11-year-olds in 1984 who had experienced one year of intervention, and 11-year-olds born in 1985 who had experienced two years of intervention; similarly for other ages. This procedure was necessary since levels of being bullied tend to decline with age, so a decrease in frequency from 11 to 12 to 13 years could be due to age alone rather than the intervention. Age-equivalent comparisons avoid this difficulty; they are potentially susceptible to historical trends – perhaps Norway was different in 1985 from 1983 in a general way which affected bullying rates – but that Olweus rejected as unlikely to any very significant extent. Olweus' findings were clear and encouraging (Olweus, 1991, 1993b). Over the two years, rates of reported bullying fell by about 50 per cent. This was true for boys and for girls, and for a variety of measures of bullying.

There has been a second evaluation, carried out by Erling Roland in the Rogaland county of Norway around Stavanger (Roland, 1989, 1993). Roland monitored thirty-seven schools over three years, from 1983 to 1986. His results were somewhat different. He did not find any clear decrease in rates of bullying over this time period – indeed on some measures there was a small increase. However, Roland did assess the extent to which schools had actually made use of the pack and materials provided. He reported a positive correlation: schools which had used the pack the most actively did have better results and a modest decrease in bullying.

Both these findings have been reported fairly widely; though both also deserve better documentation than is currently available. Is it possible to reconcile these two somewhat discrepant sets of findings? One possible explanation is differences in measurement, a possibility favoured by Olweus. In his own study, exactly the same procedures were followed at all measurement points, and this would not have been so true in Roland's study since he relied on Olweus' data for the 1983 baseline.

Another explanation, favoured by Roland (1993), lies in how much support the schools had. It seems that Olweus provided continuing and fairly intensive support to the forty-two Bergen schools over the two-year period; whereas Roland appears to have left the schools to select their own level of use of what was provided nationally. Thus, Olweus' more spectacular results may reflect what can be achieved with intensive input, while Roland's may reflect the result of simply providing a modest package without any further back-up.

How to measure the nature and extent of bullying

There are various ways of assessing the nature and extent of problems of bullying in schools. Each has its own advantages and disadvantages. One of the quickest methods is to ask class teachers 'who are the victims (or bullies) in your class?' This can provide useful information, but it will only be as valid as the teacher's perception of the problem. Important though this is, children's own reports suggest that many victims of bullying have not told a teacher about it, and many children who bully others report that no teacher has talked to them about it (Whitney and Smith, 1993). While some teachers may make exceptional efforts to find out about bullying in their class, the evidence is that, generally, most teachers are only aware of a fraction of the bullying which may be going on.

Another possibility is to interview children directly about their experiences and behaviour in school. This 'direct interview' method requires a high degree of trust and confidentiality if the child is going to be able to talk about being bullied, or bullying others, in a truthful way, and is in its nature time-consuming. However it can reveal rich and detailed information, and we used this method in the study of children with special needs (Chapter Nine), and also on a smaller scale to get information on the perceived effectiveness of particular interventions. It is not suitable for carrying out on a large scale.

Some teachers and researchers have found that it is less threatening to ask children about the experiences of other children in their class. Having ensured that they understand the terms 'bully' and 'victim' in a satisfactory way, one can, for example, ask them to name children who bully others and children who are bullied in their class. This might be done as part of a larger interview, asking perhaps about friendships, who likes whom and so on. This is called a 'peer nomination' method. Peer nominations are quite reliable in that one is pooling information from a number of informants (typically, 20–30 in a class); and agreement between children has been found to be reasonably good. These interviews are shorter than the direct interviews described above, but it is necessary to carry out a large number for each class. Peer nominations may be very useful – in fact, the preferred method – for case studies of a particular group of children, or class, or even a whole school (e.g. Bowers, Smith and Binney, 1992, in press; Boulton and Smith, 1994).

To make reliable generalisations about the extent of bullying in general, and the effectiveness of interventions beyond those on a very localised scale, large-scale survey data is needed. Here, an anonymous self-report questionnaire seems the most reliable and valid method. This approach was pioneered by Olweus (1978, 1991) in Norway, and his methodology has been used and adapted in other countries, including Spain, the Netherlands, Japan and Canada, as well as in our own large-scale studies in England. Olweus has established that his questionnaire has satisfactory test-retest reliability, and shows reasonable (though not perfect) agreement with peer nomination measures. The anonymity of the questionnaire is stressed and appears to be an important factor in providing pupils with the confidence to respond in a truthful way (as they perceive it). The questionnaire is suitable for children of 8 years and upwards.

Following contact with Olweus, Smith and Ahmad piloted the Olweus questionnaires in Sheffield schools in 1988/89. In addition they compared the questionnaire with the 'Life in schools' booklet (Arora and Thompson, 1987), and with other methods such as teacher nominations, peer nominations and direct interviews. They concluded that the Olweus questionnaire provided a suitably reliable and valid measure for large-scale survey use (Ahmad and Smith, 1990). Slightly different versions were available for junior/middle school children, and secondary school children. Following slight modifications suggested by the pilot work, we used these questionnaires extensively in surveys of primary and secondary schools.

The modified Olweus questionnaire

As later used, the questionnaires closely followed the design of those used by Olweus (1991), but some changes were made to suit the British context and current word usage following the pilot work (see Ahmad, Whitney and Smith, 1991). In the junior questionnaire we referred to 'playtime' and 'children', whereas in the senior version we referred to 'breaktime' and 'young people'. A large-print version of the junior questionnaire was made available for children who had reading or learning difficulties.

The following definition of bullying was used:

> We say a child or young person is being bullied, or picked on when another child or young person, or a group of children or young people, say nasty and unpleasant things to him or her. It is also bullying when a child or a young person is hit, kicked, threatened, locked inside a room, sent nasty notes, when no one ever talks to them and things like that. These things can happen frequently and it is difficult for the child or the young person being bullied to defend himself or herself. It is also bullying when a child or young person is teased repeatedly in a nasty way.
>
> But it is *not bullying* when two children or young people of about the same strength have the odd fight or quarrel.

This definition was amended from that used by Olweus (1991); it included 'sent nasty notes' and 'when no one ever talks to them' in order to emphasise these additional more psychological forms of bullying; furthermore, it specified that teasing should be 'in a nasty way'.

The questionnaires were administered to pupils, in school, by teachers who were not the pupils' usual teacher. Teachers explained to the pupils that the questionnaires were about how much bullying takes place in school; that it was important to answer the questions truthfully; that they did not have to put their names on the questionnaires and that no-one would know that it was they who had filled it in. If there were any pupils who would have difficulties in filling in the questionnaire, teachers were advised to put them separately in small groups and have someone else go through it with them (using the large-print version).

Pupils were asked to fill in the date, school and class and to give their answers to the questions by circling the letter next to their response choice. They were also told that for three of the questions they could choose more than one answer. Examples of how to do this were given and read out to the pupils to ensure that they understood. It was then left to the teachers' discretion whether or not they read out each individual question (more appropriate for junior children than senior) or let the pupils continue at their own pace. Before the questions on bullying, the definition of bullying was read out and explained. After completion, with no time limit imposed, the questionnaires were placed in an envelope and sealed. They were then collected for analysis.

There were twenty-six questions in the questionnaire. The first four dealt with the sex of the respondent; how much they liked breaktime; how many friends they had in their class; and how often they spent breaktime alone. The remaining twenty-two questions were about being bullied or bullying others during the current school term. The areas which the questions covered included:

- the frequency of being bullied, both in school and going to or from school;
- the types of bullying behaviour and where the bullying took place;
- who did the bullying: was it someone in the same class or in a higher or lower year; and was it girls or boys;
- the extent to which teachers or other pupils tried to stop bullying;
- how often pupils had informed teachers or anyone at home that they had been bullied;
- whether they had been bullied going to or from school; and if they had been bullied by anyone else other than pupils;
- the frequency with which they had bullied other pupils, both in school and going to or from school;
- whether or not they could join in bullying; and what they felt about bullies.

For all the questions about *frequency* of being bullied and of bullying others the pupils were given the following response alternatives: I haven't been bullied (taken part in bullying others) at school this term (0); it has only happened once or twice (1); sometimes (2); about once a week (3); several times a week (4). Because of the possible ambiguity of the term 'sometimes', teachers were allowed to clarify 'sometimes' as 'more than once or twice but less than once a week'.

All the questions required a choice of one response by circling it, with the exception of three questions which covered: *types of bullying behaviour*; *where the bullying occurred*; and *in which class were the bullies*. For these questions pupils could choose more than one response category.

A school information questionnaire was completed for each school by the headteacher. This provided information about the size of the school, resources for special needs, percentage of pupils coming from various social class backgrounds (by parents' occupation), percentage of pupils coming from different ethnic groups, and school location (rural or urban).

The 1990 survey results

The first surveys were on a small scale, in local schools (Ahmad and Smith, 1990; Yates and Smith, 1989; Boulton and Underwood, 1992). While limited in scope, these were sufficient to show that bullying was quite pervasive, and very probably at levels above those reported in Norway. This work was carried out during 1989–1990 and supported by the ESRC.

The first large-scale survey was carried out in twenty-four schools in Sheffield at the end of 1990. This was funded by the Calouste Gulbenkian Foundation (UK). It was intended to establish on a large sample just how extensive bullying problems were, and typical age and gender differences in this. There was also the possibility – not yet confirmed – that this survey could form the springboard for a larger intervention study, inspired by the success in Norway. The funding also enabled us to develop a 'survey service' for schools. In this, if a school was interested in establishing the nature and extent of bullying which pupils experienced, we provided a full set of questionnaires with details for their administration; the completed questionnaires were returned for analysis; and the school then received a portfolio of information about levels and types of bullying reported by pupils in their school, broken down where appropriate by school class and gender (Ahmad, Whitney and Smith, 1991).

All junior, middle and secondary schools in Sheffield were circulated with details of the survey service, which would be free, and with the possibility of further support for interventions against bullying subsequently. Over fifty schools, out of about eighty circulated, responded with positive interest. We then selected seventeen primary schools and seven secondary schools, on the basis that they should provide a geographical spread around Sheffield, and represent a reasonable diversity in terms of socio-economic background and ethnic mix. Within these constraints, we also aimed to include primary schools feeding in to selected secondary schools. All twenty-four schools received the survey materials after half-term, and gave the survey between mid-November and early December 1990. The total number of pupils taking part in the survey was 6,758: 2,623 from the primary sector and 4,135 from the secondary sector.

The results confirmed that bullying was extensive in schools. Some 27 per cent of junior/middle school pupils reported being bullied 'sometimes' or more frequently, and this included 10 per cent bullied 'once a week' or more frequently. For secondary schools, these figures were 10 per cent and 4 per cent respectively. Analyses by year group confirmed that there was a fairly steady decrease in reports of being bullied, from 8 through to 16 years, though with a possible slight increase at starting secondary school. (The small number of post-16 classes showed zero rates of being bullied).

So far as reporting taking part in bullying others was concerned, this was admitted by some 12 per cent of junior/middle school pupils 'sometimes' or more frequently, including 4 per cent bullied 'once a week' or more frequently. For secondary schools, these figures were 6 per cent and 1 per cent respectively. Analyses by year group showed that although fewer pupils reported bullying others in secondary school, year changes within junior/middle schools, or secondary schools, were not very substantial.

For those who were bullied, most of the bullying was reported to have been carried out by pupils in the same class as the victim, in junior/middle schools. For secondary schools, pupils were slightly more likely to be bullied by pupils from a different class (but the same year) than by pupils in their own class or in higher years than themselves; probably because secondary schools have more classes in a year group. Few seemed to be bullied by pupils from years below them in junior/middle schools and this was even less likely in secondary schools.

Boys admitted to bullying others considerably more than girls; boys did also report higher rates of being bullied, but the sex difference here was slight. Pupils who reported being bullied most often said it was carried out mainly by one boy; bullying by several boys was the next highest response; bullying by both boys and girls was the next; followed by being bullied by several girls; bullying reported to have been carried out by mainly one girl had the lowest average percentage. This pattern was consistent for both junior/middle and secondary schools. Boys were more likely than girls to report being bullied by one or several boys. Girls however were more likely than boys to report being bullied by one or several girls, or by both boys and girls. It was very rare for boys to report being bullied by one or several girls.

The majority of the bullying was reported to have occurred in the playground, particularly by junior/middle pupils. For secondary pupils this percentage was only slightly higher than being bullied in the classroom, or in the corridors. Reports of being bullied going to or from school were less than half the reported incidence of being bullied in school.

Most of the bullying took the form of general name-calling. Being physically hit and being threatened were the next most frequent forms of bullying in both junior/middle and secondary schools. Boys were more likely to be physically hit, and threatened, than were girls. Girls were more likely to experience verbal and indirect forms of bullying such as being called nasty names (in other than racist ways, which boys experienced more), having no-one talk to them (being 'sent to coventry') or having rumours spread about them. These gender differences were found in both junior/middle and secondary schools.

Pupils were asked if they had told either a teacher at school or 'anyone at home' (used to include children who may not have natural parents at home) about being bullied. There were three clear trends in this data. First, both junior/middle and secondary school pupils were significantly more likely to tell someone at home that they had been bullied than to tell their teacher at school. Second, junior/middle school pupils were significantly more likely than secondary school pupils to tell either their teacher or anyone at home that they had been bullied. Third, the percentage of pupils who did tell their teacher or anyone at home that they had been bullied tended to increase fairly consistently with frequency of being bullied, especially for the highest frequency of 'several times a week', though even here only about a half of secondary pupils had told anyone at home about it.

Teachers were seen as more likely to intervene to stop bullying than were other pupils. Some questions about children's attitudes to bullying suggested that about a half were sympathetic to victims (would try to help them, could not join in), about a quarter were rather neutral and about a quarter were not sympathetic.

The frequencies of being bullied and of bullying others, at each school, were correlated with other measures which might be expected to influence them on a school-wide basis: school size; average class size; ethnic mix (proportion of non-White pupils); an index of advantaged/disadvantaged areas of the school; how often pupils disliked breaktime 'very much'; how often pupils reported having 'no friends' in school; how often pupils reported spending breaktime alone 'once a week' or more; the proportion of bullied pupils who had informed teachers they were being bullied; the proportion of bullied pupils who had informed anyone at home they were being bullied; and how often they had been bullied going to or from school. There were few or no significant correlations with school size, class size, ethnic mix, having no friends in school and rates of bullying to/from school. However, there was an increased incidence of bullying problems in schools in disadvantaged areas, the mean correlation being -0.32. For secondary schools there were significant positive correlations of disliking playtime very much with bullying problems, and for junior/middle schools similar correlations for being alone at breaktime.

These results provided the largest sample to date in the UK, and permitted a first look at school variables. The survey confirmed the magnitude of a problem already strongly indicated by surveys carried out at individual schools, or small numbers of schools. The results are reported in detail in Whitney and Smith (1993).

The survey service results for each school were presented in a portfolio. This provided each school within the project with a great deal of information on the extent and nature of bully/victim problems in the school. The information enabled each school to build up a picture of the bullying behaviour reported by pupils overall as well as broken down by gender and school class, and to identify 'hot spots' for bullying. The survey service portfolio acted as both a stimulant and an important knowledge base for planning effective intervention.

Schools received the portfolio of results in April 1991. At the same time, they also received a free copy of *Bullying – a positive response*, by Delwyn Tattum and Graham Herbert, and a copy of the ACE information sheet *Governors and bullying*.

The DFE Sheffield Anti-Bullying Project

Late in 1990, the DFE agreed to fund a follow-up to the survey then being carried out. The intention was to work with most of the twenty-four schools, support them in developing interventions against bullying, monitor their work, and evaluate their effectiveness with the help of a second survey carried out two years after the first, in November/December 1992; it was also intended to develop suitable material for intervention packages capable of application in a wider context. The project was funded from April 1991 through to August 1993.

The project was directed by Peter Smith, at the Department of Psychology at the University of Sheffield, together with Michael Boulton (School of Health and Community Studies, Sheffield Hallam University), David Thompson (Division of Education, University of Sheffield), Helen Cowie (School of Social Studies, Bretton Hall College), Yvette Ahmad (School of Health and Community Studies, Sheffield Hallam University) and Sheffield LEA (Martin Gazzard, Schools Officer; Don Pennock, Chief EWO). Sonia Sharp was appointed as main research associate for the project; and clerical and administrative support was provided by Sarah Barron. Irene Whitney helped run the second survey in 1992; and Ian Rivers assisted in the analysis of results in the last six months of the project.

Twenty-three of the twenty-four schools elected to continue with the interventions offered. The main or core intervention was developing a whole-school policy on bullying; in addition, schools were supported in a choice of optional interventions, ranging from curriculum work (video, drama, literature), playground interventions (training lunchtime supervisors, improving the playground environment), to working with individuals and small groups (Pikas' Method of Shared Concern, assertiveness training). The process of intervention was monitored, and evaluated both by ongoing interviews and questionnaires, and a repeat survey two years later. Details of the methodology of this work, and the main results, are given in Chapter Two.

Linked research on the Sheffield Project

Two other research projects, funded by the ESRC and the Calouste Gulbenkian Foundation, were linked to the DFE-funded project.

Improving the playground environment

Many schools, especially primary schools, have somewhat bleak, uninteresting and unvaried outdoor play areas. Since so much bullying occurs in the playground, improving the playground environment might be a useful positive intervention. Work of this kind was facilitated by a grant from the Calouste Gulbenkian Foundation, provided to Peter Smith and to Anne Beer in the Department of Landscape at Sheffield University. This project was carried out jointly by the DFE Project Team in the Department of Psychology, and first Lyndal Sheat and then Catherine Higgins from the Department of Landscape. The project ran from October 1991 to September 1992. The funding enabled intensive work with four primary schools on the design of the playground environment, using plans developed by each school in collaboration with members of the Department of Landscape. The results are described further in Chapter Seven.

Children with special needs

For schools catering for special needs children (either special schools, or integrated schools which have special provisions for such children), the Olweus questionnaires were not so suitable. Nevertheless bully/victim problems are likely to be just as prevalent in these schools. Pilot work involved visits to four special schools in the Sheffield area to discuss ways in which the questionnaires could be adapted or other techniques developed. Consultations with headteachers in these schools suggested that for some children the questionnaires needed to be altered and simplified or administered on a one-to-one basis; in some cases observation or interviews with the children seemed to be the most appropriate method. This work was continued with a research grant to Peter Smith and David Thompson from the Economic and Social Research Council, 'Assessing, and intervening in, problems of bullying in children with special needs', which started in July 1991 and finished in October 1992; Irene Whitney was the research worker on this project. Eight schools within the main DFE project had integrated resources for statemented children, and took part. The methodology and results are described in Chapter Nine.

the Sheffield Project: methodology and findings

T·W·O

IRENE WHITNEY
IAN RIVERS
PETER K. SMITH
SONIA SHARP

As discussed in Chapter One, the large-scale survey of bullying in twenty-four Sheffield schools, carried out in late 1990, provided an opportunity for supporting intervention in these schools and evaluating the results, including a planned repeat of the survey in late 1992. The DFE provided the main funding for this work. This chapter describes the methods and results from this project.

The twenty-four schools were circulated early in 1991 with details of the project and an invitation to take part further. In the event only one junior school from the original survey was not willing to continue with interventions. This still left the project team with three more schools than planned for, but as there was a possibility of further drop-out over the life of the project, perhaps arising from factors such as change of priorities or staffing within one or two of the schools, it was decided to allow all twenty-three schools to proceed.

Comparison schools

The one school which declined to take part was willing to act as a 'control school', taking the second survey. In reality, the notion of a 'control' school is difficult, if not impossible, in this domain. Some project schools, as we shall see, did rather little, while schools not in the project were still affected by what was happening nationally (for example, they would have received the national circulation of materials including the 'Scottish Pack' (Johnstone, Munn and Edwards, 1991)) and might have taken various actions against bullying. Indeed, even the fact of having a survey done and receiving a portfolio was itself likely to produce some action. Nevertheless, it seemed desirable to have a few comparison schools which were not in the project. Besides the one junior school, we were able to use results from three 'comparison' secondary schools which had taken part in the earlier surveys and which were willing to be surveyed again two years later. Brief details of all the project and comparison schools are given in Table 2.1.

Planning the interventions

The project team met before the formal commencement of the DFE funding, to plan the broad structure of the project. It was decided to ask the schools participating to agree to a Core Intervention comprising a basic 'whole-school policy' on bullying. Previous work, including that by Foster, Arora and Thompson (1990) and Thompson and Arora (1991), had indicated that having a whole-school policy was likely to be an essential framework within which other interventions could operate successfully and maintain continuity (see Chapter Three).

In addition, some Optional Interventions which were available would be supported by project resources. Here, we selected interventions which were available at the time, targeted to bullying, and suitable in a UK context. These fell broadly into three categories: curriculum-based strategies, intervening in bullying situations, and making changes to playgrounds and lunchbreaks.

Headteachers were initially invited to the university for one whole day, in February 1991, for themselves and another school representative to work on a core framework of a whole-school policy on bullying; and to be introduced to the range of interventions available. Representatives from twenty-two of the schools attended this orientation day to launch the project. An overview of the project aims and the interventions available was provided. The school representatives were provided with details of support available for the interventions, in the summer term, via staff training days, Inset days and provision of resource materials. This orientation day was the first of a series of termly meetings held centrally to examine key issues related to whole-school policy development and which provided a forum for schools to share ideas with each other.

TABLE 2.1 DETAILS OF PROJECT AND COMPARISON SCHOOLS, AND INTERVENTIONS CHOSEN

School code	Number of pupils on roll	Teaching staff	Lunchtime supervisors	Support staff	% Entitled to free school meals	Number of pupils in survey	Change of head or acting head	Organis- ational change	INTERVENTIONS Curriculum	Work with children	School grounds
P1	240	10	4	3	8.8	192	A/H				T, e
P2	420	24	12	4	47.3	178	Ch, A/H	M to J	own work		e
P3	230	9	8	4	40.0	86			N, Q		T, e
P4	581	10	5	4	15.0	235		M to J			T
P5	150	8	3	1	44.7	100					T
P6	420	14	10	6	32.4	162			N		T
P7	394	17	10	6	33.2	142			H	P	T, e
P8	240	16	5	3	48.3	53				A	E
P9	230	14	6	1	60.4	166				A	T
P10	350	18	9	4	13.4	146	Ch	J to P	N, H, Q	P	T
P11	304	15	8	2	43.1	159	Ch	J to P	N, H, Q	A	T
P12	406	16	10	5	11.1	212		J to P	H, Q	A	
P13	174	7	3	2	36.2	64					e
P14	430	17	8	5	70.5	276		M to J	N, H		
P15	255	10	6	1	31.8	107					T, e
P16	316	12	8	5	41.8	111				A	T
PC1	198	8	4	3	7.1	99					
S1	400	29	5	9	25.0	250	Ch, A/H	-Y12	S	C	
S2	483	52	8	6	30.0	287		+Y7	S, N		T
S3	1447	100	12	32	8.2	953		+Y7	S, N	A, P	T
S4	1000	55	11	15	28.8	794			S, N	A, C	
S5	781	50	4	12	7.9	611			S, N	P	
S6	1000	64	8	11	15.5	839				P	
S7	1118	77	11	14	30.6	920		+Y7	S, N		T
SC1	729	60	5	13	27.4	333	Ch				
SC2	1179	72	6	16	10.2	623	Ch				
SC3	1000	60	8	12	14.6	786					

Key: Ch = change of head; A/H = acting head; M to J = middle to junior; J to P = junior to primary;
N = Neti Neti; Q = quality circles; H = *Heartstone Odyssey*; S = *Sticks and stones video*; A = assertiveness training; P = Pikas method; C = peer counselling;
T = lunchtime supervisor training; E (e) = improving school grounds on (or not on) Gulbenkian project.

A whole-school policy

Help for schools was provided with a series of further meetings. A half-day meeting to focus on development issues for whole-school policies took place in May 1991. Each school set its own target date for whole-school policy completion. Also, schools discussed the options they wished to pursue, and had selected these by the time of the May meeting.

In June 1991 Graham Herbert led a training session where he provided an overview of some of the processes involved in introducing a whole-school policy, in particular considering some of the difficulties involved in managing change within any school. He spent some time helping participants to identify performance indicators which would provide evidence of the usefulness of a whole-school policy on bullying. He demonstrated how each of the subject areas within the national curriculum can provide a vehicle for developing the theme of anti-bullying, and emphasised the importance of establishing an 'anti-bullying network' by building links within and beyond the school community.

In October 1991, schools representatives took part in a one-day meeting to focus specifically on issues of equal opportunities and bullying. The themes for the day included bullying and harassment which arises because of race and ethnicity, gender, class and special needs. Participants considered ways in which school policy and practice can respond to these aspects of bullying. Cecile Wright, a contributor to the Eggleston Report on race relations in schools, and lecturer in Education at Leicester University, led the latter part of the day.

In March 1992, a meeting was held on the theme of involving parents and pupils in policy development. The range of ways in which both parents and pupils could and should be involved was considered, and teachers from two schools in the project described their own practice in relation to this and in relation to policy development in general. Shortly after this meeting, each school was provided with a checklist to guide them in policy development. The checklist was developed by the project team, and incorporated advice given by the DFE steering committee.

Maintenance and review of the whole-school policy was the focus for a meeting in July 1992. Project co-ordinators explored review strategies and discussed ways of keeping the policy in practice over time. Whole-school policies from the different project schools were on display.

Optional interventions

Curriculum-based strategies (see also Chapter Four)

These were materials and activities which could be used within the curriculum, to raise awareness of bullying, enhance awareness of the feelings of victims and encourage pupils to feel able to talk about it and what should be done about it.

Video film for classroom discussion

The video film selected was *Sticks and stones* from Central Television (1990). It features interviews with pupils, simulated examples of bullying and clips from the operation of a bully court. We prepared a package to go with the video which contained ideas for discussion, drama and creative writing activities for teachers to use. Schools which selected this option received a copy of the video and materials, and were invited to attend a support meeting at the university run by Sonia Sharp. The video was used entirely at secondary level. For secondary schools particularly concerned with racial harassment another video available on loan was *White lies* created by Swingbridge Video. *White lies* was filmed in the north-east of England. It covers many racist issues and is intended to stimulate discussion amongst young White people. The video is accompanied by a resource booklet.

Only playing, Miss by Neti Neti Theatre Company

Neti Neti's play about bullying (Gobey, 1991) was available on video for schools interested in this option. Members of staff from these schools were invited to attend a half-day workshop with Frances Gobey from the theatre company to consider and try out ways of using the materials in schools. The workshop explored how drama techniques could be harnessed to develop anti-bullying work with pupils. Ways of using Neti Neti's video *Only playing, Miss* were discussed. Also available was a copy of the script which includes numerous follow-up ideas. This intervention was supplemented in the spring term by a visit from the Armadillo Theatre Company, a group of four drama students from nearby Bretton Hall College. They developed the workshop as part of a cross-curricular assignment for Year Seven pupils. The workshop tries to encourage pupils to understand that, working together, they can help combat bullying, and at the end of the workshop they devise a pupil charter to tackle the problem of bullying. They worked with secondary and primary-age pupils in some of the project schools.

Children's literature – The Heartstone Odyssey

This is a story for primary pupils which tackles issues of racial harassment and bullying (Horton, 1991). The main character, Chandra, is a dancer who is the victim of direct racist threats and violence as well as subtle social injustices. She tells her stories using her dances and is 'rescued' by some mice who become involved in a mission to combat and challenge racist behaviour. Teachers from schools who were interested in this option were invited to spend a day with Sitakumari, who organises the Heartstone Foundation. This training day helped teachers develop ways of using the materials through 'story circles', dance and mime. Participants went on to look at work produced by pupils reading the book, to discuss how the magazine 'Stonekeeper' can be used effectively and to talk about important issues for them when using the materials.

Pupil involvement through Quality Circles

The concept of the Quality Circle comes from industry where the circles are used to involve employees in solving problems which they feel reduce the effectiveness of their work. More recently this technique has been adapted for use in education (Cowie and Sharp, 1992). A group of interested persons meet together regularly to identify common problems, evolve solutions and present these solutions to 'management' (the class-teacher or senior management team or governors). The participants are introduced to useful skills and strategies for problem-solving and effecting change: skills for generating ideas, observation and data collection, developing strategies or solutions, and communication both within the circle and when presenting to management. Staff from the schools who chose this option were invited to attend a series of four training sessions, where they were introduced to Quality Circles and given the opportunity to participate in a circle. There was also input on how groups work and how individuals behave in groups. These sessions were developed and presented by Helen Cowie and Sonia Sharp.

Intervening in bullying situations (see also Chapters Five and Eight)

The aim of these approaches is to work directly with pupils involved in bully/victim problems.

Assertiveness training for victims

These techniques aim to encourage pupils to interact with others in an assertive rather than aggressive or submissive way. They also encourage development of conflict-resolution skills, ways of improving self-esteem and enhancing social skills in joining in games and making friends. For schools interested in this, teachers were trained by Enid MacNeill and Tiny Arora, Educational Psychologists, both of whom had used these techniques frequently in schools (Arora, 1991). The training sessions covered basic assertiveness techniques which might be helpful in coping with or preventing bullying as well as guidelines for teachers on how to run groups for children. The emphasis was on establishing small, safe groups which might include some victims of bullying and other children with poor social skills. A further session was on 'How to set up a support group for victims of bullying'. The aim of this workshop was to enable the participants to consider the various issues related to setting up a victim support group, including selection, preparation, contents and evaluation. It provided a mixture of inputs about practical and theoretical aspects, small and large group discussions and practical experiential work.

Working directly with bullies

Anatol Pikas, a Swedish psychologist, visited Sheffield in June 1991 to train project members and teachers in his method of working directly with bullies. This method, 'The Method of Shared Concern', employs a carefully structured script to guide discussion with each pupil involved in a bullying incident (Pikas, 1987, 1989). It aims to stop the bullying behaviour and encourage tolerance. The training sessions took place over a half day, and were preceded by an introductory lecture. Pikas explained the philosophy underpinning his method and highlighted some important prerequisites for using it – organisational considerations as well as personal qualities and attitudes. Through the workshops, he went on to detail the stages of his technique and demonstrated how quick and non-threatening this approach can be. Most participants felt that they needed more training and so a further one and a half days of training were provided in the autumn term. Anatol Pikas visited again in November 1991; since then, project members (Sonia Sharp, Peter Smith and Helen Cowie) have run workshops on his approach.

School tribunals or bully 'courts'

This approach was advocated by Kidscape as part of a whole-school approach to bullying (Elliott, 1991). Pupils are elected to sit on a 'court' with one or more members of staff. When an incident of bullying is reported the 'court' listen to all parties concerned and then make a decision as to what action should be taken in response to the incident. Staff from schools who chose this option were able to attend a half-day training session with Michele Elliott (director of Kidscape). She began by introducing Kidscape and by describing how 'bully courts' arose from pupil suggestion. She detailed some of the guidelines that they have developed through their work with courts, in particular the need for a 'contract' with pupils and parents which is part of whole-school policy. Participants were shown a clip of the video *Sticks and stones* and then in groups role-played the court which might have followed on from that incident. Michele Elliott suggested that giving children the opportunity to practise this themselves prior to establishing a court was a helpful training mechanism for use in class. Although two schools in the project showed initial interest in this intervention, no school actually set up a bully court.

Peer counselling

In two schools, pupils established a 'listening line' for other pupils (Sharp, Sellars and Cowie, in press). This involved pupils from across the age range undertaking some training in basic counselling skills. This was provided by Sonia Sharp and Helen Cowie. The pupils worked in small teams, comprising two or three 'counsellors' and one 'receptionist'. Each team was on duty one lunchtime per week and the pupils also attended their own support and supervision meeting on another lunchtime. The supervision was provided by a specific member of staff and there was also always a teacher 'on call' for the duty team each day. The pupils did not intervene in bullying situations themselves – they were purely a listening service.

Making changes to playgrounds and lunchbreaks (see also Chapters Six and Seven)

The aim here was to improve the quality of children's breaktime and playtime experiences, bearing in mind the large proportion of bullying which had been found to occur in playgrounds.

Working with lunchtime supervisors

Schools were offered a range of activities within this intervention. These included: raising the status of lunchtime supervisors; training lunchtime supervisors; encouraging positive behaviour in the playground; improving the quality of play; building relationships between supervisors and pupils; building relationships between supervisors and teachers; responding to aggressive behaviour in the playground; and improving provision for wet playtimes. Within each there were a number of practical strategies which schools chose to implement. Some, such as training lunchtime supervisors, were held centrally. Others were negotiated individually with schools. Schools also received copies of some booklets which provide useful ideas for work in this area.

An initial training session for project co-ordinators, lead by Mike Boulton and Sonia Sharp, considered why it is important to look at the playground and some of the difficulties of distinguishing between bullying or aggressive behaviour and normal rough-and-tumble play. The methodological difficulties of this intervention were explained and the participants discussed various strategies and suggested ways in which they would be implemented and improvements they felt could be made to them. This was followed up by training lunchtime supervisors at certain schools. The lunchtime-supervisor training comprised two morning meetings lead by Sonia Sharp and Mike Boulton, during which supervisors were provided with basic information about bullying and some strategies for prevention and management of difficult behaviour, including bullying. In two schools, additional support was provided by Gill Fell, from the Society for a Less Violent Environment (SALVE). She worked with supervisors within their schools to identify specific problem areas and to develop possible solutions.

Redesigning the playground environment

For schools with uninteresting outside areas, a radical possibility is to redesign and improve the playground environment. An all-day session on the playground environment was led for interested schools by Lyndal Sheat. This work was extended by means of a grant from the Calouste Gulbenkian Foundation to support work on playground design, mentioned earlier in Chapter One and described further in Chapter Seven.

Choices of optional interventions

Choices of optional interventions were made by May 1991, and a great deal of the relevant Inset training and provision of resources was done in June/July 1991. All of the interventions, with the exception of bully courts, were tried out in at least two schools. Some schools wanted to include the interventions as part of their whole-school approach to tackle bullying so that they had a cohesive drive against the problem. Others supplemented the interventions with materials they themselves developed or discovered. Details of which options were chosen, by school, are given in Table 2.1.

Reasons for choices

There were some frequent reasons for schools selecting certain interventions. These were:

- interventions based on important issues within the school (mainly the playground intervention, but also use of *The Heartstone Odyssey* where tackling racism was considered a priority);
- regarding drama as an effective way of tackling issues such as bullying (use of Neti Neti Theatre materials);
- interventions considered helpful in widening staff experiences and providing training skills which staff did not already possess (assertiveness training for victims and the Pikas method);
- schools were already tackling an intervention in some way and felt the project would add a useful extension to their initiative (for example, two schools had already raised funds to work on improving the playground).

Less frequent reasons included: interest and motivation of staff towards specific interventions; relevance for pupils; the educational value of the interventions; feeling in control of the timing; feeling a need to respond to survey results; it would be applicable throughout the school; it would provide good material for tutorial time; it was viewed as positive; it would enhance the aims of the school; it could be immediately put into action; and it would be an effective response to an incident.

Frequent reasons for not choosing an intervention were:

- feeling they were inappropriate for their age group;
- being unclear about what an intervention would involve;
- feeling an intervention would take too much time;
- being uncertain how effective an intervention would be.

Less frequent reasons included: staff felt they could not undertake everything; no staff interest; not a whole-school approach; not appropriate for existing structure; already using similar materials.

The schools during the Sheffield Project

Sheffield schools had undergone a major review during 1991/92, with the abolition of the middle school system. The financial situation within the LEA also led to rationalisation in most schools and many lost staff in the spring or summer term 1992. This had an obvious effect on staff morale. Within the project, three schools changed from being middle schools to junior schools; and three junior schools were amalgamated with adjacent infant schools (see Table 2.1). Related to this, five project schools had a change of headteacher during the process of the project (see Table 2.1). In four of these schools, the headteacher was the original motivating force for involvement in the project. Fortunately, the new headteachers were generally supportive of the project continuing, although this meant a shift in priorities and a reduction in momentum within the schools. Despite professional uncertainty about the future, most schools still made the bullying project a priority. These changes did, however, delay the progress of the project.

Factual data about each school was compiled to build an individual school profile. This not only included information about the structure of the school (size, percentage of children receiving free school meals, etc.) but also details relating to the degree of involvement invested in the project by the school such as number of meetings (working party, parents, staff, governors, lunchtime supervisors, etc.) devoted to the project and amount of curriculum time/assembly time spent working with pupils.

Managing the project

There were three important issues which affected the way in which the project was shaped and managed:

- the extent to which we could standardise interventions across the schools;
- the extent to which we should intervene in the process of change;
- the extent to which we could monitor the actual process of change.

Standardising interventions

From a research perspective, we wished to be able to identify clearly the mechanisms for change within the school. However, our understanding of schools as organisations made us realise that there was no way that the team could have so controlled events as to produce standard interventions in all the schools. All schools were coping with staff changes, the impact of resource reduction from current educational funding policies, varying school numbers, school mergers, meeting the national curriculum demands and the demands of the new assessment procedures. They had differing mixes of pupils, in terms of ethnic origins, mother tongue languages and social class.

Our solution to the problem was to provide a common framework for the interventions, in terms of training procedures and materials. All schools, then, began with a common baseline upon which they imposed their own interpretation and adapted the intervention to fit the needs of their own institution. This approach presented advantages and disadvantages. The obvious difficulty for the research team was accommodating the variety of interventions which emerged and the disparity of approaches; our lack of control over whether or not the interventions were introduced meant that our project design was more evolutionary than prescribed. What we were able to discern was common patterns of approach which, regardless of how each intervention was manipulated by individual schools, remained constant across the schools as a whole. From the adaptations made by schools, we were able to understand possible flaws in the interventions themselves and how they could be overcome. Finally, and most importantly for an applied research project, we were able to define how schools could tackle bullying in a way which is realistic, practical and workable within today's education system.

Intervening in the process of change

A dilemma which faced us from the outset of the project was the extent to which we should intervene. The key principle which defined the structure of the project, both for us and for the funding body (the DFE), was that the outcomes of the project should be replicable by other schools throughout the country. Other schools would not have access to an energetic research team, keen to see the project succeed. A decision was therefore taken that support by the project team would be minimised and would be based upon requests from the schools. In the initial orientation meeting, it was made clear to schools that the level of support offered by the project team would be defined by the schools themselves. The project team could offer training, information and advice but would only do so if asked. In this way, the project was similar to the usual support services available to schools via educational psychology services, behaviour support services and so on.

This format for support was helpful and clear for both schools and the project team most of the time. Problems arose when there was a communication difficulty within the school such as following a change in project co-ordinator, and this information was not passed on directly or when one person in the school knew that support was available but had not informed other colleagues. For the project team, it was hard to resist more overt direction in inactive schools or schools which were introducing approaches which were at odds with the philosophy of the project. In fact, some more direct action was taken on whole-school policy development after the first year (see Chapter Three).

It was also important to document the possible effect of 'being a project school'. Although no deliberate attempts were made to encourage special relationships between the schools, networking inevitably occurred when representatives from different schools met at training events and meetings. The effects of this were probably more beneficial for 'late starters' than for those schools who were prompt in initiating their anti-bullying strategies. There was evidence of some sharing of ideas and materials between schools.

Monitoring the actual process of change

In trying to capture as full an understanding as possible of the processes at work within the schools we wanted our monitoring procedures to be as extensive as was practicably possible, given available resources. On the other hand, we recognised that in a long-term project, over-intrusive monitoring would probably not be sustainable by the schools and also might itself have an effect on behaviour. A summary of all the monitoring procedures we used is given in Table 2.2.

Each half-term, the project co-ordinator was interviewed to keep track of developments within each school. Teachers who were involved in implementing interventions were also interviewed during each term when the intervention was applied.

Quantitative and qualitative data were collected via staff and pupil interviews as well as a parent questionnaire, all of which helped to explain why and how any change occurred. One-third of teaching staff were interviewed in all secondary schools, and two-thirds in all primary schools. In six schools (four primary and two secondary), parents were given questionnaires. These schools were selected to give a range of socio-economic background, ethnic mix, size of school and degree of involvement in the project. In two of the primary schools, a third of pupils in Years Four, Five and Six were interviewed.

Each of the interventions had its own monitoring procedure. These involved a set of specifically designed pupil questionnaires and/or interviews intended to identify whether or not the interventions were perceived to be appropriate; whether or not they led to any perceived change in behaviour and/or attitude (both personally and in peers). Staff were also interviewed to discover how they felt about the intervention, how they had implemented the intervention and whether or not they felt any change in pupil behaviour or attitude had resulted from its implementation.

In two-thirds of the schools, pupils in certain year groups were involved in half-termly lunchtime monitoring. During these periods, each pupil in the class completed a short questionnaire on return from lunchtime which asked if they had been bullied that day. These helped to identify changes over time in rates of bullying, seasonal variations in bullying behaviour and which children in particular were being persistently bullied. This information can be related to action within the schools at specific points in time.

Our major source of outcome effectiveness was the second survey of levels of bullying in all the project schools. This took place in November/December 1992, exactly two years after the first survey. A comparison between the two surveys showed what changes had taken place; these analyses are described later.

The second survey

In all, twenty-seven schools participated in the second survey; the original twenty-four project schools (one primary school, P17, was used as a comparison school since the school did not participate in the intervention programme), and three comparison secondary schools. For the project schools (and also comparison school PC1) this survey took place between late November and December 1993, two years after the first survey (one school, P5, could not complete their questionnaires until the first week of the spring term; but pupils were specifically asked to base their answers on their experiences during the autumn term). For the three comparison secondary schools, the surveys were done in March 1990/1992 in SC1, in May 1990/1992 in SC2 and in March 1991/1993 in SC3. Thus, in all cases, time-of-year effects were constant between the two surveys. Results for particular schools could be compared before, and after, the monitored interventions.

The comparisons we planned were for whole schools. In this sort of research, it is not feasible to look for changes in particular pupils; first, they get older (and are bullied less frequently, see Chapter One), and second, they leave the school! Instead, we planned to compare each whole school at two time points, rather as Olweus (1991) had compared children of equivalent ages at his two time points. However, a direct comparison of whole-school rates of bullying at the two time points was often complicated by the

TABLE 2.2 SUMMARY OF MONITORING PROCEDURES

Type of monitoring	Method of data collection	Participants	Timing	To identify
Baseline survey	Questionnaire	All pupils over 7 years old in all schools	November/ December 1990	Nature/extent of bullying behaviour
School developments monitoring	Interview	Project co-ordinator	Half-termly throughout project	Details of all school-based initiatives
School gradings	Internal meeting	Project team	Spring term 1993	Scoring of policy develop-ment process
Whole-school policy monitoring	Interview	⅓ secondary staff; ⅔ primary staff in most schools	Term following completion of draft policy	Degree of staff involvement; perceived effectiveness of policy; process of policy development
Parental involvement monitoring	Questionnaire	All parents in 4 primary schools and 2 second-ary schools	Spring term 1993	Awareness of project; degree of involvement
Pupil involvement monitoring	Interview	⅓ of pupils in Years 4, 5, and 6 in two primary schools	Spring term 1993	Involvement in project; awareness and perceived effectiveness of anti-bullying policy
Intervention monitoring	Interview and questionnaire	Pupils and staff who have experienced the intervention	During the term in which the intervention is used	Attitude towards intervention; perceived success in reducing bullying
Interim lunchtime monitoring	Questionnaire	All pupils in Years 5 and 8 in Sept.1991 in ⅔ of schools	Every lunchtime during fourth week of each half-term through-out 1991–92	Extent/location of bullying behaviour during lunchtime
Follow-up survey	Questionnaire	All pupils over 7 years old in all schools	November/ December 1992	Nature/extent of bullying behaviour

organisational changes referred to earlier. For a middle school changing to a junior school, Year Sevens transferred to secondary school a year earlier than previously. In addition, some amalgamations and catchment area changes resulted in changes in the number of classes in a year group. These changes in themselves could affect time comparisons, since rates of being bullied vary appreciably with age. To ensure comparability between both surveys, it was necessary to have equivalent numbers of classes and hence, approximately, pupils in each year group, at the two survey points.

In order to achieve this, certain class and year groups who did the survey were omitted from our calculations; in primary and junior schools these tended to be Year Sevens from our first survey and Year Three/Fours from our second survey; in secondary schools these tended to be Year Twelve/Thirteens from our first survey and Year Sevens from our second survey. Based on these adjusted figures, there were 2,212 pupils in the sixteen project primary schools and 4,256 pupils in the seven project secondary schools. The four comparison schools consisted of one primary (99 pupils) and three secondary schools (1,742 pupils). The total number of pupils was thus 8,309, ranging in age from 8 to 16 years.

The questionnaires were administered in the same way as they had been for the first survey (see Chapter One). Teachers other than the pupils' usual teacher supervised the completion of questionnaires. Confidentiality was stressed. The questionnaires differed slightly from those used in the first survey by the inclusion of two 'extra' questions asking whether the school had taken any 'action' to stop bullying and whether there had been a perceived 'change' in bullying:

Q Do you think your school has done much to try and stop bullying over the last year or so?

A Yes, a lot (+2); yes, a bit (+1); no change (0); no, not much (-1); no, nothing at all (-2).

Q Do you think that bullying in your school has generally got better or worse over the last year or so?

A A lot better (+2); a bit better (+1); no change (0); a bit worse (-1); a lot worse (-2).

These two additional questions were not asked of children in the lowest year group in each school, since they would not have been in the school for more than two months.

The headteachers of each school were again asked to fill in a school information questionnaire detailing the size of the school, average class size, location, ethnic and socio-economic mix. This was particularly relevant where schools had undergone reorganisation.

Following the analysis of results, each school received a second portfolio comparing the incidence of being bullied and bullying others with the first survey to establish whether interventions had had an effect upon the overall levels of bullying. To ensure that the comparison was accurate, those schools that had undergone reorganisation were given two sets of figures: first illustrating the change in bully/victim levels on a whole-school basis and second on a comparability basis with necessary class or year groups removed.

Interim monitoring

Although the survey provided the main source of data for the project a number of additional monitoring procedures were also employed, as shown in Table 2.2. Pupil, staff and parent questionnaires and/or interviews, usually related to specific interventions, are discussed in other chapters of this book. Additional general evidence of the effects of interventions was provided via the interim monitoring procedures. These were introduced initially to identify changes in behaviour relating to the playground interventions. However, it was soon apparent that they would be helpful as a general indicator of change and consequently all schools were encouraged to implement them.

Key year groups were identified in both primary and secondary phases; these were groups which would be present in the schools for the duration of the project, allowing us to follow up individual pupils over the two-year period. In the primary schools, pupils in Year Five took part; in the secondary schools, pupils in Years Eight and Nine were included. For five consecutive days, in the fourth week after the half term-break, these pupils completed a short questionnaire on their return to school after lunch. The questionnaire simply asked 'Have these things happened to you today?' This was followed by a list of eight bullying behaviours: racist name-calling; name-calling for another reason; direct physical bullying; damage to possessions; threat or extortion; social exclusion; rumour spreading; and 'being bullied in another way'. There were three response options available: it had not happened at all; it had happened a bit; or it had happened a lot. The data enabled us to identify exactly which pupils were being regularly bullied by their peers over time and to highlight any patterns of change.

This kind of monitoring was fairly intrusive from the schools' point of view and a few schools failed to sustain it over time. (Interestingly, some schools found that they were able to use the results very constructively and voluntarily decided to continue with the monitoring procedures themselves after the end of the project.) As only eighteen of the schools completed the monitoring, it was not practical to include the data arising from it into the general output measures. This analysis therefore remained separate from and complementary to the main data analyses.

Analysis of results

In looking at the changes in the schools over the two-year period, we examined three main aspects of our data.

- What had the schools done? We devised a number of measures of each school's *input* into the project, in terms of time and effort invested in anti-bullying interventions.
- What had the schools achieved? We similarly devised a number of measures of each school's *output*, in terms of improvements or not in indicators of bullying.
- Why had schools varied? Here we looked at relations between input and output measures, that is whether schools which did more, achieved more; and at differences between primary and secondary schools, as well as particular factors affecting individual schools.

What had the schools done?

To estimate the effectiveness of the interventions, schools were scored on the time and effort put into both Whole-School Policy Development and Optional Interventions.

Scoring of Whole-School Policy Development

The process of policy development was divided into four areas: consultation; content; communication; and implementation. The time spent on it was also assessed. These areas approximately matched the whole-school policy process in action. A grading system was devised to provide a consistent scheme for comparing schools and for relating statistically the process they underwent with changes in levels of bullying and other related behaviours. The system recorded not only whether or not schools had achieved particular aspects of the development process, but also the degree of effort invested in doing so. If information about the schools' activities relating to whole-school policy development was present in policy but was omitted in the interview data, it was still scored. The grading was intended to be based on the fullest possible picture of the schools' activities during each monitoring programme. Each school could score up to sixty-five marks for the development process, plus an additional eight marks for the amount of time the policy had been completed (two points per term). The criteria for grading within each of the areas are set out in the Appendix, at the end of the book.

The research associate knew each of the schools well and was aware of the identity of each of the schools being graded. Two other graders remained unaware of the schools' identities during the grading, each school only being identified by a number. Trial moderation meetings were held several months before the final grading, which served to give practice to the graders and to finalise the scoring scheme. When the interventions had finished, final gradings were carried out. Each person scored the schools individually and then the scores were compared. Inter-marker reliability was established at 0.78.

All twenty-seven schools could be scored as having made some steps towards producing a Whole-School Policy (WSP) over the two years. Details of all the WSP scores for each school are given in Table 2.3. We first looked to see if the various aspects of WSP were associated – were schools which scored highly on one aspect likely to score highly on others? Overall, this was indeed the case. Most of the scores denoting the various aspects of WSP development were found to correlate well with each other across schools; average correlations were 0.35 in primary schools, 0.48 in secondary schools. Figure 2.1 shows all the significant or near-significant correlations; it appears from these that time spent was a more relevant factor (had higher correlations with communication and consultation) in secondary schools, probably because the secondary schools, being considerably larger, needed more time to consult and communicate effectively. Scores on all these aspects of WSP were added to give a WSP total score which could range from 0 to 73.

Staff involvement

As part of the evaluation of whole-school policy development, extensive interviews with teaching staff were carried out in each school. In primary schools, these interviews took place with two-thirds of staff, randomly selected; in secondary schools, one-third of teachers were included. The interviews sought information on the perceptions of the individual teachers of the development and implementation of the school's policy. Teachers were asked to describe exactly how they had been involved in the process of policy development. This information was then coded on a four-point scale. To score four points, a teacher had to be involved in extensive discussion and debate about the policy, taking an active role throughout the development process. Most project co-ordinators scored four points. To score three points, a teacher would have been involved in fairly extensive discussion at

(a) Primary

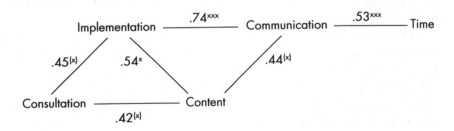

(b) Secondary

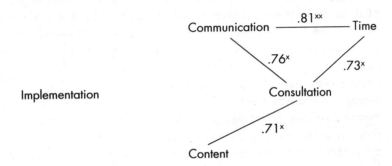

Figure 2.1 Correlations between aspects of whole-school policy for (a) primary (N = 17) and (b) secondary (N = 10) schools ((x) = p <.10; x = p <.05; xx = p <.01; xxx = p <.001)

the consultation stage but would not feel absolutely integral to the process. To score two points, the teacher would have been involved in only limited discussion at the consultation phase (perhaps one staff meeting) and would have commented on the policy document at draft stage. To score one, the member of staff would have known the policy was being developed and been offered the opportunity to comment on the draft document but not have taken up this opportunity. To score zero, the member of staff would have been unaware that a policy had been developed. The scores were summed and divided by the number of people interviewed in that school to derive a 'staff involvement' score for each school.

This measure only correlated weakly (not significantly) with the other measures of WSP (correlations with WSP Total were 0.32 for primary schools and 0.27 for secondary schools). Since it appeared to be measuring

TABLE 2.3 WHOLE-SCHOOL POLICY SCORES BY SCHOOL

School (primary)	WSP Consult.	WSP Content	WSP Commun.	WSP Implem.	WSP Time	WSP Total
P1	13	6	0	3	2	24
P2	8	3	0	2	2	15
P3	21	15	5	6	4	50
P4	19	11	1	1	2	34
P5	11	1	1	1	2	16
P6	13	8	0	1	2	24
P7	4	7	3	0	8	22
P8	19	1	0	0	2	22
P9	15	5	7	6	8	41
P10	23	15	0	3	2	43
P11	22	20	7	6	6	61
P12	6	3	1	2	6	18
P13	8	14	1	3	6	32
P14	14	4	0	0	8	26
P15	9	18	3	2	6	38
P16	14	9	3	2	8	36
Project mean	13.7	8.8	2.0	2.4	4.6	31.4
PC1	5	4	2	1	2	14
Total mean	13.2	8.5	2.0	2.3	4.5	30.4

School (secondary)	WSP Consult.	WSP Content	WSP Commun.	WSP Implem.	WSP Time	WSP Total
S1	6	9	0	2	4	21
S2	21	13	5	3	8	50
S3	15	20	0	3	2	40
S4	21	16	6	6	8	57
S5	18	8	7	3	6	42
S6	3	5	0	4	2	14
S7	7	9	1	4	2	23
Project mean	13.0	11.4	2.7	3.6	4.6	35.5
SC1	8	7	3	4	4	26
SC2	3	0	2	1	4	10
SC3	16	0	5	5	4	30
Total mean	11.8	8.7	2.9	3.5	4.4	31.3

TABLE 2.4 OPTIONS SCORES BY SCHOOL

School (primary)	Curriculum	Direct B/V	Play-ground	Options total
P1	0	0	7	7
P2	1	0	0	1
P3	4	0	19	23
P4	10	0	3	13
P5	0	0	5	5
P6	3	0	10	13
P7	4	2	16	22
P8	0	4	2	6
P9	8	4	10	22
P10	12	2	2	16
P11	11	8	11	30
P12	8	3	3	14
P13	0	0	4	4
P14	9	0	6	15
P15	0	0	22	22
P16	0	4	9	13
Project mean	4.4	1.7	8.1	14.1
PC1	0	0	0	0
Total mean	4.1	1.6	7.6	13.3

School (secondary)	Curriculum	Direct B/V	Play-ground	Options total
S1	8	1	0	9
S2	0	0	10	10
S3	16	12	3	31
S4	14	8	0	22
S5	6	8	8	22
S6	0	6	0	6
S7	6	0	0	6
Project mean	7.1	5.0	3.0	15.1
SC1	0	0	0	0
SC2	0	0	0	0
SC3	0	0	0	0
Total mean	5.0	3.5	2.1	10.6

something rather separate, it was not added to WSP total but analysed separately.

Scoring of Optional Interventions

For scoring, the options were grouped under three general headings: *curriculum*, *direct work with pupils* and *playground*. *Curriculum* reflected work done in the classroom through reading books (*Heartstone Odyssey*), watching videos, drama workshops (Neti Neti and Armadillo Theatre Companies) and Quality Circles. Schools received a score for *playground* interventions if they had taken some action to enhance the environment of the schoolyard or if lunchtime supervisors had participated in training sessions held by members of the research team. *Direct work with pupils* involved in bullying behaviour included assertiveness training for bullied pupils and the Pikas Method of Shared Concern, and peer couselling.

Schools were graded on a scale of A to E according to the amount of effort they put into the implementation of each intervention, during each of the four intervention terms.

A Very thoroughly; a lot of time and effort has gone into this. It has been given a high priority; difficult to see how we could reasonably have done more. (Score four)
B Quite thoroughly; considerable time and effort has gone into this. It has been given some priority; however more could certainly have been done. (Score three)
C Some time and effort has gone into this, but it has not been given a very high priority. We have had a go at it, but a lot more could have been done. (Score two)
D We were only able to put a very small amount of time and effort into this. It has had a low priority and probably does not represent a fair assessment of what might be achieved. (Score one)
E It was not possible to implement this intervention at all. (Score zero)

These grades were based upon assessments made by the schools themselves and then scrutinised and sometimes modified by the project team based on our own records and interviews. Inter-rater reliability averaged 0.67. Details of all the Option scores are given in Table 2.4. The Options Total is the sum of these, ranging from one to thirty-one (and zero in the comparison schools).

Total input scores

Scores for the WSP Total and Options Total inter-correlated highly (0.78 for primary schools, 0.67 for secondary schools). Thus, we felt justified in taking a Total Input measure, simply adding together the score for WSP Total and the Options Total.

What had the schools achieved?

Using the comparable, age-equivalent samples from the first and second surveys, we selected certain items or composite measures which could be taken as indicators of success in tackling bullying. These are described below.

Being Bullied Three items relating to perceived frequency of being bullied were included in this indicator:

- the likelihood of being bullied oneself during the term; here, we combined *all* the responses 'I haven't been bullied at school this term' in the questionnaire (seven items; two-point scale on each) and then calculated the mean number of responses as a percentage;
- the frequency of being bullied oneself during the term (one item, five-point scale);
- the number of children in the class who had been bullied (one item, seven-point scale).

Bullying Others Three corresponding measures of those pupils who had bullied others were examined:

- the likelihood of bullying others during the term; here, we combined *all* the responses 'I haven't taken part in bullying others at school this term' in the questionnaire (three items, two-point scale on each) and then calculated the mean number of responses as a percentage;
- the frequency of bullying others oneself during the term (one item, five-point scale);
- the number of children in the class who had bullied others (one item, seven-point scale).

Breaktime Experiences We also wished to know if there had been a change in the number of pupils who reported being alone at breaktime:

- frequency of being alone at playtime (one item, five-point scale).

Bystander Behaviour We were also interested in whether there had been a change in the 'attitudes' of pupils towards bullying:

- how likely were they to not join in bullying others (one item, five-point scale).

Perceived Role of Adults Encouraging children to tell an adult if they had experienced bullying was perceived as a key element in enabling staff to tackle the problem. We were therefore interested in identifying changes in:

- how often teachers were seen as stopping bullying (one item, five-point scale);
- how likely a bullied child was to tell anyone: teacher or someone at home (two items, two-point scale on each);
- how likely a bullied child was to tell a teacher (one item, two-point scale);
- what proportion of children who had taken part in bullying others had been talked to by a teacher about it (one item, two-point scale).

TABLE 2.5 OUTCOME MEASURES FOR EACH SCHOOL

(a) Primary schools

School (primary)	I haven't been bullied	Been bullied (freq.)	Number been bullied	I haven't bullied others	Bullied others (freq.)	Number bullied others	Alone at break time
P1	+5.0	−15.4	19.3	3.7	−13.2	9.3	−2.6
P2	+9.5	−15.0	3.2	12.2	−15.1	−9.6	3.1
P3	+34.9	−36.0	−10.4	50.6	−63.5	−14.0	29.3
P4	+6.6	−12.0	5.7	7.3	−8.1	−4.9	9.4
P5	+81.4	−54.2	−29.7	28.2	−43.8	−41.4	19.4
P6	+16.8	−17.9	−23.8	16.8	−41.8	−29.3	3.5
P7	−5.4	17.0	−8.3	−7.0	16.0	4.0	4.9
P8	+9.4	−24.7	1.3	−14.6	−5.6	2.4	1.9
P9	+28.8	−23.2	4.9	−13.2	30.8	5.8	11.6
P10	−6.1	−1.0	32.2	−7.8	22.5	27.8	4.4
P11	+13.8	−8.4	−8.9	−3.5	12.2	−7.2	−4.6
P12	−7.3	2.8	7.3	2.5	−20.7	5.6	−2.7
P13	+23.2	−29.4	−5.2	46.1	−37.2	−15.4	14.5
P14	−1.9	19.0	−2.3	−12.2	31.0	−0.9	−1.2
P15	+22.2	−13.5	11.4	9.0	−32.7	−5.1	8.4
P16	+74.9	−14.9	−3.8	0.3	−17.2	16.9	7.1
Project mean	17.39	−14.18	−0.44	7.40	−11.65	−3.50	6.65
PC1	−24.3	11.5	44.2	−34.2	44.8	55.5	−4.3
Total mean	14.94	−12.67	2.18	4.95	−8.33	−0.03	6.00

TABLE 2.5 cont.

School (primary)	Not join in bullying	Teacher stops bullying	Tell someone	Tell teacher	Someone talked to you	School taken action	School bullying changed
P1	6.7	−7.3	28.1	49.7	14.9	0.54	0.50
P2	−5.3	1.9	5.0	4.9	−39.4	0.76	0.17
P3	18.9	30.0	−1.9	15.3	−1.6	1.73	1.18
P4	12.9	9.6	−2.0	8.4	4.3	1.03	0.49
P5	5.3	−45.6	6.4	−13.3	−2.7	1.21	0.85
P6	13.8	5.1	−11.5	−5.1	−22.9	1.16	0.91
P7	−10.8	4.3	−9.3	−2.0	−14.1	1.01	0.47
P8	−6.6	−10.1	−2.4	−11.6	10.5	1.21	0.88
P9	−4.9	−13.1	1.7	10.5	41.4	0.90	0.73
P10	−4.2	13.0	22.2	54.8	−14.3	1.40	0.97
P11	−10.6	−22.7	−2.5	−16.5	−12.3	1.45	1.04
P12	9.9	23.3	16.6	65.5	20.8	1.10	0.63
P13	14.9	1.9	14.0	0.3	−1.2	1.16	0.44
P14	−6.7	−14.2	−11.7	−18.9	29.6	1.04	0.41
P15	18.1	32.4	−6.9	−23.4	−3.2	1.47	0.94
P16	−3.3	−17.8	−18.8	−15.0	68.7	1.59	0.84
Project mean	3.01	−0.58	1.69	6.48	4.91	1.17	0.72
PC1	−13.3	−8.3	15.9	11.8	30.2	0.96	0.38
Total mean	2.05	−1.04	2.52	6.79	6.39	1.16	0.70

(cont. on p. 46)

Perceived Action and Change Finally, we examined pupils' perceptions of what had happened in their school generally over the last year or so, using the extra questions described above from the second survey only:

- whether the school had done much to try and stop bullying (one item, five-point scale);
- whether bullying in school had generally got better or worse (one item, five-point scale).

Differences between the first and second surveys for the output indicators

We calculated change scores for the above variables, comparing first and second surveys. For the first twelve of these output measures, we calculated percentage change over baseline. The last two measures had no prior baseline,

TABLE 2.5 cont.

(b) Secondary schools

School (secondary)	I haven't been bullied	Been bullied (freq.)	Number been bullied	I haven't bullied others	Bullied others (freq.)	Number bullied others	Alone at break time
S1	+3.7	−7.8	−4.0	3.2	12.8	3.0	2.0
S2	−35.1	11.1	8.0	−3.2	−21.2	−0.8	−2.4
S3	+3.8	−7.7	−5.7	3.3	−10.0	−1.0	−0.3
S4	−3.6	4.4	15.5	−3.2	−2.6	−0.9	−2.0
S5	+4.9	−20.5	7.9	−0.6	−7.4	−4.3	1.7
S6	+5.7	−22.7	−13.7	12.0	−37.2	−18.4	1.1
S7	+4.06	−4.4	−2.1	2.1	−16.7	3.1	0
Project mean	−2.36	−6.80	0.84	1.94	−11.76	−2.76	0.14
SC1	+8.7	−13.4	N/A	23.0	− 38.0	N/A	−2.0
SC2	−10.4	13.7	N/A	−1.4	10.4	N/A	−0.9
SC3	+8.0	−19.6	−10.0	3.5	−21.2	−2.6	−1.9
Total mean	−1.02	−6.69	−0.41	3.87	−13.11	−2.19	−0.47

School (secondary)	Not join in bullying	Teacher stops bullying	Tell someone	Tell teacher	Someone talked to you	School taken action	School bullying changed
S1	−1.3	7.4	0.3	−6.3	−11.3	1.02	1.82
S2	22.0	−3.0	19.4	13.9	23.0	1.12	0.85
S3	0.6	4.5	18.5	25.9	37.9	0.58	0.53
S4	7.2	5.2	15.5	79.1	12.9	1.13	0.81
S5	0	3.5	14.0	60.8	99.2	1.39	0.85
S6	20.8	−17.6	10.0	31.4	43.9	0.62	0.63
S7	13.9	−0.8	4.5	22.5	63.7	0.89	0.64
Project mean	9.03	−0.11	11.74	32.47	38.47	0.96	0.88
SC1	8.2	−3.3	0.1	29.9	−1?.2	0.03	−0.09
SC2	−10.8	−3.7	1.7	−1.6	4.1	0.31	0.24
SC3	1.8	0	−1.1	−1.4	59.3	1.00	0.92
Total mean	6.24	−0.78	8.29	25.42	32.05	0.81	0.72

so we report the mean scores at the second survey, which ranged from –2 to +2 (see above). Table 2.5 shows the scores on these fourteen indicators, for each school.

Table 2.6 shows the mean raw scores on the same variables, at T1 (first survey) and T2 (second survey), for our project sample (N = 23), and our total school sample including comparison schools) (N = 27). This table also shows the t-value and probability level for the percentage difference scores between T1 and T2 on one-sample t-tests. These significance tests take schools as a unit; a lack of significance implies that not all schools improved on this measure, but would not deny the significance of change in any individual school (which would be based on number of pupils).

Being Bullied Project schools showed a significant increase in pupils who had not been bullied, and a significant decrease in the frequency with which pupils were bullied. This change is appreciable in the project primary schools, averaging around 15 per cent, and ranging up to 80 per cent (Table 2.5a). In the secondary schools however there was not much change (Table 2.5b); although five of the seven project secondary schools showed an increase in pupils who had not been bullied, the average becomes a decrease due to a large decrease in one school, S2. There was no significant change in the number of classmates who were reported to be bullied.

Bullying Others Most schools showed positive changes on all three indicators – an increase in pupils who had not bullied others, and a decrease in the frequency of bullying others and in the number of classmates thought to bully others. Only the result for frequency of bullying others was significant across schools, however; here, the change averaged about 12 per cent for both primary and secondary schools.

Breaktime Experiences Surprisingly, in most schools (especially primary) more pupils reported spending breaktime alone at the second survey. (This may reflect the experiences of reorganisation which many schools went through, see Table 2.1.)

Bystander Behaviour Project schools showed a significant increase in pupils reporting that they wouldn't join in bullying others at the second survey. This was more marked in secondary schools, where the increase averaged 9 per cent.

Perceived Role of Adults There were no significant changes in perceptions of teachers stopping bullying. However, project schools showed increases in pupils telling someone, and especially teachers, if they were being bullied, and in reporting that someone had talked to them if they had bullied anyone. These increases were modest in primary schools, but very substantial, around 30 per cent, in secondary schools (Table 2.5a,b).

Perceived Action and Change Scores for Perceived Action and Change could

TABLE 2.6 MEAN SCORES FOR OUTCOME MEASURES AT THE TWO SURVEY POINTS, AND SIGNIFICANCE LEVELS

Input measures	Project schools N = 23				Whole sample N = 27			
	Mean scores				Mean scores			
	T1	T2	t-value	prob.	T1	T2	t-value	prob.
I haven't been bullied	50.6	53.9	2.12	0.05	51.2	53.8	1.88	0.10
Been bullied (freq.)	0.9	0.7	3.40	0.01	0.8	0.7	3.21	0.01
Number been bullied	3.9	3.8	0.02	NS	3.8	3.8	0.42	NS
I haven't bullied others	65.9	68.3	1.65	NS	65.8	67.6	1.34	NS
Bullied others (freq.)	0.5	0.4	2.26	0.05	0.5	0.4	2.00	0.10
Number bullied others	3.5	3.4	1.09	NS	3.5	3.4	0.25	NS
Alone at breaktime	3.1	3.2	2.76	0.05	3.1	3.3	2.40	0.05
Not join in bullying	1.9	2.0	2.20	0.05	1.9	1.9	1.74	0.10
Teacher stops bullying	1.5	1.5	0.12	NS	1.5	1.4	0.30	NS
Telling someone	69.3	72.3	1.84	0.10	68.1	71.1	2.07	0.05
Telling teachers	47.0	50.5	2.32	0.05	45.9	49.6	2.55	0.05
Someone talked to you	32.8	35.4	2.22	0.05	31.8	34.7	2.58	0.05
School action	N/A	1.1	17.06	0.001	N/A	1.0	13.99	0.001
School change	N/A	0.8	11.04	0.001	N/A	0.7	9.97	0.001

vary from – 2 to +2. In fact all the mean scores for each school were positive (above midpoint). In the project schools the Action scores ranged from 0.54 to 1.59, and the Change scores from 0.17 to 1.82. In all but two schools, however, Change scores were lower than Action scores.

Why had schools varied?

Project schools and comparison schools

We only had one primary comparison school, PC1. It had done less whole-school policy work than any project school (Table 2.3). It had relatively low Perceived Action, and the lowest Perceived Change score, from pupils. It also had the worst or near-worst scores on all the change measures of being bullied and bullying others (Table 2.5a). Thus, on these main measures, it appears to have done less than most project schools, was perceived to have done less by pupils, and has had considerably less impact on bullying; in fact, bullying had generally got worse in this school (though there was an increase in the likelihood of bullied pupils telling someone, or bullied pupils being spoken to). In general this supports the implication that the results in the project schools are due to the interventions.

In the secondary schools the picture is more complicated. Two schools, SC1 and SC3, had done some work on Whole-School Policy, within the range of project schools (Table 2.3). SC3 had high scores on Action and Change too, though surprisingly, SC1 had very low values. These schools had as good or better results as project schools on indicators of being bullied and bullying others, and in addition SC1 showed many more bullied pupils telling teachers, while SC3 had many more bullying pupils being talked to. In most respects, therefore, these schools were like project schools in terms of input and output. School SC2 was more like a traditional control school, with the least work on Whole-School Policy (Table 2.3), and low Action and Change scores. It also had amongst the worst results on the indicators for being bullied and bullying others. As with the results for school PC1, this supports the general finding relating intervention to positive outcomes.

Relationships between Input and Output measures

To what extent does the amount of effort put in by a school (Input) predict results obtained (Output)? To examine this we calculated a correlation matrix between Input and Output measures. To limit the number of correlations, we used for Input measures (1) Input Total (the sum of Whole-School Policy Total plus Option Total), (2) Staff Involvement and (3)

(a) Primary schools

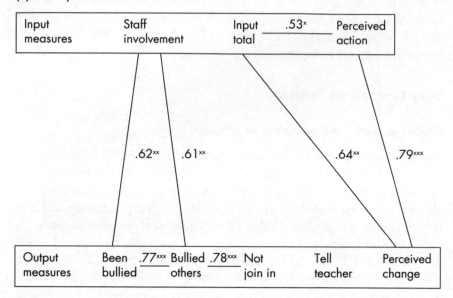

(b) Secondary schools

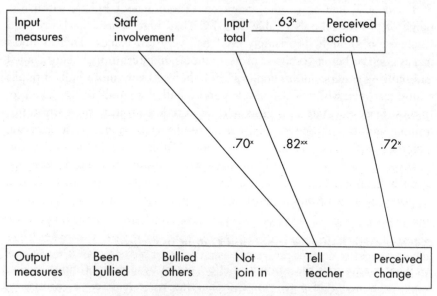

Figure 2.2 Correlations between aspects of input and changes in bullying indicators for (a) primary (N = 17) and (b) secondary (N = 10) schools (x = p <.05; xx = p <.01; xxx = p <.001)

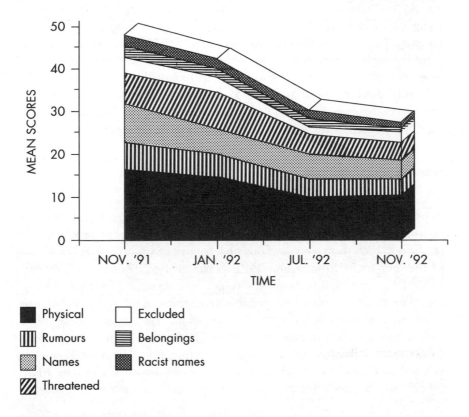

Figure 2.3 Changes in seven types of bullying behaviour, over four terms, from playground monitoring

Perceived Action. We used as Output measures (1) Been Bullied, (2) Bullied Others, (3) Not Join In (bullying), (4) Tell Teacher (if you are bullied) and (5) Perceived Change.

Figure 2.2a shows the significant correlations (those above r = 0.48) for the primary schools. The Input Total relates significantly to Perceived Action, and to Perceived Change. Thus, schools which did more judged by our ratings, also did more judged on pupil ratings, and were thought by pupils to show more improvement in bullying generally. However, this did not predict to the other Output measures, even though three of these (Been Bullied, Bullied Others and Not Join In) were quite highly related. However the other Input measure of Staff Involvement did correlate significantly with the Been Bullied and Bullied Others changes.

Figure 2.2b shows the significant correlations (those above r = 0.63) for the secondary schools. The Input Total relates significantly to Perceived Action, but not to Perceived Change (the correlation is only 0.22). Thus, schools which did more judged by our ratings, also did more judged on pupil ratings; but only the latter predicted to whether pupils thought there was improvement in bullying generally. These did not predict to the Output measures of Been Bullied, Bullied Others and Not Join In (which were not related significantly, correlations of around 0.5); however, the Input Total did relate strongly to increases in pupils Telling Teacher if they had been bullied. The Staff Involvement measure also predicted this quite strongly.

Interim monitoring

The analysis of results from the playground monitoring – the short questionnaires given daily for a week, each half-term, to certain year groups – provided another source of information on change. Here, the results for the ten days in each term were accumulated, to give composite scores over each of the four terms from winter 1991 to winter 1992. Analyses of variance (ANOVAs) were used to examine changes over time for each type of bullying. The results indicated appreciable reductions in all types of bullying. These were statistically significant for four of the eight, namely direct physical violence ($p < .01$); threats or extortion ($p < .001$); being teased repeatedly ($p < .0014$); and having nasty rumours spread ($p < .011$). A graphical portrayal is given in Figure 2.3. Mean figures for a large subset of this data (those schools which pursued playground interventions) are given in Table 6.1 (Chapter Six).

An average reduction in bullying behaviour of 46 per cent occurred between the first monitoring period in November 1991 and the final period in November 1992; only about 15 per cent of this reduction will be due to age (see Chapter One). This data also allows us to pinpoint when the change occurred. For all forms of bullying, the biggest reductions occurred between the latter part of the spring term and the first half of the summer term. The consistency of this across schools which were active in the project suggests that it is most probably the interventions being implemented which were having an effect. The least active school which took part in the monitoring, by contrast, experienced an increase of 8 per cent in reported bullying at this time. Furthermore, this period coincides with the most active period in whole-school policy development in the schools and this is discussed in Chapter Three.

Summary of findings

The results strongly suggest that the interventions had a positive impact, though the nature of the impact varied between primary and secondary schools. In general, schools improved on most measures of bullying – relating to reports of being bullied, bullying others, not joining in, telling someone if you were bullied, having someone talk to you if you bullied others. However, the main impact on the likelihood and frequency of being bullied was in primary schools, with some schools getting quite substantial reductions. These effects were smaller in secondary schools, which did however register substantial increases in the proportion of bullied pupils who would seek help, for example by telling a teacher.

Are these changes due to the interventions? Before accepting this possibility, we should consider another possible explanation – that the situation would have got better anyway. Perhaps children are better behaved in 1992 than 1990! This may seem unlikely; but the analytic design used here (as in the similar design used by Olweus, 1991) is potentially susceptible to these 'historical' effects. If this latter explanation had any validity, however, we should expect improvements irrespective of what schools had done. This is contra-indicated by two kinds of data.

First, the changes are better in the project schools than in comparison schools which did not do much work on bullying (here, we count schools SC1 and SC3 as being more like project schools, in that they did quite a lot of work on bullying policies after they had received their first survey results). This suggests that the improvements in project schools are not just due to historical effects – indeed, if anything, PC1 and SC2 register the problem getting worse in schools which are doing little about the problem. Having only two comparison schools of this type obviously limits the extent to which we can generalise.

Second, the correlational analyses illustrated in Figure 2.2 show some significant Input–Output relationships; that is, those schools which made more effort with intervention achieved more reductions in bullying. It is worth noting that our own codings of school Input Total (based on teacher reports and our own records) correlate significantly – in both primary and secondary schools – with Perceived Action (the pupils' perception of how much the school had done). These are quite independent sources of information, and their agreement supports the validity of both measures.

In primary schools, *both* these Input measures also predict the amount of change generally perceived by pupils (Perceived Change); while in secondary schools, the Input Total measure predicts strongly increases in bullied pupils telling teachers (Tell Teacher), which, as we have seen (Table 2.5b), is where the main improvements in secondary schools are found.

As compared to the general measure of school bullying assessed by Perceived Change, the measures Been Bullied and Bullied Others are indicators of personal experiences of bullying, and of perceptions of bullying in one's class. These do not correlate so significantly with the Input measures, although they do both correlate with Staff Involvement in primary schools. That the other correlations are not significant is surprising, but there is one plausible explanation: that schools which have taken a lot of action against bullying may have brought about heightened awareness of what bullying is amongst their pupils and thus led more pupils to recognise that they were experiencing some form of bullying which they might previously have discounted.

How can we test this last hypothesis – that more active schools may 'dampen down' the apparent reductions in perceived bullying, by making pupils more aware of the phenomenon? We think we can support this argument. Specifically, our reasoning would be that:

- there are average decreases in personal reports of being bullied, and bullying others, probably as a result of the interventions (supported by our results);
- those schools which have taken a lot of action on bullying raised awareness about it in their pupils, such that the reported decreases in bullying are less than they would otherwise have been (a hypothesis);
- this would lessen the correlation between school input measures and these output measures (a deduction from our hypothesis, consistent with our results);
- these output measures (personal reports of bullying/being bullied) would then not show a strong correlation with the other output measure of 'telling a teacher if bullied', which is more objective in nature (supported by our results);
- the output measure of 'telling a teacher if bullied' would relate to school input measures (supported by our results, in secondary schools).

On this interpretation, the reductions in measures of being bullied (and perhaps of bullying others) in Table 2.5 are genuine. But they possibly under-represent change, due to increased sensitivity in pupils to what bullying is and can include; and perhaps even a greater willingness to report it in the questionnaire (as well as tell a teacher). This under-representation of change would be greater in schools which have done more, thus reducing these Input–Output correlations below significance level.

The suggestion that some of these survey results underestimate actual change would also be consistent with the finding that our other assessments produced generally larger indications of change. This is true of our playground monitoring (see above and Chapter Six) and our detailed interviews with selected pupils (see Chapter Nine). Both these produced reductions in measures of being bullied of the order of 40 or 50 per cent. These assessment methods have their own problems, as they are longitudinal, sampling the same children some time later, and are thus liable to be confounded by age (specifically, the general reduction in likelihood of being bullied, with age, see Chapter One, and Whitney and Smith, 1993). However, after allowing for an average reduction of 15 per cent for age effects (Whitney and Smith, 1993), this still leaves an estimated 'real' reduction of 25 or 35 per cent, appreciably larger than the survey average of around 15 per cent.

In summary, there is considerable evidence of success in the actions of schools against bullying, though this varies greatly between schools and takes a somewhat different form in primary and secondary schools. If primary schools put effort into policy development and anti-bullying work, this will be perceived by pupils. Pupils will soon perceive a change in general bullying, and self-report levels will fall especially when all staff are involved in the work. In secondary schools, staff involvement and general effort will first have an impact on the willingness of bullied pupils to seek help from a teacher. Also, school action will be noticed by pupils, and they will consider that general levels of bullying are falling.

The reductions in bullying we have found are not so substantial, on average, as those reported by Olweus (1991, 1993b). There could be several explanations for this, some of which are considered in Chapter Three. Equally, the reductions we found are more substantial than those reported by Roland (1993), or, provisionally, by Pepler, Craig, Zeigler and Charach (1993) in Canada. We will learn more about the possibilities in UK schools when the project directed by Graham Smith (1991) in Wolverhampton reports back. However, the Sheffield Project clearly replicates Olweus' (1991) evaluation of the Norwegian intervention campaign in one respect, and the most important respect: *schools can take effective action against bullying.* Now that this has clearly been shown, and a variety of resources are available to schools, the onus is on schools to use these appropriately. This does not remove responsibility from families to provide a caring upbringing for children; nor from the wider society to provide a safe environment in which children need not feel a need to be violent. Unless these conditions too exist, it is unlikely that schools can totally eliminate bullying behaviour. But they can have an effect. *Schools can reduce bullying.* In doing so, they are likely to bring about a general improvement in the climate of the school. And these are very worthwhile objectives.

T·H·R·E·E

the role of whole-school policies in tackling bullying behaviour in schools

SONIA SHARP
DAVID THOMPSON

Establishing a whole-school policy on bullying behaviour has been recommended as a core intervention by several writers on anti-bullying projects. Olweus (1991, 1993b) was concerned with changing school climate through development of a set of clear rules and active involvement by teachers and parents. Besag (1989) recognised the need to develop a 'school system' which would prevent and respond to bullying behaviour. In the pack prepared for Scottish schools by Johnstone, Munn and Edwards (1992) it states that 'the single most important thing a school can do to prevent bullying is have a clear policy to which staff, pupils and parents are committed'. In this chapter we discuss the ways in which whole-school policies are helpful in preventing and reducing bullying behaviour, focusing particularly upon the policy development process schools need to undertake to achieve such change. First, we examine some of the evidence which establishes the important role whole-school policies play in tackling bullying.

The case for whole-school policies

Whole-school behaviour policies and bullying

Bullying behaviour is a form of aggressive behaviour and as such any approach to it should dovetail with existing behaviour policies. In understanding how school policies can affect pupil behaviour, much can be learnt from research from the last fifteen years into behaviour and discipline.

In the early 1980s Galloway, Ball, Bloomfield and Seyd (1982), Tattum (1982) and Grunsell (1980) pointed out how easy it was for the general behaviour of staff and existing procedures to encourage anti-authority identities amongst young people, and indicated the type of across-school policies and procedures which would reduce this effect. Schostak (1982) came to very similar conclusions when considering the issue of absenteeism from school, identifying truancy as a pupil response to the poor general quality of experience of their school life. Specifically he noted poor relationships with staff, few chances to take initiatives and actively participate in school, and little personal autonomy in the activities which typically took place. Gilham (1984) advocated an organisational approach when dealing with disruption in school, and provided several useful examples of how changes in school practices could contribute to increased effectiveness of management strategies. Mortimore (1980), one of the co-authors of the 15,000 hours study, suggested having a common staff policy on pupil behaviour to encourage consistency, use of effective rewards across the school, and creating a pleasant working environment where pupils are encouraged to participate in school activities.

The work of these researchers and many others contributed to the understandings developed for schools by the Elton Report (DES, 1989), which again argued for a multiplicity of procedures involving pupils and staff at many levels, and for these to be clearly set out in a school policy to encourage good behaviour and discipline in schools. Establishing good behaviour and discipline, like effective responses to bullying, involves most members of the school community, needs clear expectations as to what is and is not acceptable, and needs everyone to understand the principles upon which the practices are based.

Current understanding of the nature of bullying

Looking at the problem in terms of the school as an organisational unity, we know that bullying behaviour is resistant to change, because it can last for years and is difficult to detect and suppress. We know that it is dependent on the behaviour of a large number of people for its continuation. The peer group may feel helpless to challenge the bullying or may perceive it as 'normal'; the bullied pupils acquiesce because they see no other option possible. Adults too may unwillingly accept the bullying as an unavoidable part of school life – uncertain if anything can be done about it, reassured by its relatively infrequent eruptions into the school life in an unambiguous

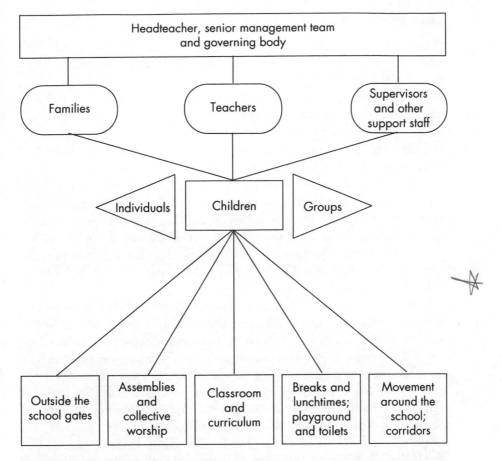

Figure 3.1 Levels of implementation of a whole-school anti-bullying policy

way, but acknowledging that it does exist and being quite concerned about its results in extreme cases. Clearly, if anything is going to change, the aim must be to influence the behaviour and attitudes of all these people. These attempts to change have to be expressed at a number of different levels – the general principles of what behaviour is acceptable in school, the specific guidelines to staff and pupils as to what actions to take when bullying behaviour is suspected, and focused programmes to support the bullied pupils and discourage the bullying pupils on an individual basis (see Figure 3.1). In other words, the school needs to have a whole-school anti-bullying policy where everyone in school has been involved in rehearsing the reasons for the change and the procedures by which it can be achieved.

Case studies of individual schools

Prior to the Sheffield Project, there had been a few studies of individual school initiatives which had been evaluated and shown to produce a reduction in incidents of bullying. One of these was a comprehensive school in Kirklees, where one of the research team had been involved with the local educational psychologist in helping the school monitor the effects of various interventions initiated by the senior management of the school. This particular case study had been described in a number of articles (Arora and Thompson, 1987; Arora, 1989; Foster, Arora and Thompson, 1990), and one of the main messages from the school staff was that a whole-school policy was essential if the school's actions were to be effective. This was because there were a number of ways in which bullying incidents needed to be approached, involving different members of staff and with implications for a number of existing management and pastoral procedures. In practice, the only way they could be co-ordinated was to have an explicit whole-school policy from the onset.

In East London, the Home Office funded an anti-bullying initiative in a secondary school in a high crime estate (Pitts, 1993). The aims of this project were to reduce violent victimisation by a process of organisational development. The central principle of this organisational change was based upon a move towards a more anti-bullying culture. Again, this was achieved through policy formulation based upon consultation and discussion amongst staff and pupils, the introduction of a consistently applied sytem of rewards and sanctions and overt concern about violent behaviour in all its forms. It was supported further by a community-wide initiative in Crime Prevention so that bullying behaviour was tackled on every level both inside and outside the school.

School-based research

There have been a number of recent studies which emphasise the establishment of a whole-school anti-bullying policy as an essential ingredient for successful intervention. The national campaign in Norway provided the first large-scale study of school interventions. As described in Chapter One, Olweus (1991, 1993b) monitored a sample of forty-two primary and junior high schools which had been involved this campaign. Although Olweus does not directly refer to the Norwegian intervention programme as comprising a 'whole-school policy' or a 'whole-school approach', some general features of the Norwegian schools' anti-bullying campaign could be seen to parallel policy development elsewhere. The intervention was explicitly multi-level (school, class and individual), and was aimed at actively involving the whole-school community, i.e. school staff, pupils and parents. The key principles of the intervention programme included providing a clear definition of acceptable and unacceptable behaviour in the minds of both pupils and staff and the implementation of non-hostile and non-physical sanctions should such unacceptable behaviour occur (Olweus, 1993b). He found that schools who implemented this kind of consistent, whole-school approach experienced marked reductions in levels of bullying behaviour and a general improvement in the 'social climate' of the school.

Roland (1993) also monitored the long-term effects of the Norwegian intervention campaign in a group of schools in Rogaland. He found that those schools which had established 'stable routines' for responding to bullying had more long-term and positive effects on levels of bullying. He emphasises the importance of an integrated approach to bullying and general behaviour management which provides a system for intervention.

In the UK, there have been two substantial projects investigating ways of tackling bullying in schools. The Sheffield Project is discussed fully in Chapter Two and will also be referred to in the remainder of this chapter. A similar project was carried out in Wolverhampton, funded by the Safer Cities Project (G. Smith, 1991). Using the same design as the Sheffield Project, schools were invited to select a range of interventions and were offered training and support in implementing these. Schools which concentrated on the development and implementation of a whole-school anti-bullying policy and which introduced other kinds of interventions as part of this policy were more successful in reducing levels of bullying within their school.

Another international project, this time based in Canada, investigated the effects of anti-bullying strategies in four schools. This small project (Pepler, Craig, Zeigler and Charach, 1993) used both quantitative and qualitative evaluation methods to identify the effectiveness of an intervention programme aimed at the whole school, the classroom and the individual pupil. After six months there were only small changes in levels of bullying in the schools despite a reasonable amount of work in the classroom and in the playground. The schools had developed comprehensive behaviour policies. However, Pepler, Craig, Zeigler and Charach (1993) point out that first, the behaviour codes did *not* specifically address the issue of bullying. Second, these guidelines were *given to* staff rather than *developed by* them. The process and style of policy development undertaken by these Canadian schools therefore differs from the kinds of policies developed by more successful schools in the other projects. These differences may account for the contrasting results, although a more extensive and longer-term investigation would be needed to confirm this.

These projects have been evaluative studies and have involved a range of styles of intervention strategies. Individually, none of these studies is able to definitively separate the effects of the whole-school policy from the effects of other more localised interventions targeted at the classroom, the playground or the individual pupil. This lack of distinction between interventions is due in part to the diffuse boundaries between what is part of the whole-school policy process and what is not. Most schools we have worked with have used anti-bullying techniques and materials as a way of implementing their anti-bullying policies rather than as discrete and separate interventions. By attempting to define tightly the different components of the intervention process for research purposes, unnatural boundaries have been created in what is really a 'whole-school' phenomenon and as such cannot be dissected in a minute way. The cumulative evidence arising from the various projects referred to in this section suggests that it is indeed the development and implementation of a whole-school anti-bullying policy which brings about change in levels of bullying. The other interventions may assist the process of reducing bullying behaviour or may help individual pupils but in the absence of a policy are unlikely to have a significant or long-lasting effect on pupil behaviour or the social climate of the school.

The Sheffield Project

All of the sixteen primary schools and seven secondary schools in the Sheffield Project undertook to develop a whole-school policy against bullying (see Chapter Two). Two-thirds of all staff in the project primary schools and one-third of those in project secondary schools were interviewed to gain a perspective on how they had been involved in policy development and implementation and how this had affected them and the school. The helpfulness of the policy in guiding staff action and in raising awareness about bullying was apparent throughout the interview data. The views of many staff are summarised in the following quote:

> I think it needs to be tackled as a policy rather than just piecemeal, which kept it under tabs initially – when I was first teaching you could deal with it individually, but I think it [bullying] has become such a powerful force now so the whole-staff approach – I applaud the decision to take this on board. Now we have got a school policy, everybody is doing the same thing. There is a lot more back-up.

Key characteristics of whole-school anti-bullying policies

It is clear from the body of school-based research currently available that some schools are more successful than others in achieving change. The range of improvement in levels of reported bullying varied dramatically from school to school regardless of where the study was carried out. In some schools, levels of bullying actually increased (Roland, 1993; Chapter Two). Certain key characteristics can be identified within successful behaviour and anti-bullying policies.

Establishing a whole-school anti-bullying policy

We discerned four specific stages of a cyclical process which successful schools in the Sheffield study undertook in establishing their whole-school anti-bullying policy. These were:

- identifying a need for policy development;
- policy development;
- implementing the policy;
- evaluation.

Each stage is linked by specific action. This action can be described as a series of steps. The need for policy development is established through awareness raising and information giving. Policy development is achieved via consultation and formulation. Implementation depends on training, communication and monitoring. Evaluation is achieved by repeated surveys and review. The thoroughness with which each stage is addressed will affect the long-term success of the policy in action.

Identifying the need for a policy

Motivation to change is a key factor in mobilising staff and governors to take action. Motivation will increase commitment. In relation to the problem of bullying, the media have helped to focus public and educational attention on the extent of bullying in schools (see Chapter One). Understanding of the serious effects of bullying on individual lives has encouraged schools to reflect on their own practice and brought about a shift away from perceptions of bullying as 'harmless fun' or 'character building'. It has also become accepted knowledge that all schools have some degree of bullying behaviour and this has led to an expectation that 'good' schools will make efforts to tackle the problem. This expectation has been reinforced by the Education (Schools) Act 1992 which sets out the framework for school inspection. From 1993, school inspectors will be required to specifically evaluate school policy on bullying behaviour and seek evidence that it is put into practice.

Most schools are anxious to reassure families and governors that they offer children a safe and happy learning environment. Recent legislative change offering families choice of local provision has increased competition between schools and therefore placed greater emphasis on 'image'. Being able to demonstrate to families that the school takes positive action against bullying behaviour is a successful selling point for any school. The effects of bullying behaviour on children's well-being and learning were described in Chapter One. Clearly, schools which address the issue of bullying behaviour success-fully should experience an improvement in pupil achievement and attendance over time.

The personal experiences of staff can also motivate action against bullying. In one of the earliest staff development programmes run by the Sheffield Project, the teachers and headteachers present were asked to reflect on their own experiences of bullying. Every one of the forty-five people present could reflect upon a personal encounter which had been based on a bullying rela-tionship. In discussion about the effects of such encounters, everyone present talked in terms of negative emotions such as distress, shame, despair, help-lessness. Like this group, a proportion of staff in any school will be motivated to do something about bullying because they themselves understand the unpleasantness of being bullied, the discomfort of bullying others or the dis-tress of being a witness to bullying behaviour.

Within the Sheffield Project, the Norwegian Project and the Canadian Study, access to specific knowledge about levels of bullying behaviour pro-vided a stimulus for concern about bullying amongst the school staff (Olweus, 1993b; Pepler, Craig, Zeigler and Charach 1993). In the Sheffield schools, the reactions of staff to their individual school's survey results were a mixture of surprise and concern. Presented with facts about bullying behaviour in their own school, the majority of staff agreed that time should be spent tackling the problem.

In summary, there are a number of ways in which senior managers can motivate staff to take action against bullying. Unity of concern will lead to agreement that policy development should take high priority within the school. This in turn will reduce the likelihood of superficiality in con-sultation and increase staff commitment to spend time developing and implementing the school's policy. Senior managers, therefore, are advised to increase staff awareness and understanding of how tackling bullying behaviour will enhance school effectiveness overall. The responsibility of the school managers is to lead the school to identify a need for an anti-bullying policy.

Policy development

Effective policy development depends upon thorough consultation. Formulation of the policy document draws from the ideas and suggestions arising from consultation. In the Norwegian schools, each class of pupils devised its own 'anti-bullying charter'. In the Sheffield study, those schools which had involved all staff meaningfully and purposefully in the whole process of policy development had the biggest decreases in bullying behaviour. The overall 'staff involvement' rating from the final evaluative teacher interviews correlated 0.54 (p <.01) with the decreases in reported levels of being bullied and 0.48 (p <.02) with the compiled responses for reported bullying generally. Schools not only consulted with teaching staff, but also with pupils, families, lunchtime supervisors, caretakers and clerical staff and governors. A primary school teacher describes the benefits of consultation:

> the thing doesn't have to be finished and perfect from the beginning – it grows and develops – and everybody contributes so it becomes *our* policy so people have a share of it.

The value of involving the broader school community, especially pupils, is described in the following quote from a secondary school teacher:

> and the kids were consulted. They felt really good about that. We actually talked about the fact that this identified it as a really important document for the school...they took it as a really important task and came up with all sorts of comments...this has been different and good. I'm really pleased that the parents are now going to be drawn in on this.

The consultation process depended on structured discussion prior to policy formulation as well as opportunities to comment on draft documents. Consequently, the schools set aside curriculum time to consult with pupils; used existing committees and meetings to enable discussion between teaching and non-teaching staff and governors; and arranged family meetings to involve parents. A popular forum for policy formulation was a multidisciplinary working party. This would consist of family representatives as well as lunchtime supervisors, teaching staff and pupils. The working party's role was to collate the information gathered through consultation and then draft the policy document. Having recirculated the draft document for comment, they were responsible for amending the policy and finalising it. In some instances they were instrumental in communicating the final policy. In one or two schools, there was a tendency for the working party to undermine the consultation process: the viewpoints of the one or two staff, parents or pupils present to be assumed as generalisable. It is important that this kind of working party retains a co-ordinating role in the consultation process rather than becoming a replacement for it.

If, through awareness raising and consultation, the roles and responsibilities of staff and pupils in relation to bullying behaviour are clearly defined, then everyone should know what bullying is and what they should do about it. This certainty is likely to lead to a heightened awareness in detecting bullying behaviour and greater confidence in dealing with it. The bullying policy is therefore more thoroughly implemented. Two teachers, interviewed for the Sheffield study, describe why they found the consultation and formulation stage so helpful:

> The discussions have been the most useful – definition of bullying and so on. It is so hard to think of good strategies on the playground in the heat of the moment.

> I think the best session we had was when we sat down as a whole staff in small groups. We talked about what we thought bullying was and what we could do about it. It really brought out the cynics and the genuine concern – into an anger: why should these people get away with making other people's lives a misery? There was so much energy to do something about it.

Another reminds us of why unconfident teachers might avoid tackling bullying behaviour:

> I think if you make the effort to have a bullying policy it focuses you on things like name-calling which get swept under the carpet a bit, because it's very difficult to know how to deal with it.

Implementing the policy

Before they are able to implement the policy, staff and pupils may need specific training. For example, if the policy requires bullying pupils to be counselled, staff may need training in counselling skills; if pupils are required to challenge bullying behaviour, they may need to be taught assertiveness techniques. One teacher talked about how unprepared he felt to discuss the issue of bullying with pupils:

> It's no good saying 'Right, read that then talk to the kids about this.' It just doesn't mean anything – you need to talk through the issues –

because it's not clear-cut. There hasn't been enough discussion of what the issue is about – it's just expected that you know and you don't.

Another said:

I should be most reluctant to take it along to the pupils . . . all I can do is express my horror and disapproval. . . . I feel powerless – and I feel I have no support.

At a minimum, teachers need to feel confident that they understand the nature of bullying behaviour. They also need to feel conversant with methods for tackling it preventatively through the curriculum and strategies for responding to it when it occurs.

Once the policy is finalised, it needs to be communicated and recommunicated. Assemblies, tutorial work, staff meetings, family meetings: all can be used to remind people of the policy. In the busy climate of today's schools, it is too easy for a policy to be forgotten over time. Many staff who were interviewed in the Sheffield study made references to the problems they faced keeping the anti-bullying policy fresh in the minds of colleagues and pupils:

I think to begin with, when we were first setting it up it was a very high profile policy. I think the danger is not so much among the people who have done it – keeping it going with the children – it's the new children coming in and new staff coming in. It's making sure everyone is aware of it.

It's something that's going to have to be kept to the fore – so that it filters through – rather than it's something that we've done – and that's it.

I can see it [the bullying policy] absolutely lost in September with appraisal. I think it might get squeezed right out when people get stuck into that . . . it's starting to become a word – to think 'Oh yes, we did bullying six months ago.' I think we shall actually have to institutionalise it – slot something into our in-house in-service days, or into staff meetings . . . but we spent yesterday afternoon just talking about the school development plan – and I'm ashamed to say that this [the bullying policy] didn't get mentioned. I didn't mention it – and she [the headteacher] didn't.

This is important. In all areas of your life you can start something, and then it is not maintained and even a good project can slowly die . . . everyone concerned with this policy needs to be reviewing it, projecting it, reminding people about it, because bullying is always going to be there.

Maintaining the profile of the policy is important but this has to be done by the majority of staff. Troyna and Hatcher (1992) illustrated how pupils in one primary school gained confidence in anti-racist messages promoted through assemblies and perceived that the headteacher implemented the school's anti-racist policy but felt let down by the majority of staff because they failed to put it into practice. Roland (1993) found that, just three years after the national anti-bullying campaign, the majority of schools he followed up in Rogaland area had failed to maintain any systematic policy in practice. In these schools, levels of bullying had remained the same or deteriorated. By introducing a monitoring system for incidents of bullying, senior managers can identify which staff are implementing the policy and which are not. Failure to implement the policy should be followed up. It may indicate a need to change the policy; alternatively, staff may need additional support in implementing it or reminding to put it into practice.

Within the Sheffield Project, most schools used both assemblies and the curriculum to promote the policy and to encourage co-operative behaviour. This was achieved by approaching the issue from a slightly different perspective for each year group, thus avoiding 'over-saturation' but at the same time regularly reminding pupils of the school's anti-bullying values. In a group interview with some primary school pupils, we were reminded of how important it is to maintain the high profile of the policy:

Well, our teacher did lots of work on bullying last term but now he's forgotten and so have we.

In contrast, we hear from a group of Year Six pupils for whom anti-bullying has been a regular classroom theme throughout the project:

Bullying . . . yeah, we've been doing bullying for two years . . . it's our job to stop it happening . . . it's really important.

Evaluation

and then it's the courage to get out there and try it and if it doesn't work to say 'It doesn't work.'

and how do you actually monitor that what you have been doing has had the desired effect? You can feel 'this is working' but how do you know unless you've got the evidence?

(Comments of two primary school teachers)

Establishing the effectiveness of a school policy in practice is essential for long-term maintenance of the policy. As a social phenomenon, bullying behaviour can be redefined over time as the school population shifts and changes. If a school drives against bullying in one form or in a particular location, then rather than eliminating it entirely, the bullying may simply alter. Evidence of this kind of shift emerged from the data collected for the Sheffield Project. In both primary and secondary schools there was a reduction in bullying behaviour occurring in corridors, playground and classroom (see Chapter Two). There was, however, an overall increase of 4 per cent in bullying 'elsewhere'. Similarly, with types of bullying behaviour: despite a reduction in those forms of bullying defined by the schools and by the project, there was an average increase of 3 per cent of pupils reporting being bullied 'in another way'. Clearly, the next task for these schools is to identify where 'somewhere else is' and what 'in another way' means, so they can begin to address these particular forms of bullying with the same degree of success.

Evaluation can also be rewarding for members of the school community. Most of the schools within the Sheffield Project were concerned by the findings of the first survey that the majority of pupils were not telling staff in the school when they were being bullied. Rigby and Slee (1993) similarly found that in Australian schools only 33 per cent of pupils who were being persistently bullied would tell an adult. In response to these results, most schools will set themselves the objective of creating a safe climate where children will feel encouraged to tell if they are being bullied. In the Sheffield Project, monitoring showed that most achieved success in meeting this objective. A similar emphasis was placed on changing pupil attitude towards bullying, in particular, encouraging pupils to actively challenge bullying behaviour rather than colluding with it or joining in. If we compare the results of the first and second survey for the pupil population as a whole rather than by school, by November 1992 there was an overall increase of 14 per cent in the number of primary and secondary pupils who say they would help a bullied pupil. Similarly, 20 per cent more secondary-aged pupils and 8 per cent more primary-aged pupils would 'definitely not join in' bullying another pupil.

Evidence of how the school policy has been effective, and how it has not, can help the school refine and enhance its anti-bullying policy in action. Unfortunately, the very nature of bullying behaviour as a phenomenon embedded and hidden in peer culture means that adult perception of change is not always reliable. Schools will need to use rigorous ongoing recording systems backed up by regularly spaced surveys if they are to be certain of what they have achieved. One school in Sweden which established effective anti-bullying procedures not only has a working group to overview reports of bullying behaviour but also repeats the Olweus survey at the beginning and end of each academic year to enable them to monitor trends in bullying behaviour within the school.

Supporting the change process

There are two main sources of support for schools involved in this kind of change process. Internally, senior managers and headteachers can demonstrate their commitment to policy development by providing a sense of direction; by allocating appropriate time and resources for policy development; by confirming roles and responsibilities of pupils and staff. Externally, support agencies such as educational psychologists, behaviour support teams, educational welfare officers and advisory teachers may be able to offer expertise, information and opportunities for objective discussion about the progress of the school in achieving its aims.

Senior management

In the Sheffield Project, it was possible to identify the way in which active promotion of the need for policy development by the senior management team assisted the process of policy development. In some schools, all staff perceived a common aim and understood the process they would undertake to achieve it from the outset . Committees, staff/governor/family meetings were made accessible; flexibility in timetabling enabled involvement of pupils, lunchtime supervisors, etc.; financial support for training was made available. The senior managers synchronised the development process with other features of the school environment and calendar to ensure a balance between efficiency and thoroughness. In schools where such support was superficial or simply not present, policy development was slow, arbitrary and usually dependent upon a small group of concerned individuals. Consequently, consultation was rarely thorough; communication was patchy and implementation confined to a particular section of the school. Here are comments from one primary school teacher and one secondary school teacher about the frustration of trying to promote change without senior management support:

> I think the majority of staff are concerned about it and are interested in having a common approach to sorting it out. The feeling is that there is a difference at the top with how things are dealt with and that doesn't help – I'm confused. I think there's a lack of commitment.

I really think the Head doesn't recognise the problem being as big as it is. I think bullying is a major thing for children and I feel like staff are bullied to start off with by the Head and the Deputy . . . if management don't even realise it's an issue you're on a non-starter.

It's like wading through treacle . . . it's so frustrating. Every week it [the bullying policy] is on the senior management meeting agenda and every week it gets pushed to the end and we run out of time. Something more important is always there to take up the time, it'll be the end of the century before it gets to a staff meeting or governors . . . we've been doing this for a year and we're getting nowhere.

The high profile of senior management in providing a clear sense of direction and a commitment to implementation is essential for success. Without such leadership, the policy is likely to founder or be fragmentary in its effectiveness, possibly causing disillusionment and distrust amongst staff, pupils and families.

Support agencies

For schools in the Sheffield Project external support was provided in three main ways:

- a training programme consisting of some 'expert' input on policy development and a series of focused discussion meetings to enable sharing of ideas amongst schools (no financial support for cover was offered);
- termly visits from a research associate, who was an educational psychologist, to discuss the school's progress and offer advice or information as appropriate;
- access to project team members to assist with school-based training or meetings for staff, families or governors.

The project team had to decide how prescriptive they should be in specifying the appropriate content for a whole-school policy, to ensure that schools did develop effective policies and that there would be a degree of standardisation of policy across all the schools in the study. To this end, we worked with schools to identify a common framework for policy development at the outset of the project. This was followed by a suggested summary of steps in whole-school policy development . However, we did not attempt to standardise more than this. There were several reasons for this decision. A central aim of the study was to encourage all the schools to take as much ownership as possible of the process of creating a whole-school policy, believing that the most effective policies would emerge when a high proportion of staff felt involved in the development process. If schools or individual staff members did ask for further help in working out their policies, the research team would be happy to give it, but the initiative had to come from the school.

Furthermore, although we had a good idea of the core principles, we did not have the detailed knowledge of the individual schools, their personalities and their existing procedures to be sure that a standard recommended package would in fact be the best for that particular school. The DFE had specified that the outcomes of the project should be as generalisable as possible – so an underlying principle of all the training was that only that amount of training and structure would be given as would reasonably be expected to be accessible for any school in the country under existing training provision. If the research team had exerted a great effort to achieve as much standardisation as possible this would inevitably have resulted in an inflexible training process for the schools in the Sheffield Project which was not necessarily possible to replicate elsewhere. The team had to relate to each school as a separate institution, and provide the type of training and support appropriate for each individual school inside the limits of time and resources available.

Training

The training programme comprised six meetings, spread over the year. In the first, as mentioned above, the project team and the school representatives discussed and agreed on important features of successful policy development. A wide variety of in-school procedures were mentioned by the participating staff, and the research team, in summarising the day, emphasised the key principles they felt emerged from the discussions – the principles of consultation with as wide a variety of people in the school community as possible, of creating a school ethos where the children felt safe to talk to adults, of taking care to communicate the policy resulting from the consultation as widely as possible, and including procedures for reviewing and monitoring the effects of the policy.

The next training session focused specifically on the process of whole-school policy development, drawing upon the experiences of an acknowledged expert in this area. The remaining four meetings developed central themes: equal opportunities and bullying; consultation; communication and maintenance; evaluation and review. The same members of staff, usually the project co-ordinator in each school, attended each meeting. Feedback about the meetings indicated that they were useful as a forum for sharing ideas, clarifying direction and motivating staff to be innovators on return to school.

One primary school teacher described how she had been encouraged by hearing about the progress of other schools:

> I got to be very stuck with it [the policy] and what loosened that stuckness was the meeting where other schools just said what their policies were and the process they had gone through, and I felt 'That's easy, we're there, we've done it.' It had become too big and what I realised from that meeting was: keep it simple.

School visits

The termly visits by the research associate were mainly intended to enable the project team to monitor the progress made by the school. The same person visited the schools throughout the project. The visit usually involved discussion with the project co-ordinator and lasted between half an hour and forty-five minutes. Each visit was tape-recorded and later transcribed. During the discussion, the research associate ascertained what action had been taken in relation to the whole-school policy and additional interventions; answered any questions the project co-ordinator might have and identified what steps the school were intending to take next. The process of review and clarification was perceived as helpful by the majority of schools. Additionally, schools reported that the very presence of someone regularly visiting the school and asking questions about policy development and implementation acted as a spur for action.

Assistance with school-based training

Different members of the project team were able to provide advice and training relating to whole-school policy development and intervention strategies. Seventeen of the twenty-three project schools took advantage of this offer, inviting team members to lead training events and meetings for staff, families and governors. The maximum amount of time allocated to this kind of training within the project schools was fifteen hours, achieved through a combination of training days and twilight meetings. In relation to whole-school policy development, the training sessions usually began with sharing facts and figures about the nature and extent of bullying generally and then relating to that particular school. Discussion of the range of responses available to schools led to the first stages of consultation. Schools were helped to plan how they would proceed with broader consultation, policy formulation, implementation and evaluation.

This school-based training enabled a wider cross-section of the school community to develop skills and acquire knowledge about bullying behaviour. The level of individual contribution to the development and implementation of the policy can be enhanced by such opportunities.

The value of supporting the change process

Without internal support, any school-based project will fail to thrive. However, how important is external support in assisting the change process in schools? Some schools will be strong enough to manage the change process independently. We have seen examples of these kinds of schools in our work within the UK. Roland (1993) points out three schools in Rogaland which have themselves developed and maintained an effective anti-bullying approach. Nevertheless, these were three schools out of forty-one! In the Sheffield study we found that there were some schools which progressed fairly independently whereas many needed more support and more direction. The more successful schools were those who were proactive in seeking support. They themselves had identified their needs and they subsequently sought advice and training from appropriate sources.

The rate of change

How quickly can a school develop and implement a whole-school policy on bullying behaviour and how soon does this begin to change behaviour and attitudes? Clemmer (1992) points out that for organisations made up of between 100 and 1,000 individuals, 'permanent and pervasive cultural change takes at least two to three years to really *start* taking hold'. He suggests that five to six years is a reasonable time-frame for substantial change to take place and warns that many organisations fail to make effective change because they underestimate the time and effort involved.

On average, both primary and secondary schools within the Sheffield Project spent twenty-six hours on policy development. This was unevenly spread over four terms. A typical plan was for the first term to be spent on planning, preparation and awareness raising; the second on consultation; the third on formulation, redrafting and ratification; the fourth on publicising and implementation; and the fifth or sixth terms on evaluation. Only thirteen of the project schools had completed their policies by the end of July 1992. The remaining ten were still in the final stages in the last (fifth) term of the project, prior to the repeat survey in November/December 1992.

Regardless of when or how quickly schools proceeded, school staff perceived changes from the first stage of policy development. Three-quarters of the one hundred and sixty-five teachers interviewed referred to the awareness raising and consultation as bringing about change in their own attitude and behaviour. For example:

> I was on yard duty and a fight broke out. I approached the scene and as I separated the boys, I asked, 'What is going on here?' I heard a murmur from one of the pupils standing by . . . I didn't know who it was . . . he said, 'It's always happening.' Alarm bells rang and I followed the situation up . . . sure enough one of the boys had been bullying the other for the whole term. . . . I'm sure that before I would not have picked up on that, I'm more sensitive to the possibility of something being bullying than before.

> I suppose our playground has changed. . . . I don't think you'll find a lot of teachers standing around gossiping on our playground – you would at one time but not now.

> The discussing it with the class, it's become an issue which it wouldn't have been. We've all been subjected to it happening – coping with it at an individual level but the discussions with the class have made me think about it in a way I wouldn't have done before.

> The most significant part was possibly the initial impact – and the in-service training – that raised everybody's awareness to it [bullying]. That was very significant I think because we were more aware of what was happening in school. And for a time it almost seemed to increase. I don't know if that was because we were more aware and we were actually trying to handle things and deal with things, or whether that amount of bullying had been going on but we'd just treated it in a different manner.

The correlation between school gradings for consultation (which included awareness raising) and pupil perceptions that the school were trying to take action against bullying were highly significant (0.52; $p < .01$). In secondary schools, this also correlated significantly with increases in pupils telling someone when they had been bullied (0.64; $p < .05$). Awareness raising and consultation were perceived by both staff and pupils as important factors in increasing understanding of bullying and in signalling commitment to take action against bullying. They also seem to be linked with the beginnings of cultural change within the schools.

Interviews with pupils about the impact of the whole-school policy on their school indicated that, on the whole, things had got better.

> It's been good because I think it's, like, scared people. People who have

> been bullying other people, picking on people – it's scared them that they're going to get caught for it and I think it's worked really.

> It's much better now . . . they [the teachers] do care about bullying . . . they go on about it all the time and if you get caught even name-calling they tell your mum and dad.

Staff too perceived changes in pupil attitude and behaviour:

> I think the improvement has been with the children who are more aware of things . . . who realise what they are doing is anti-social . . . it's reached some children certainly and they are willing to turn round and tell someone else that they are wrong.

> I think some children are a little bit more confident. I think some children now can name behaviour for what it is. They don't just come and say 'He's just hit me' – they perhaps say 'I've just been bullied.' They understand what is happening.

> They're [the pupils] very open about coming and telling me things now if they feel picked on . . . there's a solidarity in the form helping each other in situations now . . . they don't feel that it's something they can't talk about.

From the Sheffield Project, we can see that changes in behaviour and attitudes begin to take effect during the preparatory and development stages of the process, which involves the whole-school community in awareness raising and consultation. This is evident not only from the interviews but also from the interim lunchtime monitoring (see Chapters Two and Six) which highlighted the summer term 1992 as a significant time for change in levels of bullying. This time point does coincide with policy development in most schools. Furthermore, as already mentioned, of all the features of policy development monitored, staff involvement in the development process correlated significantly with changes in levels of bullying behaviour. The extent to which pupils felt involved in policy development was not monitored, but our findings suggest that that this too may be a significant factor in precipitating change. In summary, it is probable that it is not only putting the policy into practice that matters, it is also the process of arriving at the policy formulation in the first place which makes a difference.

Differences between primary and secondary schools

The extent of change in levels of bullying did vary from school to school. We have already demonstrated that much of this variation will be due to the way the school approaches the process of policy development and implementation: role of senior management, the degree to which staff are involved in consultation. Certainly, we can see that any school *can* make a difference to levels of bullying through establishing an anti-bullying policy, but do certain types of school have to do more than others? Roland (1993) and the Sheffield study reported different outcomes of intervention for primary schools and secondary schools. This difference may result from a combination of size of school and age of pupil. The smaller schools generally experienced a greater degree of change relative to effort. Size of school and degree of change in levels of pupils reporting being bullied correlated significantly (p <.03). This finding might account for the more consistent reduction of bullying recorded in schools reported by Olweus (1991, 1993b), since average pupil population in Bergen was only two hundred pupils per school (figures courtesy of Bergen Education Department). Another difference between the Norwegian and English education systems relates to the ages of pupils within the schools. In Norway, children stay in the same school between 7 and 14 years of age; in England, the transistion between primary and secondary occurs at age 11 or 12.

For most educationalists or occupational psychologists, the notion that change may be achieved more quickly in the primary sector, or in smaller schools, will hardly be surprising. With smaller numbers of staff, pupils and families to bring together, the whole process of policy development and implementation can be facilitated; the smaller group size enabling more thorough discussion and debate about important issues. The implementation of the policy will be more visible in a small school community, therefore becoming a deterrent at a faster rate. However, size is not always a distinguishing feature between primary and secondary schools. Other cultural and organisational differences arise reflecting teaching practices and timetabling, hierarchical and administrative management styles, staff training, physical environment and so on.

As described in Chapter Two, in the Sheffield primary schools there were generally much more noticeable changes in levels of pupils reporting being bullied – the largest difference being 54 per cent. In the secondary schools, changes in levels of reporting being bullied were much more modest, even increasing in some cases. However, levels of bullying others fell more dramatically, with an average reduction of 13 per cent.

The big changes in secondary schools, however, were not related so much to levels of being bullied or bullying others. The changes in the secondary schools demonstrate a much more marked culture and attitude shift amongst pupils. On average, 38 per cent more pupils would tell a teacher if they were being bullied. The more the secondary schools have done about bullying, the greater the increase in numbers of pupils who would tell someone (0.82; $p < .01$), with some schools doubling the numbers of pupils who felt confident enough to talk with staff about the problems they were experiencing. Fifteen per cent more pupils would try to help someone who was being bullied; 31 per cent more pupils say they definitely would not join in bullying another pupil.

It may be that these kinds of changes are forerunners to a reduction in levels of bullying behaviour, only follow-up studies will establish this. The secondary schools may only now be reaching stages which the primary schools passed through at an earlier point in time, the slight changes in levels of reported bullying being effected by heightened awareness amongst pupils. Alternatively, differences between primary and secondary school culture may have lead to differing outcomes between the two sectors.

Difficulties in developing a whole-school anti-bullying policy

Over the course of the Sheffield study, some difficulties faced by schools in developing the policy became clear. Some of these were:

* managing the leadership of the project;
* change of personnel during the project;
* reluctance to involve one or more significant groups in the school community;
* lack of existing trained staff ;
* uncertainty as to the reaction of the general public.

Managing the leadership of the project

As a change process, the introduction of anti-bullying policies requires leadership as well as management. Frequently the particular school staff with personal commitment to the policy were found at different places in the school hierarchy, from heads to young main-grade teachers. Successful policies could be established with leadership arising from any of these roles, with the proviso that if the active personnel were not in the senior management team, then someone from the team needed to take a specific managerial responsibility for supporting the progress of the policy through the school committee structure. This would involve such tasks as ensuring that relevant items on meeting agendas were not delayed by time pressures, that access to training was supported by necessary finance, that discipline procedures judged appropriate in cases of bullying after the policy was established were consistently applied across the school, and that appropriate secretarial support was available when needed. A further task was to enable the process of establishing the policy to be presented and supported by the governors, and subsequently by the parents of the school pupils. By themselves, these managerial tasks need not take too much time, if the necessary documentation and other material are prepared by the actively committed more junior members of staff; but if they are not carried out, those other staff rapidly become disillusioned and the progress grinds to a halt. Our findings and the evaluative study by Thompson and Arora (1991) suggest that one of the key factors in the success of the policy is the clearly visible support for policy development by the head. The confidence shown in the school procedures by the children, particularly the bullied pupils, was highly influenced by their belief that the head supported the project and would in turn support the teachers directly involved lower down the school.

Change of personnel during the project

This is a persistent managerial problem in schools. Clearly, new staff need access to the documentation of the policy, clear discussion of resulting school procedures so far as it affects their supervisory and disciplinary roles, and access to whatever training they need as it becomes available. In some study schools it was common to find new teachers who said something like, 'I only joined the school at Christmas and I don't know anything about the project.' Without involvement of new staff in the implementation of the policy, over time the policy will cease to be effective.

Reluctance to involve one or more significant groups in the school community

One of the results of the evaluation of the process of implementation of the policy across the twenty-three schools was that some schools appeared very reluctant to involve the pupils, the parents or the non-teaching staff. This was in direct contrast to some other schools which appeared not only to involve the three groups, but to gain great support from doing so.

The pupils in particular were universally supportive – which might be expected, as they in many ways had the most to gain. Eighty-three pupils in two primary schools were interviewed to ascertain the extent to which pupils were affected by the whole-school policy development process. These primary schools were selected because they were very similar in terms of pupil numbers and background, but they did differ on the extent to which pupils had been directly involved in their school's anti-bullying approach. In the school where pupil involvement had been more extensively encouraged, 74 per cent of pupils interviewed knew what the school's policy on bullying was and its implications for their behaviour. In the other primary school, where tackling bullying had remained mainly an adult responsibility, only 31 per cent of pupils knew what the school was trying to achieve and how this related to their behaviour.

Involving parents might have seemed difficult logistically if the school did not have well-established parental contact procedures. However, schools which attempted to involve parents extensively for the first time found the project provided a good opportunity for the establishment of such procedures, as parents are supportive of establishing anti-bullying policies, across all social groups. The results of a parent questionnaire sent out to six project schools indicated that the schools had been reasonably successful in communicating with families that they were attempting to develop a whole-school anti-bullying policy. The return rate for the questionnaires was 41 per cent; 64 per cent of the parents who responded were aware of the work within the school and 79 per cent knew that they could become involved in the process if they wished to, although only a quarter had actually done so.

Lunchtime supervisors feel that bullying is something they should be concerned about, and are usually very pleased that the school is preparing a policy. The effectiveness of implementation of the policy certainly depends crucially on their involvement and understanding of the issues, as lunchtime is one of the commoner times when bullying occurs.

Lack of existing trained staff

Lack of training tends to act as a brake on the willingness of staff to undertake any new procedures in school, by reducing their confidence that they can perform effectively. Some of the processes involved in implementing the policies did require some training; others were natural extensions of existing basic skills of teaching and managing children and of organisation within the school. Three of the most relevant areas of pre-existing training were training in group-work methods of handling pupils, training in counselling skills for detailed work with individual children (Knox, 1992), and some aspects of management training such as project management and staff development. The project team in Sheffield did undertake to provide introductory training in the specific intervention strategies and in implementing a whole-school policy for schools in the study, and this kind of outside support from LEA Psychological Services or other advisory personnel would be useful to identify early on in the planning stages of the project. The availability of such support is useful in encouraging staff to think seriously about devising and implementing a policy.

Uncertainty as to the reaction of the general public

Part of this uncertainty arises from the fear that when the local community and media see the school devising the policy, they will tend to conclude that 'the school has a problem with bullying'. For example, the headteacher of one school spoke about his concerns:

> when other schools, who we are in competition with, say they do not have bullying to their parents what are the parents going to think? So we have a big problem. It's not just our parents, it's also our possible clients – parents of children coming from infant schools and the parents have to decide whether to send their children to junior or middle schools. So the parents that come here come knowing what is happening and what goes on and are in the main very supportive, our problem is with parents who aren't here, they don't know, they see that word 'bullying' and then they are told by other headteachers that there isn't any bullying in their school. It's very difficult to change their minds.

This probably was more of a genuine difficulty in the past, before the media publicly made discussions on bullying more acceptable. Some schools aimed to make the anti-bullying policy a part of their 'public relations' programme, actively pointing out how bullying is minimised in this particular school and how parents are involved in that. Parents often have anxieties about bullying in secondary schools when children are about to transfer from primary, and myths amongst top junior children are notorious. A clear policy which reassures parents and children can enhance a school's attractiveness quite considerably.

Future research issues in Whole-School Policy Development

The Sheffield Project had little chance to see how schools continued with their policies after they had been developed. The most obvious research issue is whether policies are evaluated and maintained over time, and how to help or encourage schools in this. Such information is unfortunately also lacking from the Bergen evaluation (Olweus, 1991, 1993b). We just do not know how short-term the effects of either the Norwegian interventions, or our own, are likely to be. Roland's three-year follow up in Rogaland (1993) demonstrates that the effects of an anti-bullying initiative can, if unsupported, be short-lived; case studies of individual schools, on the other hand (for example, Foster, Arora and Thompson, 1990) show us that steady effort over time yields positive results.

One specific element which has immediate importance for evaluation and maintenance is the extent and type of the monitoring necessary in the long term. The most obvious combination of monitoring techniques depends upon recording the main incidents, and their duration, in conjunction with periodic surveys. Nevertheless, the detailed arrangement of these elements is far from clear. For example, would class-based or year-group-based surveys be adequate for survey purposes, and would they give significantly greater motivation to the programme by involving the pupils effectively? Where is the point at which repeated surveys become habitual, and pupils' responses become more random?

Conclusions

A whole-school policy on bullying, if properly implemented, will reach all pupils in the school and most members of the school community. By contrast, most individual intervention strategies (as described elsewhere in this book) will have a more limited impact in terms of pupils reached, and the length of time for which they are effective. The consistency of response and the intensity of preventative work needed to bring about change in pupil and staff attitudes and behaviour are only likely to be achieved through a concerted whole-school approach with firm leadership and commitment from senior management.

To do this effectively requires a considerable investment of time and effort by everyone within the school community, in particular staff and pupils. First, the need for a policy must be firmly established. Then, involvement of the school community in the development phase is essential. The effort to implement the policy must continue over time with schools finding new and imaginative ways of re-promoting the school's anti-bullying values from year to year. Unless the policy is monitored and evaluated, the gains made may be lost in the future.

The rewards of such effort are tangible. The reduction in bullying achieved through the implementation of a whole-school anti-bullying policy can be identified within the first year in most cases. The reduction may be substantial in primary schools. In secondary schools the first signs of change may relate to reporting of bullying instances or to an increased willingness to help others. Improved relationships between staff, pupils and parents should emerge from the policy development process in either the primary or the secondary phase.

tackling bullying through the curriculum

HELEN COWIE
SONIA SHARP

Introduction: the co-operative curriculum

While a whole-school policy is vital for creating a framework in which incidents of bullying can be dealt with effectively over the long term, it is also important to consider preventative work of a positive kind, so that incidents are less likely to occur in the first place. In this chapter, we argue that a curriculum which is rooted in co-operative values can create the kind of context where bullying is unlikely to flourish. Indeed, fostering such a climate might be part of a whole-school policy. In addition, such curriculum work can help raise awareness and empathy, important aspects of the first stage of policy development (see Chapter Three).

Classes that are working co-operatively will be characterised by a predisposition to examine and be responsive to different contributions from fellow group members. The teacher will ensure that many tasks are designed in such a way that they can only be done by collective effort; furthermore, that all members of the class or the working group consider it worthwhile to engage in these tasks together. Effective co-operation relies on a shared understanding of various social rules and procedures, and should reflect values such as: reasonableness, orderliness, openness, freedom to take risks with ideas, equality and a respect for others (Cowie and Rudduck, 1988, 1990). Here are some examples of pupils working co-operatively:

The teacher has just read *Charlotte's web* to the class. The children are very moved when Charlotte dies. The teacher takes time to explore the feelings which have arisen. The children are able to share some of their own experiences of loss.

Rachel, aged 9, has written a story but she is not very happy with the ending. She consults with her writing group for their opinion. The children meet regularly in this group and are used to giving and receiving constructive criticism.

Some Year Six pupils have become very concerned about not having an area in the playground where they can sit and talk quietly. They call a class meeting to discuss ways in which the problem can be solved fairly.

A group of pupils in Year Ten approach the Deputy Head with a proposal to set up a voluntary helpline for fellow pupils who are feeling victimised. They ask if they can organise a training day in which they learn about basic listening and support-giving skills.

The examples are all very different in content, but what do each of the activities have in common?

- the pupils are working together rather than individually;
- there is a concern to use a range of resources which different individuals or groups have to offer;
- an atmosphere of trust has been created in the classroom;
- there is a general ethos of respect for each person;
- the activity involves direct and meaningful communication among the participants;
- the activities offer opportunities for the practice of skills of co-operation.

Most importantly, the teacher has created structures in the classroom which facilitate the occurrence of co-operative activity. In other words, the pupils have regular opportunities to experience and explore the many facets of co-operation within their own school community.

Values of trust and respect for the person

Fundamental to the co-operative curriculum is a commitment to values of trust and respect, which enable children to develop in their understanding of self and others. Why are these values essential? If children's experiences of social interaction involve caring relationships, they are more likely to be emotionally strong and self-confident. Supportive relationships in a peer group are important for healthy emotional development. Positive social relationships create a sense of self-worth and acceptance which the isolated child is unlikely to experience. This sense of self-worth is likely to extend into adult life. Co-operative activity can promote the flow of communication by encouraging participants to share ideas and experiences in an atmosphere which is friendly and accepting. Where care has been taken to build up trust in the group, pupils can learn to give and receive honest feedback about one another, and can discover how they are perceived by their peers. And although the role of the adult facilitator is crucial, a large part of the work comes from the power of the peer group to promote personal awareness and to enable individuals to develop a sense of identity.

The emotional security of members of the group can be enhanced in a number of ways and the methods are well known in lessons specifically concerned with personal and social development (PSE). The emphasis on change might enable, for example, a child who was previously shy and unforthcoming to develop social skills in the safety of the group. Or the victim of bullying in the playground might, in the safety of the group, share feelings of distress and experience the support of peers. This co-operative approach emphasises the teacher's need to promote, both in herself and in the pupils, qualities of empathic understanding, acceptance and genuineness, in order to create a climate which values personal growth.

A sense of community

The direct experience of learning and working in a co-operative classroom can give pupils a chance to become responsible thinkers with not only a positive sense of self but also a concern for their own community since, through genuine conversation and dialogue, children can be led beyond their initial positions, based on their own experience, to recognise that the world view of others may be radically different. The dialogue extends beyond the classroom walls to broader issues such as world peace, conflict resolution, gender and race. Proponents of the co-operative curriculum aim to create a positive climate of goodwill in the classroom which will give pupils a secure base for solving problems, for confronting controversial issues, for facing difficulties in their social relationships and for developing a sense of ownership of their class and school community.

We can see how the co-operative curriculum creates a forum where pupils begin to have direct experience of empowerment. This has its responsibilities; and as with any empowerment, the power can be misused. But in the co-operative classroom there are structures which create opportunities for pupils to challenge anti-social behaviour at all levels, whether it occurs in a small group where one member is overbearing and domineering, or whether it concerns concerted action to combat bullying in the school at large. From this perspective the pupils are learning that they have power to challenge accepted ways of doing things which nevertheless seem unjust. Change here goes beyond individual personal growth and begins to address the possibility of being an active and responsible member of one's community, for example through heightening awareness of issues around community action and social change.

An example might be the power of groups to challenge prejudice against Black pupils or to explore gender issues in their own classroom and in their immediate community. In a co-operative classroom, where the ground rules of equality of opportunity have been established, there is scope for the negotiation of change (Cowie, 1994; Salmon and Claire, 1984; Salmon, 1992; Cowie, Smith, Boulton and Laver, 1994). This is confirmed by evidence from the USA (Johnson and Johnson, 1989) that a sense of self-efficacy is more likely to be promoted by working in groups than by either competitive or individualistic methods. Children in co-operative groups come to believe that they will be effective in taking action to solve problems and develop a sense of personal control and empowerment.

Reframing experience

The co-operative classroom can also be the setting for pupils to learn to tolerate different perspectives on the same issue. This does not mean that they never disagree – they often will in the course of debate – but rather that they learn to listen and reflect as they hear the very differing views of other members of their class. Collaborating pupils, through the process of working together, can help one another to increase understanding. There is strong evidence (Brown and Palinscar, 1989; Bruner, 1986; Donaldson, 1978; Vygotsky, 1978) about the links between learning and social processes. Talk plays a central part in the learning process and it has been claimed that there are some cognitive processes which can only take place when the pupil is actively engaged in meaningful communication with peers and adults in his or her social environment. Bennett and Dunne (1992) and Dunne and Bennett (1990) have made systematic investigations of the ways in which social processes influence children's performance on specific types of task. They stress the need for educators to understand the social context where learning takes place and, with communication as a central feature of their approach, point to the role of task-related talk in enhancing pupils' capacity to learn. They argue that children become much more proficient at developing their own ideas and at reaching informed conclusions when they are involved in well-structured group work of a co-operative kind.

The power of the group

We now consider how important the peer group is in maintaining either co-operative or bullying behaviour. Within any bullying situation it is possible to work directly and individually with the pupils involved (see Chapter Eight), but powerful methods for preventing bullying occurring in the first place are those which involve the whole peer group: the bullies, the victims and the bystanders.

For most children it is important to feel accepted by their peer group. The making and breaking of friendships can figure largely in their daily experiences of school, and the feeling of group membership can underpin their happiness there. When talking to pupils involved in bullying gangs it is often fear of what the rest of the group would say that hinders pupils in changing their behaviour. In the survey carried out by Whitney and Smith (1993), 18 per cent of pupils said that if their friends were bullying someone they would join in. A comment made by a pupil during interview provides us with an insight into why this occurs:

> I think it's like because if somebody's bullying them – you don't want to be friends with them . . . because everyone will tease you for being friends with them . . . so everybody'll join in the bullying.

Half of the pupils in the same survey said that other people – both children and adults – ignore bullying behaviour. Research into bystander behaviour (Latane and Darley, 1970; Latane and Nida, 1981) shows that as the number of bystanders present at an incident increases, so the likelihood of somebody doing something to help the situation decreases. They call this trend the 'diffusion of responsibility'. The only exceptions are children under 9 years of age. Above this age, the decision to take action is often inhibited by social concern about 'what other people will think'. If intervention in a bullying situation is encouraged and valued by the school community, pupils are more likely to challenge bullying behaviour than remain inactive.

The school profiles which were developed through the bullying survey (Whitney and Smith, 1993) showed clearly that within a single year group there can be classes with disproportionately high levels of bullying whereas in other classes there is scarcely any bullying at all. What is the difference between these classes that leads to such a marked contrast in the levels of bullying behaviour? We would suggest that a major contributing factor would be the class 'ethos': the atmosphere generated collectively by the pupils in that class which supports or colludes with bullying and other forms of aggressive behaviour.

There are two powerful ways in which pupils can indicate support for bullying behaviour. First, pupils can passively support the bullying behaviour by ignoring it or by remaining silent. These pupils can maintain the victim's role by avoiding the bullied pupil(s) or by not inviting them to join their social group. They can socially reinforce the pupils who are doing the bullying by co-operating with them, being friendly towards them or by not saying anything to them about the bullying behaviour. They can even help to enhance the reputation of the bullying pupil by gossiping about bullying incidents.

Second, pupils can support bullying behaviour in a much more active way. They can do this by: verbally encouraging the behaviour; preventing the pupil being bullied from escaping the situation; shielding the situation from adult view; acting as 'look out' or warning the pupils who are bullying that an adult is approaching; generally assisting the pupil to bully by holding the pupil being bullied, or holding coats or bags; directing the bullying behaviour, e.g. 'Go on, put her bag down the toilet!'; acting as a messenger for the pupils who are bullying; laughing or smiling at the bullying behaviour; writing graffiti confirming the role of the pupil as victim or bully; refusing to give information about the situation even when asked.

This ethos can most effectively be changed in classes where the values of co-operation are promoted through the curriculum. Each of these two types of support for bullying can be challenged where pupils are working in a co-operative classroom. If it is not challenged, then gradually, over time, the pupils begin to believe that 'every class is like this'. They begin to believe that the behaviour of the bullies is impossible to change and out of their control. This feeling of helplessness spreads and can include teachers; thus the downward spiral of bullying behaviour is perpetuated and consolidated.

It is possible for an anti-bullying climate to exist within a class group where the group norms are oriented towards co-operation and tolerance. It does not mean that everyone in the group needs to be close friends but rather that the individual and friendship groups do not gain status through aggressive or dominant behaviour. Peer approval will be given for non-aggressive behaviour; unacceptable behaviour such as bullying will meet with rejection or challenge.

The pupils who spend much of their time in this kind of atmosphere are likely to feel confident that they can control bullying behaviour. Pupils who do indulge in bullying behaviour are likely to feel uncomfortable because they are breaking the group norms; they are also unlikely to receive a fearful or satisfactory response from their chosen victim. Pupils being bullied are more likely to seek support from their other classmates because they will expect to be supported. Research on implementing co-operative group work in junior school classrooms has shown that it can reduce the extent of victimisation of vulnerable children, even in difficult classroom conditions (Cowie, Smith, Boulton and Laver, 1994). This is not to say that such implementation will always be easy. Children who enjoy bullying others may dislike co-operative activities and make the creation of a co-operative classroom more difficult (Smith, Cowie and Berdondini, 1994).

The co-operative curriculum includes in its aims a commitment to encourage pupils to be more active in challenging and preventing bullying behaviour themselves. A detailed consideration of using co-operative group work activities in junior school classrooms has been given by Cowie, Smith, Boulton and Laver (1994). In the following sections of this chapter we illustrate other ways in which teachers have successfully tackled bullying through the curriculum. We describe interventions drawn from the Sheffield Project and from elsewhere. First, we consider the Quality Circle, where pupils in co-operative groups learn skills and strategies for tackling bullying in their own classrooms and playground. Next we look at drama, role-play and video work where pupils use improvised dramatic role-play as the basis for extending role repertoire, exploring unhelpful or destructive behaviours in the safety of a co-operative group and creating new possibilities for responding to bullying situations in new ways. Finally we show how story-telling and narrative give children a heightened sense of self and a greater sensitivity to others as they hear how characters in a narrative encounter oppressive, bullying behaviour and how they learn to challenge it. Sensitive use of literature engages the imagination and encourages co-operation as children respond at an emotional level to the story and relate what they hear to their own experience.

The Quality Circle method

The Quality Circle (QC) idea comes from industry but its methods and techniques can easily be adapted to school settings (Schofield, 1986; Cowie and Sharp, 1992). Essentially the QC consists of groups of people – of around five or six pupils each – who meet together regularly, usually weekly, and who are trained by someone with experience of QCs to identify common problems, analyse them, evolve solutions and present these solutions to 'management' – in this case a panel of adults, such as the headteacher, school governors, parents. The members of the QC are introduced to appropriate skills and strategies for problem-solving and effecting change: skills for generating ideas, observation and data collection, developing strategies for solutions, and communication, both within the circle and when presenting to management. A fuller and more detailed account of how QCs work in practice can be found in Cowie and Sharp (1992, 1994).

The QC follows a particular cycle:

- forming the group;
- brainstorming the problem;
- prioritising the problem;
- investigating the problem/doing research;
- identifying causes;
- suggesting solutions;
- presenting the problem and solutions to management;
- monitoring and evaluating the outcome.

The QC is distinctive because it gives participants the opportunity to acquire a range of skills which facilitate a problem-solving approach to social life. The ground rules of the QC, which are explored during the group-forming phase of the cycle, actively discourage behaviour which is domineering or destructive or which discriminates against group members. As the group works together to research an issue and to generate ideas for finding solutions to the problem, there is an opportunity for satisfaction in experiencing at first hand the creativity of team work and for acknowledging that a solution can come from any member. The members of the QC are taught specific skills which will facilitate this approach to an issue like bullying (see Figure 4.1). Thus the techniques of the QC affirm democratic values by demonstrating how constructively people can work together when there is an atmosphere of trust and a willingness to acquire accurate information on the topic under investigation. Members of the QC are also made familiar with techniques for conflict resolution through debriefing and regular group evaluation sessions (Cowie and Rudduck, 1990).

Members of the QC learn skills which will serve them well in other areas of the curriculum. They are taught how to carry out small research investigations through surveys, through interviews, through questionnaires and through systematic observation. They learn how to put their findings into readily accessible forms, such as bar charts, pie charts, flow charts, which can convey the information economically and effectively. When the QC comes to the point in the cycle where the presentation to management occurs, group members are given training in communication skills. They learn to structure a talk, to shape the argument, to present key points in a visually attractive way, to deliver the talk with confidence and to handle questions with ease. Here are some of the outcomes of QCs in a number of classes:

- a lunchtime games tournament to reduce boredom;
- a survey on bullying in the whole school;
- a booklet on bullying written by the QC and disseminated to other classes;

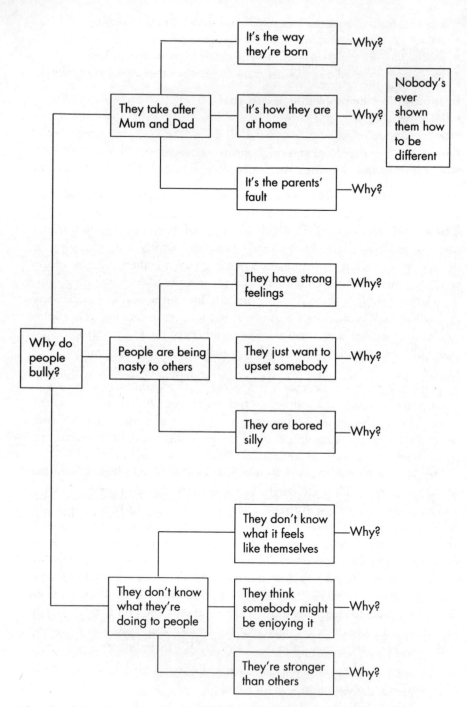

Figure 4.1 An example of a Why? Why? diagram: a 10-year-old's responses to the question 'Why?'

- a play on bullying devised by pupils and shown to other pupils;
- the QC taught younger children co-operative games;
- special discussion groups with a particularly high-bullying class;
- the QC established a gardening team to improve the school playground.

By using the techniques of the QC, members develop in their own ability to relate effectively to one another. In addition, they have opportunities to experience the process of playing a part in the management of change. Thus the QC method aims to give young people a sense of ownership of their own school community. This will stand them in good stead in their future roles and responsibilities as adults.

Evaluation of Quality Circles

The effectiveness of the QCs was evaluated in the Sheffield Project through observation of QC work in practice as well as teacher and pupil interview and questionnaire (Mellor Smith, 1992). This small-scale but intensive evaluation study involved three classes of primary pupils, aged between 9 and 11. The interview and questionnaire schedules were designed to establish how pupils and teachers responded to the QC process; what they had learnt from the QCs about themselves and about working with others; how the QC approach had affected their attitudes to bullying behaviour and their own behaviour. In addition, we were interested in learning from the teachers how appropriate the QC structure had been as a curriculum method.

The three teachers were enthusiastic about their pupils' responses to QCs. Typical comments were:

> The children started analysing their behaviour, reactions and feelings.

> The issues became more deeply involved as the QC progresses. The children raised implications within those issues and those for the future.

> The children are encouraged to think logically about the problems. They learn to work in groups. When problems have been addressed, they learn to present their solutions and thus gain valuable social skills.

> I must admit, I was a little cynical at first. . . . I didn't quite believe that primary school children could really cope with this kind of approach . . . but they showed me up. . . . I learnt just how mature they can be . . . it's made me feel very differently about this kind of co-operative work. . . . I would like to learn more.

The pupils too enjoyed the challenge of addressing real issues in their own school community. In a survey of fifty-seven pupils' attitudes towards participation in a QC (Mellor Smith, 1992), it was found that 97 per cent liked the experience and 95 per cent felt that the QC group had worked well together. Over half of those who took part stated that they had become more aware of bullying and that they now tried to stop it; 69 per cent said that they were more careful about what they said and did to others at school.

Typical responses were:

> QCs show that we can take an active role in preventing bullying.

> They help pupils to improve their own environment.

> They make you more aware of the damage that bullying can cause.

> You learn what other people are good at. Things which you didn't know about before.

> It feels as though you are really in charge . . . we stop bullying . . . we've been doing it for two years . . . it makes the school better.

In interviewing pupils about their experiences of the QCs, their sense of involvement, their commitment to the co-operative processes of the QC method and their motivation to be involved in solving a 'real' problem were clearly evident. As Walker (1989) writes: 'Creative energy arises from taking initiative, *not* from being given choices.'

Although we have no evidence to suggest that QC work will stop bullying behaviour on its own, our research indicates that it enables pupils to explore the issues meaningfully and provides them with a clear structure to formulate and implement their own solutions. It certainly raises awareness about the problem of bullying and helps the pupils to understand and reflect upon their own behaviour and attitudes towards others. Its basis in the co-operative learning style promotes a non-violent, constructive approach to problem-solving. Although it does not directly teach pupils how not to bully others, it teaches the interpersonal skills which are essential for non-violent behaviour: communication, co-operation and problem-solving (Walker, 1989).

Although QCs could be used in secondary schools, and have been in the USA (Schofield, 1986), in our study the approach was mainly introduced in the primary sector. Discussion with teachers about why this was so indicated that the more flexible nature of the primary curriculum made it easier to incorporate into the teaching day. The QC process combines a number of curriculum areas, in particular English, maths and science, and therefore is particularly suited to the integrated curriculum of the primary school.

To enable the QCs to be successful, both the school and the class teacher need to be committed to enabling the pupils to take a participative role in school management. This means that the adults in the school community must be prepared to share power and decision making with the pupils by respecting and recognising the value of their solutions. Tokenism will undermine the purpose of the QCs and will quickly demotivate the pupils. The constructive energy which evolves through the QC work we have observed comes from the pupils' perception that they are centrally involved in solving a real problem rather than looking to the teacher for the right answer. In bringing QCs into the classroom, the teacher trains the pupils in the QC techniques but from there on the pupils themselves define, investigate and find solutions to the problem. The teacher and the school management must be committed to facilitating the implementation of the pupils' solutions wherever possible.

Four factors have been identified which hinder the progress of quality circles. These are:

- the QCs run out of problems to solve;
- lack of support/enthusiasm from managers;
- lack of change or failure by management to implement QC recommendations;
- QC members' self-interest inhibits involvement, usually because the managers do not share gains made by implementation of the QCs' recommendations.

Ledford, Lawler and Mohrman (1988) note that QCs often stay parallel to an organisation – an added extra – rather than an intrinsic feature. Although these potential difficulties have been identified in QCs in industrial settings, it is possible to apply their conclusions to an educational context. The more the QCs become part of a participative management procedure, enabling pupils, teachers and even parents and governors to work in partnership towards making the school more effective, the more likely they are to be successful. Although within our experience we have only encountered schools which have formed pupil QCs, there is no reason why mixed QCs with open membership could not become part of the school system.

Using drama, role-play and video

Drama teachers have long been aware of the potential of drama and role-play for helping pupils to gain an understanding of their own lives, to increase their capacity to explore the hypothetical, to learn about how other people think and feel, and to come to terms with disturbing emotions like anger, fear and hate. Not only does this learning take place within the safety of a role-play situation, but also there are other people involved in the process, whether as participants or as onlookers. There are a number of outcomes. Participants in a dramatic enactment become more integrated as a group; there is a heightened sense of group consciousness; participants have shared in a response to an emotive issue such as bullying; participants are able to work through the consequences of different lines of action in the safety of a role-play. Thus drama creates a context in which the teacher can enable pupils to face up to difficult or disturbing emotions and, because they are in role, they are likely to feel safer in exploring them.

Spontaneous role-taking is an activity which emerges early on in life. Pre-school children in their play will readily take roles which reflect familiar everyday experiences (parent and baby; doctor and patient; shopkeepers and customers). They can also be observed to explore less familiar situations through the medium of role-play as they enact explorers in space, or cops and robbers. Role-play enables them to venture into the world of fantasy and make-believe as they enact monsters, witches, princesses and daleks. But it is also rooted in reality. Children and adults continue to observe their own lives as a series of episodes often with a 'text' and with actors, supporting cast and an ending. The skills of role-taking and empathy develop throughout child-hood and can be charted in the continuing interest in creating imaginative stories. Through characters and events, children at primary school and beyond continue to experiment with roles and to explore new situations imaginatively. It is one important way of becoming socially aware. It can also be a safe way of exploring disturbing experiences. Glove-puppet plays have been used with very young children to disclose painful experiences of victimisation or abuse (for a moving account of this see Musgrave, 1988).

Drama teachers (Jennings, 1986) believe that we do not grow out of role-play but can continue to respond to situations which give us the opportunity to empathise with the feelings of another person, explore the outcomes of our actions, experience what it might be like to be treated in certain ways, and get feedback from others in role as we act out a range of emotions. Furthermore, since drama engages the emotions, it is a method which is likely to be motivating and enjoyable. As children grow older there develops a new capacity – the ability to reflect on what they have just done.

There is no one way of facilitating role-play. In fact, there are conflicting theories within the discipline of drama in education itself (see, for example, Bolton, 1989). Most would agree, however, that the teacher must be firmly 'at the helm' and that at points the teacher needs to stand back from the situation in order to observe, reflect and interpret the interactions which are taking place. Some drama teachers would be content simply to share this perspective with their pupils or to remain in the role of neutral chairperson. Other drama teachers would argue that the teacher needs to be actively involved in the role-playing exercises in order to model the activity and illustrate possible responses. The category of drama which is most relevant to our theme of bullying covers a broad range of approaches, from sculpting work (introduced by Boal, 1979) to psychodrama (developed by Moreno, 1964). Essentially, participants in this mode are not concerned with performing a play but rather with exploring and responding to ideas about relationships.

Heathcote (1980; see also Wagner, 1979) argued that pupils can engage with roles through a combination of information about the situation and an appeal to self-knowledge. Drama requires co-operative work since everything is done in the context of others in the drama:

> In a classroom, each individual must agree to be open to others and to stay with the challenge of responding relevantly if the imagined moment is to take on the texture of real experience. Ironically, by disciplining themselves to respect the rules of drama, the participants become more free to discover all of the possibilities within the art form. (Wagner, 1979, p. 147)

Pupils are not being trained to be professional actors; nor does the role-play lead to a performance. What the teacher aims to do is to expand their understanding of life experience and develop their capacity to take the perspective of other people. Pupils in role 'get inside' different characters and experience how it might be to find themselves in a particular situation.

Gobey (1991) points out that drama enables pupils to move more quickly than, say, classroom discussion to a position where they can challenge the view that bullying is simply an immovable fact of life – that 'bullies and victims are just like that' or 'it's the way they're born'. The Neti Neti Theatre Company has broadened pupils' definitions of bullying to include 'the use and abuse of power at school, persuasion tactics, teasing, name-calling, excluding, and physical bullying' (Gobey, 1991, p. 71). The members of the company use intensive mime work to enable pupils to express feelings of hurt, rejection and fear while in role, and so to understand how people feel when they are the victims of different forms of bullying. In addition, through enactment, the pupils discover that to an extent behaviour is a matter of personal choice and responsibility. Again, by trying out different roles and situations the pupils learn that behaviour can be changed.

In the Sheffield Project teachers worked either from the video *Sticks and stones* (Central Television, 1990), the video *Only playing, Miss* by Neti Neti Theatre Company (1990; Casdagli and Gobey, 1990) or with the Armadillo Theatre Company. Those teachers who used *Sticks and stones* were supplied with a pack of possible follow-up activities prepared by Sonia Sharp; teachers who used the Neti Neti video attended a workshop run by Frances Gobey from the Neti Neti Theatre Company to investigate ways in which drama activities can be used to explore the issue of bullying with pupils. The Armadillo Theatre Company worked with individual classes in some of the schools.

Here is an example taken from the work of the Armadillo Theatre Company (Meddis, 1992), a theatre in education project whose aims were to highlight the problem of bullying to school pupils, help them to recognise it, give them a sense of responsibility for the fact that it was happening in their school community, and suggest possible solutions. The four members of the company enacted a short play about Mark (the victim), Ian (the bully), Nikola (a spectator) and a teacher. Note that the short play can just as effectively be an extract of video, such as the materials of the Neti Neti Theatre Company (Casdagli and Gobey, 1990; Gobey, 1991; Housden, 1991).

Each character introduces him/herself to the audience. At appropriate points the actors step out of the action and explain, in role, what they think of the situation while the other actors stay 'frozen'. For example, Nikola, explaining (out of role) to the audience how bad she feels about Ian's unpleasant bullying of Mark, establishes an empathy with the audience which becomes very significant later on in the workshop when the rest of the class begin to work out their own solutions to the problem. She has also established that this device is acceptable in the role-play.

This dramatic episode is unresolved so that the children are faced with the task of finding their own solutions. The collective experience of watching the short drama is the basis for all that follows in the workshop. They are then given an opportunity to come to an understanding of how this particular way of relating could come to be and how it might be changed. This understanding does not emerge without some effort and the teacher needs to allow time for reflection. But the use of drama gives the opportunity for identification with the characters and creates an opportunity to enter into the context though sympathetic re-enactment.

In the early stages of the drama, the members of the company (or the teacher where video is being used) stepped firmly into the action in order to get the participants involved. But once the pupils have begun to develop their own ideas the adults no longer need to play a prominent part in the role-play itself. Rather, at critical points they should stop the action in order to focus the pupils' attention on issues which have arisen in the course of the enactments. Both in and out of role the adult facilitators demonstrate sensitivity to the feelings of the participants, such as shyness and embarrassment. When the topic is bullying, it is quite possible that a number of the participants will be experiencing painful emotions and it is essential for facilitators to be proactive in showing concern and awareness. They must also leave time for individual reflection and for collective response-sharing in order that the full impact of the experience can be internalised by the pupils. As Egan and Nadaner (1988, p. 253) put it: 'The exercise of re-enactive imagination enriches moral development. Moral development involves understanding both people and values.'

Evaluation of drama, role-play and video

Eight schools in the Sheffield Project helped to evaluate the videos and role-play activities – four primary and four secondary. A total of 568 pupils completed a short questionnaire two weeks after they had experienced the videos or the drama workshop to establish to what extent they had understood the central themes of the curriculum work and to what extent they had changed their attitudes and/or behaviour about bullying after watching the video or being involved in the play. A sub-sample of four classes of pupils (ninety-five children) and their teachers were also interviewed.

The teachers found the videos useful as a stimulus to discussion. They all rated them as good or excellent for this purpose. They did not feel that watching the videos alone, or being part of the workshop, actually changed bullying behaviour. They did feel that the materials needed to be reinforced by the implementation of a clearly defined and well-disseminated school policy about bullying behaviour.

Drama activities were perceived as very valuable in allowing children to rehearse responses to bullying behaviour, to train them how to be actively challenging to bullying behaviour and to make them feel more powerful in the face of bullying. This kind of work allows the teacher to introduce and explore feelings and emotions with pupils. One teacher reported finding two of the pupils most frequently involved in bullying incidents 'particularly helpful in giving insights into the experience of both bully and victim'.

The importance of managing the videos and the drama work in a constructive way was emphasised by another teacher, who said:

> It needed extremely careful handling as some children . . . only one or two . . . identified with the bully and copied his behaviour and body language. If not used carefully, this kind of material could have a less than desirable effect on a certain kind of child seeking powerful status or image who is not really a bully but could become one if she or he is still immature.

Indeed, both Armadillo Theatre company and Frances Gobey (Neti Neti Theatre Company) are careful not to allow children they do not know well to enact the role of a bully. They prefer that either an adult takes on the role or the 'empty chair' technique is used whereby an imaginary character is built up by the group and represented by an empty chair. This strategy ensures that the role of bully is not glamourised nor is an individual in the group labelled. It avoids stereotyping based on physical appearance or gender as well.

Interviews with pupils demonstrated that they had learnt that by doing nothing about a bullying incident they reinforced the power of the bullying pupils. The action they took when confronted by a bullying situation depended on what they had been encouraged to do by the teachers in these role-play situations. The lessons learned from these activities have wider applications (cf. assertiveness training, see Chapter Five). One girl approached her teacher and said: 'That was so good. I am always getting pestered to lend my things and now I know how to say "No".'

The pupils' responses to the interviews and the questionnaires indicated the effectiveness of these materials for raising awareness amongst pupils about the problem of bullying if they are introduced and followed up in a meaningful way. Eighty-one per cent of pupils said that they had found the curriculum work interesting and half reported that the work made them feel very strongly about bullying. Some of these pupils felt so moved by the video and ensuing drama work that they instigated their own pupil-based action groups against bullying. In one school (S1), this took the form of a pupil anti-bullying group which eventually played a major role in writing and publicising the school's anti-bullying policy, and in another (S4) the pupils devised a play about bullying which they showed to the rest of the school, the feeder schools and a parents' group. These same pupils proposed a counselling service be established (described in Chapter Five). It must be pointed out that the pupils' energy and enthusiasm was matched by their teachers'. This mutually supportive relationship provided and maintained motivation for action.

Fifty-seven per cent of pupils said that they were more aware of bullying since watching the video and that they were more likely to intervene if they encountered bullying behaviour; 64 per cent of the pupils felt that these materials had encouraged them to be more careful about their behaviour towards others, although the extent to which this increased consideration of others lasted depended on the thoroughness with which the issue of bullying was explored and the extent to which the anti-bullying ethos of the school as a whole was reinforced over time. In one school, where there was no follow-up work and no attempt to develop an effective anti-bullying policy, many pupils' responses to the video and theatre workshop were summed up by one pupil who said:

After, all they [the teachers] said is 'That's what can happen when you're bullying' and 'Don't do it'. It did work but a couple of weeks after it didn't 'cos then Terry started bullying again.

If the co-operative curriculum is not reinforced regularly, thereby maintaining a high profile in the children's minds, then pro-bullying attitudes can soon be re-established. As one child commented: 'Our teacher did a lot of work about bullying last term and things got better . . . he's forgotten now though and so have most people.'

Literature

Literature can be a useful way of raising awareness of bullying, and increasing empathy for those who experience it. Consider this extract from *The Heartstone Odyssey*, and how it is used:

> One of the men reached up and grabbed the inspector's jacket, pulling him down. 'I told you, Paki, we don't take orders from your kind.' . . . Snuggletoes (the youngest mouse) could stand it no longer. Perhaps he hadn't been on adventures before, but he wasn't going to sit and watch this. With one jump he was off the table, across the carriage, and beside the old lady. 'Can I borrow one of your pencils please?' he said. 'Of course,' whispered the old lady, 'but be careful.' 'No', said Snuggletoes, he'd seen enough of being careful. . . . Snuggletoes took a big scoop of ice-cream from the tub and balanced a spoon across the pencil like a see-saw. Then he climbed on to the edge of the tub and jumped down, stamping on the spoon as he landed. The ice cream flew through the air and hit the man straight in the face. He jumped back in surprise and let go of the ticket inspector. . . . 'Vermin, I'll get you for that and your Paki friends.' The two men got up and began to lurch down the carriage.
>
> (Kumar, 1985)

The children listen to the story, write down some immediate responses to it and then form into groups to discuss what it meant to them. Here are some of their comments:

- When Chandra was on the train and some men started calling her names. . . . I think it is cruel to call people names because I have been called black bastard and nigger . . . it makes you feel really bad.
- I understand what it felt like 'cos someone wrote graffiti on my wall.
- I feel like nobody. They hang around with all the big'uns and show off. . . . I feel like nobody 'cos I'm just there.

The responses of these pupils indicate how powerfully stories can affect us. They report physical sensations, emotional reactions of fear, anger and hatred, expressions of empathy with the characters ('It made me sad when Chandra . . .') and reminiscences of similar experiences of their own ('It reminded me of when I was bullied . . .' or 'I suddenly remembered that . . .'). This passage combines all the elements which children report as being so engaging for them in a story like this: humour, action, mystery and making them 'feel sad or angry'.

Can this kind of experience actually facilitate change in the listeners? Does the reading of literature have the power to make people lead better lives? By building on this fundamental need for stories, are teachers able to help children to address important personal issues in their lives? Protherough (1983) points out that reading of itself does not make people better. However, he argues, the stories which we shape around our own lives arise out of our accumulated responses to real events and to those which we experience in imaginative fiction. 'The actual and the fictional are inseparably interlocked within us' (Protherough, 1983, p. 15). So, the teacher invites children to respond to literature less as a way of telling moral tales than to help the children to develop a sense of self and to offer some new perspectives on how it might be possible to relate to other people. Protherough actually checked this out with readers of 11 years and upwards when he asked them directly what they thought about favourite works of fiction. These young readers reported that they often imagined that they were one of the characters or that they were in the places where the events of the story took place. Some reported that they were trying to make links between the world of the book and their own life experiences with comments like: 'I put myself in their position and see if I would think or do the same as them', or 'When I read, the things which pass through my mind are similar experiences of my own.' These children seem to be using the story in order to test out their thoughts and feelings. In a sense the reader's values and experiences are in a process of interaction with those portrayed in the story.

Educators have not always viewed stories in this way. In the nineteenth century it was actually considered by some to be harmful to read imaginative stories to young children. Tucker (1982) describes how one Victorian educator, Mrs Trimmer, criticised the use of fairy stories because 'they fill the heads of children with confused notions of wonderful and supernatural events'. A similar viewpoint appears in the Board of Education (1927) *Handbook of suggestions for teachers* in which the authors are cautious about the value of exercises in invention such as fairy tales which illustrate 'merely the unrestrained play of the fancy and the love of make-believe'. In the present day there are still educators who deliberately exclude imaginative activities from their curriculum on the grounds that the school's domain is the real rather than the imaginary. Others might admit that stories are enjoyable but they are not to be taken seriously in the education of the child.

From an opposite stance, some educators have argued that the symbolic images of fantasy can help children to work through emotional conflicts (Guggenbhul, 1991). They would argue that themes of the imagination deal with real emotional issues in the child's life and give children the opportunity to resolve inner conflicts. The emphasis in this type of work is on allowing pupils to listen to stories which describe situations or problems which are universal. They are encouraged to supplement the story with their own fantasies – by making up new episodes or by enhancing a scene. Once the story has been told, the pupils explore the images evoked by the story through art or drama. Often the pictures or role-plays produced by the children relate to their own lives and situations. Guggenbhul writes: 'The children unconsciously find their own personal theme and visualise it by painting it or drawing it. They become aware of new aspects when they act out their theme.' The teacher helps pupils to do this by discussing the emotions and meanings portrayed in their work with them. Group discussion draws out parallels between the story, the images elicited through the art or drama and the conflicts faced by the children themselves. Through the discussion, the pupils move from the imaginary to the reality and are then able to apply the lessons learnt from fiction to their own lives.

A more moderate stance taken by many English teachers postulates a direct link between the world of the imagination and the social reality of the child's life (Britton and Pellegrini, 1990). Hardy (1977, p. 14) argued that narrative is the 'continuation of the remembering, dreaming and planning that is in life imposed on the uncertain, attenuated, interrupted and unpredictable or meaningless flow of happenings'. She sees narrative as a fundamental way of organising experience which is part of everyone's life. Like Applebee (1978) and Britton (1977) she claims that narrative mediates between the person's individual needs and the constraints of reality. This approach to narrative confirms the self-reports of children yet avoids the extremes of focusing too heavily on deep-seated emotional conflicts in the child. It is also confirmed by research by psychologists on the purposes and effects of social role-taking (Light, 1980).

From this perspective readers are themselves constructing and reconstructing the story which they read or hear. No two will re-create the story in exactly the same way. At the same time, there will be common themes running through. Meaning is something which emerges through the reader's interaction with the text. And in fact, when children were asked to talk about books which they had liked it was the emotional impact which was remembered: 'Kizzy made me look differently at new children in school', 'Black Beauty upset me when the animals were tortured so' (Protherough, 1983, p. 38).

The Heartstone Odyssey

The Heartstone Odyssey, which grew out of the oral traditions of India, was written with the precise aim of combating racist bullying. It is a story which is meant to be told and listened to, rather than individually read. Through the characters and events in the story, all children are given an opportunity to consider bullying in a different way. There are opportunities for sharing responses; there are also events in the text which show assertive strategies for standing up to bullying whether as a victim or as a bystander. All children who listen to the story are given insights into ways in which they personally relate to others in an imaginative world of good mice and evil crows.

Racism is, unfortunately, a feature of UK culture which reaches into our schools. Studies of racism amongst school children (Kelly, 1990; Cohn, 1988) show that racism is an issue which no school can ignore. Troyna and Hatcher (1992) disturbingly describe the racist harassment and bullying that most Black pupils experience in mainly White primary schools and also demonstrate how this intimidation extends beyond the school gates. Additionally, they emphasise how hard this kind of bullying is to detect by teachers and other adults within the school. Gillborn (1992) explores how schools themselves, perhaps unintentionally, can undermine the rights of Black pupils by their responses to and interactions with pupils in and around the school. However, Troyna and Hatcher (1992) also argue that even pupils who engage in racist behaviour can hold anti-racist views and that schools can build on these attitudes to encourage an anti-racist ethos within the class-room and around the school. Although not an answer to racism in isolation, *The Heartstone Odyssey* can form part of a curriculum approach to tackling the problem.

The Heartstone Odyssey allows children to come face to face with the nasti-ness of racism and the dangers of racial stereotyping from the earliest pages of the book. This is set within a context of inequality and injustice in its broader sense. Through discussion of the story, teachers can establish a forum where pupils can talk openly about the unjust and violent treatment which some groups of people encounter in their everyday lives, including their own experiences. The cruel realities of racist bullying and harassment are exposed through the narrative in an honest way; but the message of the story is clearly communicated – such behaviour and attitudes can be challenged and can be changed.

Evaluation of *The Heartstone Odyssey*

Horton (1991) describes how *The Heartstone Odyssey* could be used as a powerful medium to help tackle bullying in the primary school classroom. She points out the importance of using the materials carefully, allowing sufficient time for the pupils to express their ideas and thoughts as the story unfolds. She also suggests that although the text is long, teachers should not be tempted to cut out parts of the story in case the full impact of the story on behaviour is weakened.

Within the Sheffield Project, the materials were used almost entirely in primary schools, usually in 'story time'. The materials were used in classrooms with a mainly White population as well as classes where many of the pupils were Black. Teachers reported that young Asian girls in particular seemed to identify with Chandra and her experiences. On the whole, girls enjoyed the story more, probably because the main character is female. However, as the story progressed, the combination of action and mystery gradually engaged the boys as well.

All pupils in the classes completed questionnaires asking for their responses to the story. Thirty-nine per cent of the pupils could remember the kinds of strategies used by Chandra and the mice and felt that they could try these anti-bullying techniques out if they were being bullied. Two pupils who were being bullied at the time of the interviews said that when they were being bullied they remembered the story to help them feel more confident. When asked what they had learned from *The Heartstone Odyssey*, pupils responded:

Don't bully.

Don't call names, don't be a racist.

Don't torment people with a different colour skin.

To know what black people went through in the slavery days.

White people can mix with black people.

Don't let other people persuade you to bully.

Contrary to Horton, we found that classes responded well to the story being cut or amended in some places. The story is long, some teachers spending two terms reading it to their class. In particular the teachers stressed the importance of reading and re-reading the book prior to using it with the pupils. They felt that it was better to summarise some parts of the story but found that the majority of pupils understood the text. Fourteen per cent of pupils found the story difficult to follow and these were all boys.

Obviously teachers intending to use these materials need to ensure that the story is accessible to all pupils and adapt their story-telling technique accordingly. The story is written in a particular style which reflects the oral story-telling traditions of India; activities can combine the oral nature of the story with visual representation by dance. The Heartstone Organisation recommend that teachers explore the story and identify the characters within it through art, drama and dance. They provide guidance for teachers who wish to do this.

Three classes in the project schools (one Y4, one Y5, one Y6) were closely monitored (Shah, 1992), with all of the pupils being interviewed. From these ninety-three pupils, twenty-seven were selected for more thorough interviews and monitoring. Of these twenty-seven, nine were nominated by both themselves and their teacher as bullying others, nine had been bullied and nine had not been involved in bullying or being bullied at all. These pupils were interviewed at three time points: in the first week of the story being read; once the pupils had reached Chapter Six of the story; and six weeks later. The pupils who were involved in bullying others liked the story least, perhaps because the story emphasised the inappropriateness of their behaviour amongst their peers. Nevertheless, most of them reported that they stopped bullying others whilst the story was being read and this change in behaviour was corroborated by their peers. All of the nine pupils who said they had been bullied reported that the bullying had stopped since the class had been reading the story.

In the three classes, all of the children reported that they would tell someone if they had been bullied, and 67 per cent would tell a teacher. These levels of 'telling' are higher than levels found in other surveys, where pupils usually tell someone at home rather than a teacher and many pupils do not tell anyone (Whitney and Smith, 1993). Perhaps pupils in these classes feel more confident to tell someone because bullying has been placed upon the classroom agenda through its inclusion in the curriculum.

In the classes where the pupils seemed to have gained most from *The Heartstone Odyssey*, the teachers had spent time exploring the meaning of the story through drama and dance and had held discussions about racism. The way in which the story is presented and its themes explored relates to the effectiveness of the materials as a tool for tackling racist bullying and harassment.

Tackling bullying through the curriculum: some general issues

By tackling bullying through the curriculum, schools can open a discourse with their pupils about the nature of the problem. This raises awareness about what bullying is and can enable teachers to gain insight into the types of bullying behaviour which pupils in their school experience.

The extent to which these approaches change pupil behaviour seems to depend on the level of interaction the approach requires and the thoroughness with which the materials are explored. Approaches which involve pupils regularly and over time, such as *The Heartstone Odyssey* and Quality Circles, seem to have a more positive effect than those which are by their very nature confined to short-term exploration within the curriculum, such as playing a single video.

The importance of spending a reasonable amount of time on social issues such as bullying has been emphasised by our findings, and the teachers in the project schools felt they never had enough. It seemed that this was particularly a problem for teachers using the videos and role-plays. As one teacher who had used the Neti Neti video and drama activities said:

> Boys particularly remain verbally pretty hopeless at resolving conflict, expressing feeling, asking assertively and sensitively. I wish there was time to do three times as much work like this. For many of the more assertive girls this work has given them a concrete tool for action, and they are already using it.

empowering
pupils to take
positive action
against
bullying

F·I·V·E

SONIA SHARP
HELEN COWIE

 ## Introduction

This chapter continues to develop the theme of preventative work to reduce bullying behaviour, but from a slightly different perspective. The three interventions described here empower pupils themselves to take action against bullying behaviour. Once the pupils have been taught the appropriate skills, they are entrusted by staff to act appropriately. Adults provide initial training, support and supervision.

The interventions are:

- collaborative conflict resolution;
- peer counselling;
- assertiveness training.

All three interventions build on the essential skills of effective communication, in particular, active listening and assertion. The reader will discern the similarities between the three approaches, especially the underlying principle of problem-solving which recognises and respects human rights.

Whilst particularly helpful for pupils who are experiencing bullying behaviour, these are useful skills for *all* pupils to learn and practise. Although children may not encounter bullying behaviour, they are likely to experience disagreement or dispute within their day-to-day lives. They may be coerced or manipulated into doing things they do not want to. If they themselves do not experience such pressures, their friends or classmates might. Training in these basic skills can help children to resolve such situations themselves and offer support and assistance to their peers.

In addition to providing individual pupils with a set of strategies to apply to difficult situations, these interventions offer them opportunities to contribute directly and positively to their school community as well as to the broader social context of our society. Essentially, each of these interventions is based on fundamental principles of citizenship which will be applicable throughout society and not just within the school setting.

Schools are now required to set education within the context of the spiritual, moral, cultural, mental and physical development of pupils and of society (Education Reform Act, 1988). From 1993, under the new inspectorate, schools will be evaluated on their provision for the moral development of pupils. The National Curriculum Council (1993) states that in order for schools to fulfil this obligation, pupils need access to opportunities to discuss matters of personal concern, to develop relationships with adults and peers and to develop a sense of belonging to a community. Each of these interventions offers such opportunities.

In addition to being directly taught how to implement these interventions, key issues can be reinforced indirectly if teachers choose lesson topics, stories, examples and assembly themes which reconfirm the co-operative ethos of the school and which reflect the values underlying them. The way the classroom and the school as a whole is managed can model positive conflict resolution and assertiveness and can indirectly teach children how to handle difficult situations constructively. This may require some staff to move away from more traditional disciplinary methods when handling peer conflict and disagreements. Walker (1989) points out that 'there is little value in "teaching" non-violence for one or two hours per week when the principles advocated are not put into practice on a day to day basis.'

Whether these interventions are introduced as part of the general curriculum or are offered as a support system specifically targeted at bullied pupils, pupils are encouraged to develop and implement their own solutions to the problem. Collectively, the three interventions offer pupils a choice of possible 'scripts' to apply when confronted by bullying situations. Through using them, pupils learn that they can be powerful and constructive in the face of bullying behaviour, both for themselves and for their peers.

Collaborative conflict resolution

Extensive work in schools has been carried out by the Kingston Friends

Workshop Group (Walker, 1989), an independent organisation associated with the Religious Society of Friends (Quakers). The philosophy of this group is the belief that peacemaking is necessary not only at a political level but also at an interpersonal level. Through workshops and activity packs, members of the Kingston Friends Workshop Group aim to help young people develop skills and strategies for resolving their own conflicts, in particular in relation to bullying, in a collaborative and creative way.

Kreidler (1984) describes six levels of conflict resolution. These are communication, negotiation, mediation, arbitration, litigation and legislation. He views these levels as forming a scale, moving from collaborative conflict-resolution levels at one end (the first three levels) through to legislation at the other end. Collaborative conflict resolution is characterised by the opportunity for direct communication between the disputants, and the disputants remaining responsible for finding their own solution through negotiation and mediation. The further one moves along the scale, the more the conflict is likely to escalate and the less likely it is that a win–win solution will be determined. The disputants are left powerless and possibly without their fundamental needs in the situation being recognised or met.

The focus for this section is the more collaborative end of the scale: communication, negotiation and mediation. Communication and negotiation involve the children concerned directly with the dispute or disagreement. At the communicating level they are simply talking with each other. When negotiating, they follow a structured process to find a solution. For mediation, a neutral third person may be called in. This mediator helps to find a solution but does not prescribe what they should do. She or he assists the individuals to recognise what they need and facilitates communication about this.

Two key skill areas are needed for collaborative conflict resolution. The first is to be able to express feelings and needs in a clear, direct and honest way. The second is to be able to listen carefully to someone else. Other important aspects include respect for self and others; open mindedness and critical thinking; empathy and co-operation (Walker, 1989).

Collaborative conflict resolution is not about deciding who is right or wrong in a disagreement. Some people assume that the outcome of a conflict will be for one person to 'win' and the other to 'lose', or at best for both people to give something up in order to reach a grudging compromise. However, the key idea which underpins all creative conflict work is looking for a 'win–win'. This principle is also a core assumption of assertiveness training. Approaching a conflict as if all people could win shifts attention away from the participants and on to the problem itself and how to tackle it creatively.

Negotiating a win–win solution

A commonly used model for conflict resolution is the six-stage negotiation process which leads to a win–win outcome (Fisher and Ury, 1990). It is similar to the mediation process described below, but does not involve a third party and has no written agreement and follow up.

In the 'win–win' negotiation process participants:

- *identify 'wants' and 'needs'*: say what you want and why you want it, be very specific;
- *listen*: listen carefully to what the other person says they want and need; if they are not clear about it, ask them to be more specific;
- *brainstorm possible solutions*: think of all the possible ways you might solve the problem; don't discuss whether you think they are good or bad;
- *choose a fair solution*: reconsider each idea and choose solutions which will make everyone feel like a winner;
- *make an action plan*: when you have agreed on one idea, plan how you will put it into action – decide exactly who will do what and when.

Children can be taught the skills mentioned above. They can also be taught to be assertive themselves and to listen carefully to other people. A pupil may be able to avert and de-escalate a bullying situation by applying creative conflict-resolution skills.

Choosing when to mediate

Bullying situations often arouse strong emotions which get in the way of a resolution. In fact, the problem is likely to become personalised, and once that happens it is difficult for those involved to talk to one another without breaking down into angry accusations and recriminations. If this the case then mediation is needed.

In the mediation process (adapted from Leimdorfer, 1992, p. 26), participants:

- define the problem;
- identify feelings;
- listen to the other person;
- visualise an ideal solution;
- express their own interests and needs;
- generate a variety of options;
- the parties and the mediator evaluate likely effects;
- the parties and the mediator negotiate and agree an action;
- they sign an agreement;
- they agree to meet again to evaluate the result;

- if necessary, the cycle begins again from this new starting point.

The aim of mediation is to create a situation which is better than the present one. Familiarity with the strategies of conflict resolution through mediation can create opportunities to increase trust, decrease fear and begin to co-operate over the matter. The two sides meet in the presence of a mediator, a person who will not pass judgement or assign blame but will help those in conflict come to a resolution themselves. To avoid a situation in which the bullied pupil is yet again intimidated by the bullying pupil it can be helpful for each party to be accompanied by a friend (Cawley, 1992).

Here we describe a four-question analysis which often leads to a practical outcome with which all sides are satisfied:

- What is the problem?
- How do you feel about it?
- What would you like to happen?
- What could actually be done?

What is the problem?

In this part of the process, the mediator's task is to find out what actually happened but to ensure that it can be worded in an objective way. A key issue at this stage is to distinguish between what people want and why they want it. In conflict situations, people often express their wishes (their position) rather than their needs or interests, although it is their unmet needs which underlie the conflict.

Initially the two sides may respond with accusations which imply that the problem can be located in a particular person, for example A shouts 'He broke my watch strap!' while B retorts 'He kept on showing off about his new watch and made fun of me just 'cos my parents can't afford to buy me one. He asked for it!' The mediator enables the opponents to rephrase the problem in terms with which everyone can agree, for example 'There is a disagreement about the watch' or 'We can see that A would like to . . . which conflicts with B's desire to . . .'. Once the mediator has put the conflict in this more objective form of words, it is possible to begin to tackle the problem rather than the persons involved.

How do you feel about it?

At this stage, the mediator is facilitating the search for honest expressions of emotion, including anger, fear and insecurity. The mediator must ensure that the pupils express feelings in a way which does not pass judgement on another. A good way to do this is to insist that they talk only about their own feelings ('I got angry when he kept on showing everyone his watch' or 'I feel really scared now when he comes near me') and avoid negative labels and value judgements ('He is so annoying!' or 'He has a real chip on his shoulder about his family').

What would you like to happen?

Instead of focusing on the past and exchanging accusations which go over old ground, the mediator tries to get the conflicting parties to look ahead. ('The past is over; we cannot change that. But we can do something about what we would like to happen next.')

It is useful if the mediator gives the pupils a chance to think imaginatively ('If we had a magic wand . . .' or 'In an ideal world . . .') since even if an idea is quite impractical, it can give some insight into alternative ways of reaching a solution. From this question the mediator elicits ideas from the opponents which can give each side an image of what it may be possible to achieve ('I wish I had new trainers and a digital watch like everybody else' or 'I wish I could be more popular and have lots of friends and play in the team').

What could actually be done?

This is the point where practical steps can be planned which are acceptable to all sides. The solution will not be perfect but it is often useful to look at a range of possible options in order to make a choice with which everyone can agree. Hard questions must be asked at this stage such as 'Is this a fair solution?'; 'What is the cost in terms of money, effort, time?'; 'Who is helped by it?'

Even when the action is agreed on (A might agree to help B with his football practice as compensation for breaking the strap), that is not the end of the story. It is probable that the four-question cycle will have to be gone through again at a later stage. The point is, however, that in the process of doing this there is a much greater likelihood that there will emerge feelings of trust and co-operation amongst all parties.

Evaluation of conflict resolution procedures

Collaborative conflict-resolution skills are learned and can be improved with practice. We may wrongly assume that pupils (and staff) already have these skills. DeCecco and Richards (1974) found that many of the 8,000 students included in their study ignored or avoided conflict situations.

This suppression of anger often led to a build up of tension and outbursts of misdirected violence. Johnson and Johnson (1991) found that children from the most privileged backgrounds were often unable to manage conflict in a positive and constructive manner. Their research showed that much conflict was dealt with by employing bullying behaviour: teasing and insults, put downs, or by referring the problem to someone with more authority and power to 'sort the other person out'. A quarter of children in primary schools and one-fifth of pupils in secondary schools are bullied more than once or twice in any school term (Whitney and Smith, 1993). Much of this bullying behaviour might be avoided if children were taught how to resolve their conflicts peaceably and constructively.

Evaluative studies claim that there are six key benefits for children who learn to resolve conflict effectively, either by themselves or through the help of a mediator (Johnson and Johnson, 1991). These are that

- Intellectual conflict, where there is a difference of ideas, opinions or perspectives, trains children to be more effective, imaginative and analytical thinkers and communicators. It is viewed as being constructive when pupils engage in a debate or discussion in order to address controversial issues. Conflict encourages more effective and thought-through decision making.
- Conflict is a central feature of intellectual growth – when existing concepts are challenged and then overthrown by new information and experiences. Constructively managed interpersonal conflicts enhance personal relationships and teach children to value each other.
- Certain stages of social and moral development are reached through conflict resolution.
- Conflict can stimulate interest and motivate children as learners.
- Conflict enables pupils to learn more about themselves.
- Conflict-resolution skills are skills for citizenship and leadership.

Children can be taught how to resolve conflict themselves and how to mediate for others (Kreidler, 1984; Kingston Friends Workshop Group, 1987; McCaffery and Lyons, 1993). Bryant (1992) demonstrates that children who deal with conflict calmly and constructively develop better peer relationships than those pupils who respond by being aggressive or by avoiding the situation. Where conflict resolution and mediation skills are taught in school settings, interpersonal relationships are enhanced among the pupils and between teachers and pupils. In addition, all involved in the process will have learned strategies which will serve them well when they encounter their next area of conflict.

Peer counselling

The power of peer-group influence has been well documented (James, Charlton, Leo and Indoe, 1991). Pupils have been used to assist their peers in three main ways:

- to tutor;
- to reinforce positive behaviour;
- to counsel or advise.

The focus of this section will be the last of these three peer-support systems: peer counselling. Carr (1988) writes that 'peer counsellors are people who put their caring into action by talking and listening to their peers about their thoughts, feelings and experiences. While they may give advice and other practical assistance when appropriate, they primarily encourage self-exploration and decision making.' When faced with worries, frustrations and fears, adolescent pupils are far more likely to turn to their peers than to an adult (Sharp and Thompson, 1992). When being bullied, pupils are less likely to tell a teacher than anyone at home (Whitney and Smith, 1993). Schools, then, are faced with the problem of encouraging pupils to tell someone if they are being bullied. A peer counselling service may be helpful in achieving this.

To date, most of the evaluative studies of peer counselling services have been based in Canada and North America, and none of these were specifically concerned with bullying problems. Carty (1989) investigated the effects of peer counselling on stress and social support. She found that peer counselling did indeed have a positive effect on healthy adolescent development. Henriksen (1991) trained a group of twenty-two pupils in basic helping skills. She found that implementation of a peer counselling programme over one term led to positive outcomes for both school and counsellors. Thompson (1986) similarly found that there were benefits for both school and individual pupils who were involved in peer counselling work. She found that pupil counsellors became more open to new ideas and felt more adequate.

Carr (1988) used video recordings of the counsellors, self-reports, teacher and parent reports to evaluate the effectiveness of the 'City-Wide Peer Program' in Victoria, Canada. From every perspective, the service was perceived as a success. The students demonstrated their ability to help their peers in handling complex problems as well as day-to-day difficulties. De Rosenroll (1989) postulates that peer counselling training enhances pupil relationship skills and as such could be helpful for all pupils. He points out that school-aged pupils are both willing and able to help each other and that these caring skills can be enhanced with training and support. In an earlier study, de Rosenroll (1986) examined some of the difficulties that can arise in establishing peer support services in schools. He asks whether or not these kinds of service diminish access to professional support services. Schools which are considering the introduction of this kind of service need to be certain that they are offering a broadening of support rather than using pupils to replace adult roles.

Introducing a peer counselling service in school

In reflecting on the ethical and organisational implications of such a service, three main areas emerge: confidentiality, responsibility, and training and supervision (Cowie and Pecherek, 1994).

Confidentiality

Some assurance of confidentiality is necessary if other pupils are to feel secure to use the service. However, ethically the school still has a responsibility to monitor problems faced by pupils under their care. Legally, schools have to ensure that any pupil who discloses sexual or physical abuse is responded to in accordance with LEA procedures as recommended by DES Circular 4/88 (1988). Pupils can therefore only offer a semi-confidentiality, i.e. they will not discuss the other pupil's problems with anybody other than the appropriate member of staff or within a supervision session. They will, however, be required to provide some details of the problem to the staff who co-ordinate the service and must notify these staff if any form of abuse is disclosed to them.

Responsibility

The issue of confidentiality is linked with that of responsibility. It is the school which ultimately holds responsibility for all pupils in its care. The establishing of a peer counselling service does not place that responsibility elsewhere. Schools need to establish back-up systems to ensure that they remain aware of how the service is being used and that they follow up quickly any incidents when the counsellor has acted inappropriately or when the child using the service is experiencing serious difficulties. In such cases, the onus remains with the school to take direct action. In the case study described later in this section, this matter was addressed by the establishment of a recording system which was regularly reviewed by the appropriate member of staff. This enabled monitoring of general usage of the service and follow-up by staff if appropriate.

Training and supervision

The quality of training and supervision will determine the effectiveness of the service over time. Gougeon (1989) states that initial training should not only offer essential listening and helping skills but also opportunities to practise these skills. Robinson, Morrow, Kigin and Lindeman (1991) developed a training course for secondary-aged pupils which emphasised personal growth, acceptance of diversity, self-assessment and basic counselling skills. The programme included trust-building exercises and role-play to enable skills practice. Carr (1988) offered pupils a ten-day training programme which included not only thirty hours of basic communication skills training but also thirty hours of special issues training. This was followed up by forty-five hours of supervised in-school work experience.

Schools will need to consider who offers such training – this person should be an experienced counsellor themselves and it may be necessary for schools to involve local support agents such as Educational Psychologists or other professional trainers if nobody within the school has the necessary skills. There may be parents of children who have these skills and would welcome the chance to be involved in this way. The duration of a training programme will vary according to availability of trainers and timetabling within the school. Although initial training should cover the essential skills, an ongoing long-term training programme can allow pupils to improve their practice and develop new skills over time.

Linked to an ongoing training schedule, there needs to be some provision for supervision. Most helping professions recognise the value of supervision meetings which provide a forum for discussion of practice. In this time, the counsellors can explore difficulties they encounter and consider ways of improving their counselling skills. For schools, supervision will form an essential part of the back-up system referred to earlier in this section. Without it, there is a danger that inappropriate counselling styles will become entrenched and pupils may be handling problems which are beyond their capabilities. Whilst individual supervision is valuable, small group supervision is perhaps a more feasible option in a busy school. Again, the adult offering supervision should be appropriately skilled themselves. They should ensure that this time does not become completely consumed with organisational issues and focuses on the counsellors' own experiences with clients. Organisational and management meetings should be kept separate from supervision time.

Case study: the bully line

Whilst counselling schemes have been established elsewhere to support pupils generally, it is only recently that peer counselling services have specifically tried to assist bullied pupils. Whitney and Smith (1993) highlight the problems which schools face in encouraging pupils to talk about the problems they face with a member of staff in school. Many children do not tell anyone that they are being bullied. Obviously, if schools remain ignorant of the difficulties being faced by their pupils, they are unable to take effective action.

Within the Sheffield Project, two secondary schools started to implement peer counselling towards the end of the project. Here we describe the process at one school, S4. The development of the counselling service in this school followed on from an intensive period of curriculum work on bullying. Two terms previously, the whole school – pupils, teachers, non-teaching staff, governors and parents – had been involved in developing and implementing a whole-school anti-bullying policy. The counselling service was viewed by the headteacher as an extension of the whole-school approach to tackle bullying. The idea for a peer counselling service originated from a group of pupils who had been exploring the theme of bullying for part of their GCSE drama coursework. After watching the video by Neti Neti Theatre Company, *Only playing, Miss*, the pupils decided to devise their own improvised performance on the problem of bullying. In researching for the performance, they came across a 'bully line' pupil support service set up in a school in Islington (see Keise, 1992). They were impressed by the idea and approached their drama teacher with the proposal to establish a similar scheme in their own school.

The pupils felt strongly that they could become part of the whole-school anti-bullying drive in a positive and constructive way. They argued persuasively that through offering a peer counselling service they could contribute to the school community in a way which adults could not. They pointed out that pupils sometimes did not wish to talk immediately with an adult, preferring to talk the matter over with a peer first before deciding on a course of action.

The 'bully line' became an alternative to teacher support, complementing rather than detracting from the anti-bullying strategies put into practice by the adults in the school community. The bully line aimed to offer a listening service for pupils in the school. The pupils involved tried to provide a safe place where pupils could talk freely and explore possible solutions to their difficulties. They were also able to act as advocates for the bullied pupil by passing on details of their situation to appropriate staff or by accompanying the bullied pupil whilst they themselves told someone. Their role clearly did not include intervening in a bullying situation or tackling bullying pupils on behalf of another pupil.

The involvement of the pupils in the establishment of the bully line was deliberately formalised to emphasise the importance of the role and the responsibilities of the pupils. Successful candidates were interviewed and took part in a one-day training course run by Helen Cowie, Gerard Walsh (a freelance counsellor) and Sonia Sharp. The pupils learned and practised a number of good listening skills such as refraining from interrupting, how to paraphrase, to be comfortable with silence and emotion. They were taught about body language and social distancing. They learnt that the good listener attends very carefully not only to the words which people use but also the messages and emotions underlying. She or he is attentive and does not detract from the other person's statements by interrupting, offering advice or relating their own similar experiences.

Through the day, the pupils were also assessed on their readiness to become bully line counsellors. Those who were perceived to be competent to act as peer counsellors attended a further twilight training session where all and any possible hitches or problems with the service were discussed. This session also considered the practicalities of running the service on a day-to-day basis. Those counsellors who were deemed not quite ready were invited to attend further training in basic listening skills run by a member of the school's pastoral team who was an experienced counsellor herself. They were encouraged to support the bully line by working as receptionists for the service in the meantime.

The final team of peer counsellors included pupils from most year groups, including Year Seven, and represented an even mix of boys and girls; 68 per cent of these pupils had been bullied themselves at some time in their school career. This was often what had motivated them to volunteer to be involved. As the school was split site, a bully line service was established in each building. The pupils worked together in teams of three to four members. The receptionists were also part of this team. Each team was 'on duty' on a specific day each week. Supervision was provided on a fortnightly basis by a member of staff who was a trained counsellor. By providing supervision the staff were assured that the pupils were handling cases in an appropriate way and could help the pupils continually to reflect on and enhance their listening skills.

The school monitors usage of the counselling service via recording sheets completed by the pupils after each meeting with a 'client' pupil. A named member of staff is always 'on call' to support the bully line counsellors if they need it. The counsellors are encouraged to support each other and meet specifically to share issues and concerns on a weekly basis. In addition to this, the training programme for the counsellors has been ongoing. A series of twilight meetings has provided continual reinforcement of the basic listening skills as well as introduction to new, more sophisticated counselling skills.

During the training, great emphasis was placed on confidentiality although the counsellors were advised never to promise secrecy. It was clearly not appropriate for these counsellors to handle situations where a pupil discloses sexual or physical abuse. The counsellors were given a procedure to follow should this arise.

Evaluation of the peer counselling service

The value placed on the service by pupils was investigated through pupil interview and questionnaire (Thornton, 1993). The nineteen pupil counsellors were interviewed along with sixty randomly selected pupils from Years Seven, Nine and Eleven. The service was used mostly by younger pupils, older pupils preferring to talk directly to an adult. Thirty-three per cent of Year Seven pupils said they would use the service. This was supported by monitoring the actual usage of the service which was being used mainly by Year Seven pupils. One third of Year Seven pupils had used the bully line once or twice during the academic year. Several pupils had set up regular meetings with their chosen peer counsellor and this work focused on raising self-esteem as well as discussing the problems of bullying.

Almost all of the pupils who were interviewed felt that the service was a good idea and felt that it contributed positively to the school's anti-bullying strategies. No-one who was interviewed felt that it was not a success. When discussing reservations about the service, the older pupils in the school were worried about confidentiality. Their hesitancies in using the service emphasised the need to communicate the competencies of the pupils who work as counsellors. To maintain credibility, the other pupils must feel confident in their skills.

There were some initial difficulties in the attitude of other pupils towards the bully line. The peer counsellors needed support in how to deal with hoaxers and how to cope with intimidation in the counselling room itself, such as when a domineering friend brings along a reluctant bullied pupil as a way of demonstrating power. The peer counsellors found that training in assertiveness was useful in dealing with these kinds of situation.

For the teachers, the main problem in organising the service was providing the back-up and supervision. With two sites, staffing resources were stretched and the onus on one member of staff to be available on four lunchtimes each week is untenable in the long run. It is hoped that as a result of staff training and awareness raising, staff will be encouraged to volunteer their services in an 'on call' capacity.

The service demonstrated that pupils can be effectively involved in tackling the problem of bullying and in assuming supportive roles for their peers, but also that schools must be thorough in planning how such a service might be implemented.

Assertiveness training for bullied pupils

Pupil responses to bullying behaviour can be divided into four categories: aggressive, passive unconstructive, passive constructive, and assertive. When discussing ways of responding to bullying with groups of teachers, parents or pupils, the most common pieces of advice offered seem to be either ignoring the bullying behaviour or encouraging the pupil to 'stand up for themselves'. Rarely, however, are pupils told *how* to 'stand up for themselves' unless this self-protection includes 'fighting back'. In this final section, we propose that assertive techniques and responses, as distinct from passive or aggressive ways of interacting, are an effective and empowering set of strategies which pupils can be taught to employ themselves.

Aggressive responses include any responses which aim to hurt, damage or overpower the bullying person. Typical responses may include calling names back, ganging up on the person or physically attacking them. These kinds of responses may only serve to escalate the situation or may provide the bullying pupil with justification for continuing their persecution of the victim.

Passive unconstructive responses are usually submissive or involve no reaction whatsoever. Ignoring the bullying behaviour falls into this category, as does meeting the bullying pupil's demands or standing helplessly by whilst someone damages their property. There does not seem to be any evidence that being passive in this way reduces the likelihood of bullying behaviour recurring. It may leave the bullied pupil feeling even more helpless.

Pupils can respond in *passive constructive* ways which are appropriate to the situation. Exiting quickly from a bullying situation can at times be an effective solution as is telling a supervisor or teacher or enlisting support from friends. In these passive constructive responses then, the pupil is not taking direct personal action to challenge the bullying behaviour themselves but they are taking action which might prevent it from continuing or avoid it happening, even if this involves somebody else challenging the bullying pupil for them. However, avoiding the bullying pupil may entail missing classes or making inappropriate option choices; nor is help always to hand. There is also a danger that over-reliance on these kinds of strategies can disempower the bullied pupil further. They could come to view themselves as helpless to resolve the situation, having rather to seek help from others or to avoid the situation altogether.

In responding *assertively*, the pupil will stand up for his/her rights without violating the rights of the other pupil. The assertive pupil will respond to the bullying pupil by stating their intentions, wishes and/or feelings clearly and directly. They remain resistant to manipulative or aggressive tactics. Assertive responses rely not only on verbal messages but on eye contact and body language as well.

Here is an example of an assertive response to bullying behaviour:

> Rachel pushes Sudha against the wall. She grabs her by the collar and threatens that if Sudha does not give her some money she will 'do her in'. Sudha stays calm, looks Rachel in the eye (counting to three inside her head) and says 'I don't give my money away.' Sudha repeats this statement to each of Rachel's subsequent threats, using a calm, confident tone and maintaining eye contact. Rachel walks off in disgust after her third threat – without the money!

Assertiveness training

Assertiveness training has been used as a therapeutic method for enhancing social and interpersonal skills since the 1950s (Salter, 1949). The notion of assertiveness is based on a specific philosophy of human rights. To be assertive involves standing up for one's own rights and expressing thoughts, feelings and emotions in a clear, honest and direct way which does not abuse other people's rights (Alberti and Emmens, 1975).

Zuker (1983) presented these rights as including the right to:

- be treated with respect;
- discuss personal feelings and opinions;
- be listened to and taken seriously;
- say no without feeling guilty;
- ask for what one wants;
- make mistakes;
- choose not to be assertive.

Lange and Jakubowski (1976) identified five different categories of assertive behaviour. These five kinds of assertive behaviour build upon 'basic assertion' which involves a straightforward statement describing feelings, opinions, beliefs or desires. This basic assertive statement can be supplemented by recognition of how the other person is feeling (empathic assertion); repetition and extension of the assertive statement (escalating assertion); describing contradictory behaviour displayed by the other person (confrontative assertion); describing how the individual responds emotionally or physically to the other person's behaviour and describing how she or he would like them to change their behaviour accordingly (I-language assertion).

The aims of assertiveness training for victims of bullying

Assertiveness training is usually recommended for individuals who find it difficult to stand up for their own rights, responding to difficult situations either passively or aggressively. It has been seen to increase self-confidence and improve interpersonal relationships (Hargie, Saunders and Dickson, 1991). Assertiveness training for children can lead to increases in self-esteem (Kirkland, Thelen and Miller, 1982; Arora, 1989) as well as increased usage of assertive behaviour and decreased anxiety (Rakos, 1991). Children who respond to conflict calmly and assertively are preferred by their peers (Bryant, 1992).

Research into the behaviour and characteristics of victims of bullying indicates that this group of children may benefit from assertiveness training. Boulton and Smith (1994) found that children who were bullied had lower self-esteem than those were were not bullied. Childs (1993) found that the more pupils were bullied, the lower their self-esteem. Olweus (1993c), in a follow-up study of boys identified as passive victims, noted that male victims of bullying have difficulty in asserting themselves, as young adults. He suggested that family factors may be linked to this lack of assertiveness.

The social discouraging of assertive behaviour in girls has been well documented (Sarah, Scott and Spender, 1980; Wolpe, 1988). Keise (1992), in her investigation of bullying in single-sex schools, postulates that some bullying behaviour amongst girls can be seen as a rejection of and challenge to feminine stereotyping in UK society. She writes:

> For some young women, seeking their feminine identity through the traditional routes of boyfriends, make-up and being 'good' is simply not enough. They want these things and more besides. They seek to be equal to the male members of their families and their male friends and can match fist with fist. It would seem, moreover, in some instances, that if the academic route is perceived as an impossible means of acquiring power and status then power needs to be sought by another route – and one route may be bullying.

The obvious victims of this kind of bullying, are of course, the girls who comply most obviously to the stereotyping, the least assertive girls.

Assertiveness techniques build on a standard formula and provide an individual with a clearly defined structure to use in professional or social contexts. They therefore provide the user with a 'script' which they can fit to meet their personal needs. One common feature of bullying behaviour is that it is persistent (Smith and Thompson, 1991b). Within the assertiveness group, each pupil can rehearse a script which is appropriate for their specific bullying problem. This script can provide a certain sense of security, almost a shield against the nastiness of a bullying situation. Pupils can feel more control and power, less anger or despair. They can be trained to maintain a neutrality which de-escalates the situation rather than exacerbating it.

In summary, assertiveness training for victims of bullying can help pupils by:

- broadening the range of coping strategies available to them when faced with bullying situations.
- providing opportunities to rehearse implementing assertive strategies to resolve bullying situations;
- helping them to feel more self-confident and increase self-esteem.

Gender and group membership

The issue of gender is relevant in relation to the identification of pupils as victims of bullying. Boys seem often to be over-represented in identified groups of bullied pupils. In a study by Schwartz (1993), a sample of 200 children (with an equal number of boys and girls) did not yield enough girls to include in the aspect of the research which focused on peer-nominated victims of bullying. Arora (1991) found that more boys were nominated by teachers for inclusion in a social support group for victims of bullying and, indeed, in the Sheffield Project many more boys than girls were included in assertiveness groups by their teachers. This recognition of boys who have been victims of bullying rather than girls by both peers and teachers is contrary to the equal numbers of boys and girls reporting being bullied in general surveys. Whitney and Smith (1993) found no significant difference in the frequency with which girls and boys themselves reported being bullied. The worrying implication of this is that girls who are victims of bullying may be being overlooked; perhaps because bullying amongst girls is more likely to be indirect and therefore less easy to detect; or perhaps because the role of passive bullied pupil is assumed to be 'normal' for girls. Schools which are intending to put this kind of intervention into practice will have to examine their identification process carefully.

Structure and content of assertiveness courses

The techniques used during training courses are drawn from various well-known sources (Dickson, 1982). For example, Arora (1989, 1991) aimed to teach pupils how to deal effectively with bullying and how to avoid being bullied. She included strategies to improve social skills generally, such as awareness of feelings; how to work co-operatively with others; how to maintain friendships; skills for conflict resolution as well as specific assertive strategies. She recommended that pupils spend a total of at least twelve hours within the support group, to allow sufficient time to build relationships with each other and to enable them to work effectively together.

Within the Sheffield Project, we closely monitored six groups of pupils in three schools, which ran for between six and eight weekly sessions. During these the pupils were taught how to:

- make assertive statements;
- resist manipulation and threats;
- respond to name-calling;
- leave a bullying situation;
- enlist support from bystanders;
- boost their own self-esteem;
- remain calm in stressful situations.

A more detailed account of the organisation and content of the assertiveness groups can be found in Sharp, Cowie and Smith (1994).

Evaluation of assertiveness training

Arora (1991) found that after attending twelve hours of assertiveness training pupil self-esteem had increased. Teacher ratings indicated an increase in assertive behaviour in the classroom and the pupils reported a decrease in being bullied.

In conjunction with the Sheffield Project, Tonge (1992) evaluated the effectiveness of assertiveness training groups in three schools which involved a total of nineteen children. Outcomes of the assertiveness groups for the pupils were measured in three ways:

- self-esteem questionnaires given to pupils;
- pupil interviews including responses to hypothetical bullying situations;
- teacher reports on behaviour changes.

Pupil self-esteem was measured using the Culture Free Self-Esteem Inventory (Battle, 1981). Pupils completed this questionnaire at the beginning of the first group meeting and again at the end of the last group meeting. From these scores it was possible to establish differences in pupil self-esteem before and after the pupil had completed the assertiveness training course. A follow-up of the same pupils two terms later identified how well and under what circumstances these differences were maintained over time (Childs, 1993).

A significant increase in self-esteem was evident immediately after the pupils had attended the course of assertiveness sessions. There was a slight fall back in self-esteem scores two terms later, but this was not statistically significant. In one school, the increase in self-esteem continued even after the group had been completed. In this school, the teacher who ran the group maintained support for the pupils throughout the year. In the other schools, where there was no real contact with the teacher once the group had ended, there was a gradual decline in self-esteem scores. This indicates that whilst assertiveness training groups such as these are effective in boosting pupil self-esteem, long-term maintenance of this change will depend on continuing intermittent reinforcement and support.

The pupil interviews found that 71 per cent of the pupils felt more confident as a result of the sessions (Tonge, 1992). One pupil said: 'I feel a bit bigger, instead of being little. I feel as though I can look down on them from a great height instead of them standing on the ladder and looking down at me.' Another reported feeling 'more, like, sure of myself, more positive about things than I were before'.

In the interviews, pupils were given bullying scenarios. They were asked how they would respond to these situations and their answers were categorised as aggressive, passive unconstructive, passive constructive, and assertive. A first interview was given as the groups started, a second midway and a third after the groups ended. Pupils' answers were compared to see if there had been any changes in their kinds of responses to bullying situations. The interview also enquired to what extent and under what circumstances they had used the strategies introduced in the sessions.

There was a significant change in the coping strategies preferred by the pupils. The pupils indicated an increased tendency to use constructive responses to bullying situations (especially when pupils had been given opportunities to rehearse and role-play using their own bullying situations) and a decrease in aggressive responses. They also reported a 68 per cent decrease in being bullied at the final interview.

The teacher interviews reinforced these positive findings. The form tutors/class teachers of the pupils involved in the group were asked to describe any changes in behaviour. These teachers reported an increase in assertive behaviour around school and seemed to feel that there was a general improvement in self-confidence amongst the pupils.

The follow-up interviews in the next academic year (Childs, 1993) showed that even two terms afterwards and without reinforcement, most of these pupils were still feeling more confident and that levels of bullying had remained lower than before the groups had met. Some children had remained friendly with other pupils from the assertiveness group, an informal supportive relationship having been established. Different children found different aspects of the groups helpful – for some it was techniques they could use to stop or avoid a bullying situation; for others, it was not so much responding to the bullying but being able to stay calm and positive when being bullied. More than half the pupils found they felt more confident about making friends outside the group. One pupil compared his behaviour before and after the assertiveness training: ''cause (before) I weren't talking, I were just . . . I didn't go and talk to anybody. If you go and talk to somebody, you make friends with them, don't you.'

One boy, who reported gaining little from the groups directly, was pleased that the school was at least 'doing something about it'. Other comments made by the pupils highlighted the need for balance between discussion and practice. One older and more mature pupil felt frustrated by not having enough time to talk about the problems he was facing because of the practical focus of the group he was in.

Generalisation of techniques taught in a group situation such as these is always a concern – will the pupils actually put the techniques into practice? Eighty-five per cent of the pupils said that they had applied the assertiveness techniques to situations around the school. However, this level of generalisation was not so apparent for situations outside school. The focus for most of the role-play in the groups had been in-school situations. Rehearsal for a wider set of contexts both inside and outside school may be needed. Forty per cent of the pupils also reported that although they had used the techniques sometimes, there were still occasions when they had wanted to use a particular technique but had not. In explaining this pupils commented:

> It's a bit hard sometimes . . . like, if you want to say something, the kids might go after you if you said that.

> You want to try but you're afraid of getting hit.

> I just forgot all about what I was going to do.

Obviously, in introducing the techniques there is a need to consider when a particular approach is appropriate and when it is not. Work on coping with feelings such as anger and fear is also an important component of this kind of work. Plenty of opportunities to practise can also increase confidence and familiarity.

Maintaining the changes

Whilst assertiveness training leads to a short-term increase in self-esteem for most bullied pupils and provides them with a set of strategies which are useful to them in bullying situations, schools need to do more than provide an isolated six- or eight-week 'self-help' course for victims of bullying.

First, continuation of some kind of support system, albeit not as intensive as the initial course, has proved helpful especially for pupils with special educational needs. Pupils who were offered opportunities to talk with a teacher or fellow pupils about their bullying experiences after the end of the group, maintained more positive effects of the group over time. It may be that here is a suitable juncture for the combination of different interventions. Could the support role be taken on by other pupils, for example via peer counselling? Could the tenuous group network mentioned earlier in this section be more firmly established so that whilst the formal group ends, an informal one continues? Would occasional 'booster' sessions be helpful for these pupils, perhaps on a termly basis? The involvement of parents may also provide an additional support mechanism.

Second, this kind of group work is perhaps most effective as part of a whole-school approach to tackling bullying (see Chapter Three). We can build upon this work with the individual pupil who is being bullied by establishing an anti-bullying ethos within the school. The timing of these assertiveness groups needs to be carefully orchestrated to precede or coincide with curriculum work which aims to activate peer pressure against bullying behaviour. This may deter other pupils resisting changes in the victims' behaviour.

Broader applications of assertiveness techniques

The value of assertiveness techniques is not only confined to the small, safe and specialised group setting. Many pupils experience pressure to conform against their wishes at some time in their lives and it has been our experience that most pupils can benefit from learning assertiveness techniques within the general curriculum. This kind of training broadens the pupils' repertoire and provides them with an alternative vocabulary for responding to potentially difficult situations.

In addition to providing an opportunity for pupils to learn helpful skills, it can also offer a forum for introducing the notion of children's rights into the pupil and staff agenda. Sometimes, a denial of children's rights can lead to resistance against the introduction of assertiveness techniques to the timetable. Teaching staff who tend to employ aggressive management strategies may fear that somehow their authority will be undermined through such teaching, or teachers who themselves are passive in their own professional relationships may feel uncomfortable about the notion of assertion itself.

In some schools, rather than introducing assertiveness techniques to small groups of bullied pupils or as a subject in the curriculum, teachers have preferred to use the assertiveness strategies for responding to particular bullying incidents. In this way, they feel they have something concrete to offer a bullied pupil on an individual basis. It also enables schools who have not got sufficient resources to run withdrawal groups for small numbers of pupils to implement this kind of intervention (although this will be less time/cost-effective in the long run). This intervention can involve just the teacher and the bullied pupil or can include a special friend who can then support the bullied pupil outside the training context or the child's parents who can help with rehearsal.

An extension of this individual approach applies when a teacher or supervisor comes across a bullying incident and needs to respond immediately. A common occurrence in these situations is for the adult to reprimand the bullying pupil and to comfort the bullied pupil. This kind of response can serve to reinforce the helplessness of the bullied pupil. An alternative response (Hannan, 1992) would be to demonstrate disapproval of the bullying behaviour and to support the bullied pupil in responding directly and assertively to the bullying pupil. An example of this is provided below:

> The teacher enters the classroom to find John and Nathan playing catch with Joe's bag. He is clearly distressed about this.
>
> *Teacher*: (To John and Nathan) Give Joe his bag back. You both know that you should not behave that way in this school. (To Joe) Joe, you don't seem happy about John and Nathan's behaviour. Is that right?
>
> *Joe*: (Shakes his head and looks down.)
>
> *Teacher*: OK. Joe, tell John and Nathan that you don't like it when they mess around with your bag and you don't want them to do it again. Come on, you can say it. (Teacher stands next to Joe supportively.)
>
> *Joe*: I don't like you messing around with my bag. I don't want it to happen again.
>
> *Teacher*: Good. Now, Joe – I don't think this will happen again but if it does I want to hear about it. (Turns to John and Nathan) Now, John and Nathan, I know you both do well in class and I expect better behaviour from you. Like Joe, I don't want a repeat performance. We will fill in an incident slip and leave it at that.

In this example, the teacher has responded to the situation in accordance with the school's policy for bullying behaviour but has additionally aided the pupil in being assertive himself.

The main advantage of individual encouragement of assertive behaviour and/or general classwork on assertiveness techniques is that neither relies on the teacher being a skilled group facilitator. Additionally, special arrangements for group meeting times are not necessary. However, there is no reason why a school could not use all three methods for encouraging assertive behaviour as part of its whole-school anti-bullying approach. Where staffing or timetabling restricts the possibilities of running an assertiveness group for pupils, there may be other people within the school who would be willing, and with training, able to organise and facilitate the group. Parents, governors or lunchtime supervisors could provide adult support. Pentz (1980) and Huey and Rank (1984) have demonstrated that secondary-aged pupils can, if properly trained, teach assertiveness skills to their peers.

Summary

However hard schools try to learn about the nature and extent of bullying behaviour within their community, a certain amount is likely to remain hidden within the peer culture of the pupils. By providing pupils with the skills to be assertive, to be supportive of each other, to resolve conflict constructively, schools help the pupils to help themselves.

The methods described in this chapter clearly have organisational implications attached to their implementation. Training for teachers and pupils should be provided by an appropriately qualified and experienced person. This training should not only address the basic skills necessary, but also consider issues of ongoing support and supervision for pupils who are involved. It needs to provide opportunities for pupils to practise and rehearse their different scripts and roles.

Assertiveness groups, counselling and mediation services all require space, time and administration. Where children are referred to such services, schools need to ask themselves *how* this will be done, and *who* will do it. Gender and cultural issues need to be considered in organising such systems. Monitoring of these kinds of support services is essential. Schools need to know how often, by whom and how effectively pupil support systems are being used. Information gathered through monitoring needs to be fed back to enable change and improvement. Maintenance of these interventions is important to encourage implementation over time. A one-off lesson on conflict resolution or 'saying no' may have some benefit for some pupils. However, a more determined and structured effort is required to guarantee that pupils will put such skills into practice.

Although all pupils can potentially benefit from learning about these kinds of interventions, they are more likely to be effective if they are implemented as part of a cohesive and thought-out drive against bullying behaviour. The findings of the Sheffield Project, and other studies mentioned in this chapter, indicate that these positive and empowering interventions do have value both for individual pupils and for the general ethos of the school. To maximise their effectiveness schools need to integrate them into the school organisation and be rigorous in their implementation, maintenance and review. These kinds of approaches are complemented by each other and by other interventions described elsewhere in this book.

understanding and preventing bullying in the junior school playground

MICHAEL J. BOULTON

Introduction

Relatively few writers have explicitly focused on *playground* bullying, which is surprising given that the playground is the most common location in which bullying in school takes place. This will be a focus of the present chapter. It begins by presenting data on playground bullying (and other activities) and continues by considering some of the measures that can be taken to tackle the problem of playground bullying/fighting. In so doing, it will include a discussion of the playground option of the Sheffield Project. This part of the project will be described and a brief assessment of its effect on levels of bullying, and other outcome variables, will be presented. An attempt will also be made throughout the chapter to consider both the likely benefits of each suggestion for intervention, as well as some of the possible negative outcomes, based on what we know about bullying and other aspects of the social psychology of childhood.

Children's activities in the playground

Until fairly recently, the question of what activities children spontaneously choose to engage in in the playground has received relatively little attention from researchers. Many teachers, too, appear to be less concerned with, and/or aware of, children's experiences in the playground. Some recent studies, using interview and observational methodologies, have shown that for most of the time, the majority of children are engaged in friendly sociable activities in the playground (Blatchford, Creeser and Mooney, 1990; Boulton, 1992). These activities include such things as sociable non-play interactions with peers (such as talking in groups), rule-governed games (such as rounders and football) and boisterous rough-and-tumble play.

Nevertheless, results from these studies could give a false impression of the levels of aggression/bullying on the playground. It is possible that while aggression/bullying could account for only a very small proportion of children's playground time, they could still occur fairly frequently in bouts of short duration. Similarly, a minority of pupils could engage in elevated levels of aggression/bullying compared with their peers. Indeed, interview and observational studies with children confirm that while aggression and bullying take up relatively little of most pupils' playground time, they nevertheless are experienced at one time or another by a large proportion of them, and can have a detrimental effect on their happiness and psychological well-being. Mooney, Creeser and Blatchford (1991) interviewed primary school pupils in inner London and found that 67 per cent of 7-year-olds and 50 per cent of 11-year-olds reported that they had been involved in fighting in school at some time during the present academic year. Boulton (1993a) used a similar methodology with a group of pupils from two inner city schools in a different conurbation and found similar results. Overall, 51 per cent of 8 and 11-year-old pupils had fought with another pupil during the current school year.

Self-report data such as these, especially on such an emotive topic as aggression/fighting, need to be considered with caution. Some children could either over- or under-report their involvement for reasons which are not clearly understood at present. One study of bullies and victims found that some children who may be classified as extreme victims are less likely to report being victimised in face-to-face interviews than they are in anonymous questionnaires (Ahmad and Smith, 1990). Hence, alternative methodologies should be employed to look for confirmatory evidence of the level of children's involvement in playground fighting and bullying. Boulton (1993a) directly observed a sample of 8 and 11-year-old boys and girls as they interacted on the playground. Focal sampling, recording the behaviour of individual children for periods of about forty minutes per child, showed that the mean rates for engaging in playground fighting and bullying for 8-year-old girls and boys was 2.6 and 3.7 episodes per hour respectively, and for 11-year-old girls and boys it was 1.1 and 1.4 episodes per hour respectively.

It is important to recognise that fighting and bullying are not synonymous.

Nevertheless it can be argued that they are related, not least in the sense that they can both be thought of as being sub-categories of aggression. Moreover, it is clear that both fighting and bullying can have upsetting consequences for children. Blatchford, Creeser and Mooney (1990) asked 11-year-old pupils what they did not like about playtime. They found that one in five pupils expressed worries about such things as bullying, being beaten up, fighting and people starting trouble. Boulton and Underwood (1992) found that about 87 per cent of 8 to 10-year-olds reported that they experienced negative emotions when they were bullied, and more than 80 per cent that they felt better about themselves prior to the onset of their being bullied. Imich and Jefferies (1989, p. 46) stated that

> One could hypothesize that a child who is worried about going into the playground at breaktimes and lunchtimes is at a higher risk of educational failure in terms of classroom performance; certainly, experience in working with school non-attenders suggests that what goes on out of the classroom can often be a significant factor in explaining school absenteeism.

An attitude sometimes encountered among both teachers and parents is that fighting and bullying are an inevitable and normal part of growing up and that all children 'have' to experience them. This perhaps is a matter of degree. Blatchford, Creeser and Mooney (1990, p. 171) asked:

> is there an acceptance of much higher levels of aggression ... than would ever be tolerated inside the school itself? ... are we allowing in the playground the creation of a confrontational moral code that runs counter to the spirit of co-operation and toleration many teachers strive to encourage in the classroom?

If this statement matches the reality of life in any of our school playgrounds, it would be necessary for action to be taken. In the next sections of this chapter, various issues that relate to tackling playground bullying and fighting will be discussed.

Adult supervision of the playground

In order to reduce levels of bullying and fighting in the playground, we must consider the general issue of adult supervision. Poor supervision could be one important reason why the playground is the most common location in schools where bullying takes place. Several related questions need to be addressed, including which members of a school's staff actually do the supervising, what training and support they receive in order to be most effective and how this could be improved, whether and to what extent supervisors should become more actively involved in children's playground activities than they generally are at present, and how relevant behaviour management skills may be enhanced.

Several authors have called for an examination of the way children are supervised in the playground, probably stemming from an awareness that playground supervision has not received the attention that it deserves. Certainly the level of training offered for classroom practice far exceeds that offered for managing children's behaviour in the playground. Typically, junior school children are supervised during the main midday break by female assistants, usually members of the local community. Lunchtime supervisors often find themselves in charge of large numbers of children, and in many cases the ratio may exceed fifty children to each supervisor (Andrews and Hinton, 1991). This in itself is a situation that is far from ideal, and one suggestion is to increase the number of supervisors on duty (Thompson and Smith, 1991). The general consensus would probably be that such a measure would help to reduce levels of bullying/fighting. Empirical data supports such a view. Olweus (1987) reported a negative correlation of around -0.50 between relative density of teachers during playtime and number of bully/victim problems.

However, it is clear that financial constraints would rule out significant increases in the numbers of lunchtime supervisors which headteachers would be prepared to take on, notwithstanding the relatively low rates of pay on offer. As one headteacher said, 'Of course I would like to double or even triple my supervisory staff but the money is just not there.'

Many teachers, too, would probably not receive favourably calls for them to spend more of their lunchtime in the playground. Indeed, the benefits for teachers of taking a lunch break away from pupils have been vehemently articulated by representatives of the profession.

An alternative to increasing numbers of staff on duty in the playground would be to improve some specific skills of those supervisors that schools actually employ (Birmingham City Council Education Department, 1991; Blatchford, 1989; Boulton, 1994; Imich and Jefferies, 1989; Mellor, 1991). Until relatively recently, training of lunchtime supervisors has been largely overlooked. Nevertheless, the situation does seem to be improving. Sharp (1994) reviewed the suggestions put forward in a number of training schemes, many of which provide sound practical advice. My own conversations with lunchtime supervisors lead me to believe that in the majority of cases there is enthusiasm and goodwill among supervisors for training. As one supervisor who attended our training courses put it:

We do the best that we can but its hard to know if we are doing the right thing. This is the first course I've been on and I've been doing this job for over five years. I think we can all learn a lot – there's always something new to try to help us stop the children from fighting and falling out.

A common suggestion put forward by advocates of training courses has been that supervisors take on a more active role in the organisation of children in playground activities (Andrews and Hinton, 1991; Birmingham City Council Education Department, 1991; Ross and Ryan, 1990). The rationale is that if children are involved in friendly co-operative play, they will not be involved in aggressive activities such as bullying and fighting:

> Problems will arise if children have nothing to do. Charging around all over the playground, having nowhere to sit, being cold and bored leads to aggravation. Purposeful activity will eliminate much of the trouble and keep everyone a lot happier.
>
> (Birmingham City Council Education Department, 1991)

One possibility would be to provide children with play equipment to facilitate their involvement in co-operative play. In one middle school in which I carried out research prior to the Sheffield Project, the headteacher was persuaded to invest in items of play equipment that the children could use in the playground – rounders bats, tennis balls, skipping ropes and plastic hoops. Anticipating a more harmonious group of children, the playground supervisors placed a large box containing this equipment in the playground and invited the children to help themselves. However, almost from the very first moment this action proved to be a failure. The children squabbled over possession of particular items, and even after the supervisors had intervened to sort these problems out, the children continued to argue about the most desirable locations in the playground to use the equipment. Within a couple of weeks the experiment was abandoned.

Experiences like these suggest that it may be a mistake to simply provide equipment and, at the very least, it is important for staff to think through the implications of this or any other course of action. A more systematic approach was taken by two other schools (Birmingham City Council Education Department, 1991). Prior to the introduction of the games materials, the supervisors and interested members of the teaching staff devised strategies for managing the apparatus. In part, this involved a recognition that there were insufficient items to go round for every pupil. In one school, a rota system was introduced based on year groups. There were some initial 'teething troubles' with the introduction of the equipment – children trying to use the equipment when it was not their year group's turn, bats being used to assault other pupils and skipping ropes being used to disrupt other children's games. Nevertheless, one headteacher reported that:

> after the initial problems the scheme has worked well. Parents have reported that children have talked about it at home – a sign, perhaps, that it has a been a success for them and preferable to being left to their own devices. We will be continuing, resourcing it ourselves now.
>
> (p. 9)

A related suggestion to providing play equipment is to encourage supervisors to join in the games and play activities of children in their care. Again, though, it is necessary to think through the wider implications of this course of action. While there may be important advantages in trying to keeping children occupied, there may also be disadvantages. Children may benefit in various ways from playing together in the absence of close adult guidance. I found that when children were engaged in playful activities they were often in quite large, and sometimes very large, groups. For example, boys' games of football had on average over thirteen participants, and the games of rounders played by the girls involved on average over ten individuals. Games played with so many participants could provide a real challenge to children and help develop their organisational and social skills. These advantages would be less obvious in adult-organised activities. Denzin (1977) regarded the need for children to construct their own social order as a unique feature of the playground game context. This might be a real benefit of playtime for many children, and one that may be lost if adults 'take over' playtime. It may take on even greater significance because many of the 'traditional' out-of-school play opportunities are no longer available to many children.

The social skills that may be developed in free-play contexts with other children may also provide some 'protection' from bullying, although this hypothesis is yet to be fully tested and is supported only by indirect evidence at present. Dygdon, Conger and Keane (1987) asked children to provide information about the characteristics of pupils that they liked or disliked. Popular children were perceived by peers as those individuals who exhibited more social skills in real-life encounters in general, and in play interactions in particular. For example, popular children were said to engage in socially desirable play participation and play permission, whereas children that were disliked were said to engage in these same activities in a more negative way. In turn, being liked by one's peers is associated with low levels of bullying, and conversely, being rejected by peers is associated with higher levels of bullying (Boulton and Smith, 1994; Lagerspetz, Bjorkqvist, Berts and King, 1982; Olweus, 1978).

Another 'down side' to providing too much adult supervision is that children will be given less opportunity to experience and deal with various sorts of conflict. Titman (1989) stated that 'a degree of conflict during play is inevitable and provides a valuable way for children to learn that people are different, and for them to develop skills to understand conflict and find ways of dealing with differences and conflict' (p. 106) (and see Chapter Five).

While these potential problems associated with adults pursuing a more active involvement in children's playground activities should be kept in mind, it is important that we consider some of the potential benefits. Titman (1989) presents a strong case for active adult participation in children's play, both in the playground and elsewhere, stating that 'involvement with children during their play can pre-empt and prevent problems arising and is thus a preferred management style to supervising them' (p. 107).

Titman argued that 'the role of the playworker is complex and multi-faceted' (p. 107), and she outlined some of the traits necessary for such a demanding role. These include the ability to interact and form close relationships with individual children, while at the same time being able to relate to many children of both sexes, diverse ages, backgrounds and temperaments. The adult should be able to maintain control but in a subtle way and without recourse to excessive authoritarian sanctions. Few if any of us naturally possess such qualities, and once again there would appear to be a strong case for providing training courses for playground supervisors to enable them to fulfil such a demanding role.

The above discussion suggests that we would be wise to look for a compromise between too much adult intervention (that may interfere with the benefits of 'true' free play) and too little adult intervention (that may do nothing to help reduce bullying/fighting). Research in middle schools in New Zealand supports the notion of 'limited' adult participation in the playground. O'Rourke (1980) found that adults who immediately set up activities for children when they entered the playground for recess, and who left after eight to ten minutes, were almost as effective in terms of 'take up' by children, and in reducing levels of rule breaking and fighting, as adults who started activities after the first ten minutes and played with the children until the bell. O'Rourke concluded that 'those children who are at a loss for things to do, and those who turn to mischief and fighting can be offered more rewarding and appropriate ways of participating' (p. 30). Similarly, Murphy, Hutchison and Bailey (1983) found that adult-organised games decreased the frequency of aggression, property abuse and rule violation among 5–7-year-old children in the playground prior to the start of the school day. Thus, it is possible for adults to help children organise their playground time, and encourage participation in friendly games, without children losing out on the potential benefits associated with free play.

Enhancing behaviour-management skills of playground supervisors

In order to effectively manage children's playground behaviour, it is necessary for supervisors to possess a range of some specific behaviour-management skills. Like any other type of skill development, competence in this particular range of skills can be enhanced with appropriate guidance and practice. Nevertheless, one absolutely elementary skill – the ability to actually detect whether a child is behaving aggressively – has been overlooked in most training courses now on offer for playground supervisors. Adults are faced with several problems that could impede an 'accurate' perception of the nature of children's playground behaviours.

One major problem stems from the existence of a category of play that looks superficially similar to true aggression, often referred to as rough-and-tumble play, or play-fighting. This may take up between 5 to 10 per cent of children's time in the playground (Boulton, 1992; Humphreys and Smith, 1987). The actual figure will vary with child characteristics (such as age, sex, interests) and environmental features (such as type of play area surface). Many teachers seem reluctant to accept that activities which appear to *them* to be aggressive may in fact be playful as far as the children themselves are concerned. In the words of one teacher, 'if it looks like fighting to me that is enough, I tell them to stop it'. This sort of attitude can probably help to explain why, when I was collecting data in the playground, I noticed that children were sometimes reprimanded and punished by adults (usually teachers or lunchtime supervisors) for being 'aggressive' towards another child when they appeared to me to be only playing with that child, and why, in some other cases, adults failed to step in to halt an episode of what appeared to me to be true aggression.

To a casual adult observer there does appear to be relatively little difference between playful and aggressive fighting, especially as they both draw on a common repertoire of actions, especially hitting, kicking and grappling. However, several studies suggest that prior to adolescence, the two categories of behaviour arise from distinct motivations and have different characteristics (Aldis, 1975; Boulton, 1991a, b; Costabile, Smith, Matheson, Aston, Hunter and Boulton, 1992; Fry, 1987; Humphreys and Smith, 1987; Pellegrini, 1987, 1989; Smith and Boulton, 1990). Whereas aggressive fighting involves the intention to hurt by one or other or both parties, this feature is absent in playful fighting encounters. Supervisors of children in free-play situations would benefit by being made aware of the distinction that can be made between playful and aggressive fighting.

Even for those teachers and lunchtime supervisors who do recognise the rough-and-tumble/aggression dichotomy, there may still be problems in actually distinguishing between real and mock aggression (Boulton, 1993b). I prepared a videotape of episodes of playful and aggressive fighting involving junior school pupils and showed this to forty-four adults. The adults were asked to say whether they thought each episode involved playful or aggressive fighting, and their responses were compared to a standard view based on children's perceptions of these episodes. For more than one in ten episodes, adults could be thought of as making a 'mistake', that is, they perceived an episode as playful that children themselves tended to view as aggressive, or vice versa.

Given that children spend noteworthy amounts of their time in the playground in play-fighting activities and that aggressive fighting, although taking up much less time, is still a feature of the typical junior school playground, this could be a cause for concern. Children are usually supervised in the playground by either teachers or lunchtime supervisors, and neither group is explicitly trained in how to distinguish between playful and aggressive fighting.

Nevertheless, it is true that participants in this study were not practising junior school teachers or lunchtime supervisors, and so it remains possible that experience in observing children may make adults more adept at distinguishing between playful and aggressive fighting. However, Connor (1989) provided evidence to suggest that a propensity to view ambiguous episodes as aggressive by some adults may be *increased* when the individual actually works with pre-school children on a regular basis. She imputed this tendency to 'concerns that children will get out of control or will hurt each other' (p. 215). Perhaps the tendency to err on the side of caution (i.e. by having a 'readiness' to view ambiguous episodes as aggressive) is the 'least serious' type of mistake that could be made by supervisors of children in the playground. In the short term, it would be better for an adult to step in to halt an instance of playful fighting that was mistakenly construed as aggressive than to refrain from intervening in an instance of physical bullying because it was mistakenly perceived to be playful.

Nevertheless, there may be some other less beneficial implications of this course of action. As was noted above, supervisors are often in charge of large numbers of children in the playground. By focusing on 'innocent' activities such as playful fighting, their attention might be diverted away from more obvious cases of aggression and bullying. One solution that might help supervisors in this area would be to ban rough-and-tumble play. However, some psychologists have suggested that participation in friendly rough-and-tumble play may be beneficial for some children in a variety of ways. Pellegrini (1987) suggested that playful fighting is characterised by the swopping of roles, and hence may facilitate the development of turn-taking skills. Boulton (1991b) suggested that playful fighting and associated activities may serve an affiliative function by promoting and enhancing friendships. If these suggestions are valid, then it would not be sensible for schools to ban rough-and-tumble play outright. More research is warranted on the issue of the developmental and educational significance of children's playful fighting and associated activities.

Why are (some) adults poor at distinguishing between playful and aggressive fighting? We might speculate that preconceived ideas could cloud some of our judgements. For example, an individual who does not accept that any 'fighting' can be playful is almost certainly going to infer that an episode of rough-and-tumble play is aggressive. In contrast, another individual, who perhaps participated in rough-and-tumble play as a child and received lots of pleasure from doing so, may be more likely to infer that an aggressive episode is playful.

Another reason for mistakes among adults is suggested by an examination of the actual process of making an inference about the aggressive versus the playful nature of an episode. Boulton (1993b) found that children are significantly more likely than adults to rely on the physical actions of the participants, but significantly less likely to use inferences about participants' action/intent and facial expressions. Adults who actually supervise children in the playground and elsewhere could be encouraged to avoid making subjective inferences about the actions/intentions of children, and instead pay attention to more 'concrete' criteria, such as the nature of the physical actions. Observational data (Boulton, 1991a; Fry, 1987) suggest that the actions of children within bouts of playful fighting are more likely than those within bouts of aggressive fighting to be restrained, even to the extent that punches, kicks, etc. are deliberately aimed to miss an 'opponent'. Similarly, roles within bouts of playful fighting (such as which child is restraining a partner and which child is being restrained) are more likely to be deliberately reversed compared to bouts of aggressive fighting. By being made aware of these physical differences between the two categories of behaviour, supervisors' abilities to tell them apart might be improved. This issue is covered in more detail in Boulton (1994) and in Smith and Boulton (1990).

As well as being able to correctly identify aggressive acts when they occur, supervisors also should be able to respond appropriately. A complaint expressed by some senior managers and teachers about lunchtime supervisors is that they do not always behave in ways that best resolve such problems. Many adults in day-to-day contact with children, not just playground supervisors, may benefit from a consideration of alternative ways of managing pupils' behaviour. In the lunchtime supervisor training programme implemented as part of the Sheffield Project, we focused on the rationale and likely benefits behind such strategies as trying to keep calm in the face of children's actions that are very provoking for adults, not being seen by the pupils as someone who jumps to conclusions but rather as someone who is prepared to listen to all sides before deciding what to do, refusing to be side-tracked by pupils that have misbehaved, avoiding sarcasm and direct personal criticism, labelling the behaviour but not the child as unacceptable, having a hierarchy of sanctions at one's disposal that is known to both adults and children (see below), and not using teachers as a means of controlling children.

The last point raises the crucial issue of authority, or more specifically, *perceived* authority. A common complaint of many lunchtime supervisors is that because the children do not view them as having the same level of authority as teachers, they cannot properly manage misbehaviour when it occurs in the playground. They report that children do not do what the supervisors tell them to do, and often respond with verbal insults. Even in schools that have explicitly stated to pupils that lunchtime supervisors have the same level of authority as teachers, some problems have remained.

In some cases, these problems stemmed from teachers' behaviour. For example, I have seen cases where a teacher has intervened as a supervisor was actually in the process of dealing with an instance of playground bullying, taking over the situation uninvited. In another case, a child was told by a teacher to ignore what the supervisor had just told him to do. Behaviour such as this only serves to reinforce the idea in children's minds that teachers have more authority than supervisors. Some teachers might like to consider how they interact with supervisors in front of pupils, and how this might convey unwanted messages to them and make the supervisor's job even more difficult. For this reason, we also recommended that supervisors do not use teachers as a means of controlling pupils, as was noted above.

Enhancing the social skills of children

Just as some adults may benefit from social skills training in recognising playful versus aggressive intent in children's actions, so too might some pupils. At the infant school level, Sluckin (1981) argued that 'undoubtedly a certain number of children . . . fail to distinguish and react appropriately to rough and tumble (pretend) and real aggression' (p. 40). Several studies have found that the majority of children are skilled at doing so but a small proportion might have problems (Boulton, 1993c; Costabile *et al.* 1991; Pellegrini, 1989; Smith and Lewis, 1985). Boulton (1993c) prepared an edited videotape containing episodes of both types of encounter. Children were asked to say whether they thought each one was aggressive or playful in nature, and to give reasons for their choice. Most, but not all, pupils (thirty-four out of forty-four 8-year-olds and forty-two out of forty-five 11-year-olds) showed significant agreement with the standard view of each episode. The most frequent criteria used were the physical actions of the participants, subjective inferences about actions/intentions of the participants, and whether the participants stayed together or separated after the episode.

In the USA, Pellegrini (1989) found evidence that poor decoding skills in these types of interaction are associated with elevated levels of aggression on the playground and low popularity with peers. Pellegrini examined the transitional probabilities of rough-and-tumble play leading into other activities. Playground encounters that involved children who were poor at making the distinction between play and aggression, and who tended to be unpopular with their peers, were more likely to turn into aggression, whereas those of children who were skilled in this area, and who tended to be popular with their peers, were more likely to turn directly into friendly games with rules.

A likely scenario to account for these results is that a child will try to initiate a rough-and-tumble encounter with another, but this will be misperceived as a hostile assault due to poor social skills and so will receive an aggressive retaliation. The initiator of the original rough-and-tumble overture will see the aggressive response as inappropriate (after all, she/he was only playing) and hence will feel justified in responding with aggression herself/himself. Thus, the encounter which began with one child's attempt to be playful has ended up as aggression due to social skill deficits in another (Dodge, Murphy and Buchsbaum, 1984).

Such an explanation is supported indirectly. I have found that the most common method children use to initiate a bout of rough-and-tumble play with peers is physical rather than verbal. Typically, a child will begin with a light tap, an attempt to grab their partner or other such action, rather than with a verbal initiation that is a common means by which children start many other playful activities ('Shall we play tick'?). Thus, non-verbal social skills are of paramount importance in rough-and-tumble encounters. Other research has also found a clear relationship between the way a child attributes the causes of a peer's actions and their actual response – aggressive retaliations are usually reserved for peers who are perceived to have acted with hostile intent (Dodge, 1980; Nasby, Hayden and de Paulo, 1979). This would clearly apply to both the children in the scenario described above. Dodge suggested that a child who lacks the ability to accurately detect hostile intent may come to be a disliked member of the peer group and the target of truly anti-social behaviours. This then confirms the child's view that other children are unfriendly and aggressive and, over time, these attitudes may crystallise into a paranoid world view.

The evidence and arguments described above suggest that, in some individuals, the social skills that normally ensure that rough-and-tumble play bouts *remain* playful are in some way 'faulty', and this may contribute to their becoming aggressive/bullying members of their peer group and/or victims of peer aggression. An important question, therefore, is where do these social skills come from? Abilities in this domain could be largely independent of actual experience, suggesting that they are inborn. Alternatively, these skills may be dependent to some extent on children's experiences of rough-and-tumble play and/or aggression.

Perhaps the most likely explanation is that both innate factors and social factors are important. A study that examines these issues in younger pupils is clearly warranted, not least because by banning children from engaging in rough-and-tumble play we could be taking away opportunities for them to develop social skills that allow them to differentiate between playful and serious aggression. These would be important skills during childhood as well as during adulthood.

On a practical level, there does appear to be a case for schools to try to identify those relatively few pupils who may have difficulties distinguishing between playful and aggressive fighting, and to help them develop their skills. One possibility that I am addressing currently is to use videotaped material with them, pointing out why they might be mistaken in inferring that a given episode was playful or aggressive. They might also be coached to pay attention to the aspects of bouts that socially skilled pupils attend to.

The existence of children who might mistakenly view playful actions by peers as aggressive may also mean that supervisors should not automatically discount the ubiquitous excuse of 'I was only playing'. Clearly, some children do use this excuse to try to disguise the fact that they were bullying other pupils; what might not be so obvious is that in some cases it may actually be true.

Mobilising the 'silent majority'

Several authors have put forward the view that an essential aspect of reducing bullying in school is to enlist the help of children who are not directly involved. Herbert (1989) stated that 'Perhaps the most important factor in combating bullying is the social pressure brought to bear by the peer group rather than the condemnation of individual bullies by someone in authority' (pp. 79–80). Similarly, Boulton and Underwood (1992) argued that 'Children should be made aware . . . that *everyone* has a responsibility to act either by challenging the bully directly or reporting the incident to an adult' (p. 82, italics in original).

Data on children's attitudes towards bullying in general (i.e. when it is not directed at themselves) are far from encouraging, and suggest that much work is needed to change attitudes. Rigby and Slee (1991) found that a small but noteworthy proportion of children, especially boys, admired bullies. For example, they agreed with statements such as 'It is funny to see kids get upset when they are teased.' Given that the playground is where most bullying takes place, and often this happens out of sight of adults, there are grounds for arguing that changing the behaviour of pupils who witness acts of bullying should be a priority. It is probably only after attitudes have been changed that children's actual behaviour will change in a manner that is likely to help reduce the levels of playground bullying, as well as bullying in other situations both inside and out of school.

Reducing or removing playtime

The ultimate way to eradicate playground bullying would be to reduce or even eliminate playtime altogether. Indeed, in some Australian and American schools, and some schools in the UK, the traditional afternoon playtime has been removed from the daily timetable. There are some very important issues that need to be addressed in relation to this question.

As was noted above, some writers believe that free play provides a unique opportunity for children to develop important inter-personal skills. Many of children's more traditional free-play opportunities outside of school have disappeared and so the playground remains one of the few contexts in which they can interact with large numbers of peers and develop these skills.

Over and above these considerations, it is also the case that many children greatly enjoy playtime. Blatchford, Creeser and Mooney (1990) asked 11-year-old children to state how much they liked each of the three daily playtimes. The long dinnertime break evoked the most positive responses. Overall, 84 per cent of children liked it, and 58 per cent went so far as to say that they 'love it'. Substantial proportions of pupils also said that they liked or even loved morning playtime (72 per cent) and afternoon playtime (55 per cent). Only a relatively small proportion of children expressed negative attitudes to dinner playtime (6 per cent), morning playtime (15 per cent) and afternoon playtime (9 per cent). Similarly, Evans (1990) reported that 75 per cent of teachers admitted that they threatened the withdrawal of playtime as a form of punishment, and that this was effective because most pupils did not want to lose their play break.

Another argument in favour of maintaining traditional playtimes is that it gives children the opportunity to 'blow off steam' and hence facilitates children's attention to academic school work. Pellegrini and Davis (1993) examined the effects of classroom 'confinements' of various durations on children's classroom behaviour, and concluded that children, and especially boys, were more restless while working in their seats as a function of time. The children tended to fidget more the longer they were confined, suggesting that the chance to play in the playground may help them cope with the sedentary demands of the classroom. However, the children were less attentive to their studies after vigorous playground activities than after less active social and non-social play. The latter result would seem to support the notion of reducing playtime, or at least discouraging certain boisterous activities which boys seem to favour. However, more work needs to be done on this issue, and Pellegrini and Davis themselves stated that 'boys, more than girls, are restless in classrooms, generally. Recess probably does not do much to affect this' (p. 94).

Responding to bullying and other unacceptable behaviour

Despite our best efforts, bullying/fighting will probably continue to occur, albeit at reduced rates. There is a clear need to examine the strengths and limitations of various ways of responding to them over the longer term as well as in the immediate situation. Foster and Thompson (1991) considered some of the issues surrounding adults' responses that need to be addressed if we are to efficiently discourage future occurrences. They noted that responding to bullying presents us with some special difficulties, largely because the bully accepts aggression as a viable strategy to deal with interpersonal disputes.

They stated that:

> If disciplinary action is to be truly effective, sanctions have to emerge from social pressure on the bully and be accepted by the bully as appropriate, and should not involve explicit aggression on the part of adults. The sanction has to be consistent with efforts of school staff

to establish a social climate where physical aggression is not used as a means of gaining popularity, maintaining group leadership, or influencing others to do what they are told. The sanctions against bullying have to emerge from the views of the children involved themselves, supported by the adults.

(Foster and Thompson, 1991, p. 13)

Many adults feel a strong sense of outrage when they see a child being bullied in the playground by another pupil or, even worse, a group of pupils. In the words of one middle school teacher:

I wanted to give him [a bully] a taste of his own medicine. He's always picking on Mark [a victim] even though he's been told time after time. In the end I just about kept control of myself and marched him off to see the headteacher. But I still made it clear just how mad I was.

Despite the strong emotions that bullying may arouse, we must resist the temptation to over-react or to 'bully the bully'. Social learning theory (Bandura, 1977) would clearly predict that children are likely to imitate the actions of adults, and so an aggressive response to cases of bullying may exacerbate the problem rather than help to alleviate it.

From a moral and ethical standpoint, physical sanctions are unacceptable to a growing number of adults. It also appears to be the case that many children who are involved in bullying may be classified as 'bully/victims' – that is they bully some peers and are bullied by others. It is possible that these children bully some of their weaker peers *because* they themselves are bullied by stronger pupils, perhaps to bolster their self-esteem. If so, then it would be even more inappropriate to be overly punitive with them.

This is *not* to say that we should justify their bullying in any way or that we need accept it, but rather that we should consider alternative ways of responding. Nowhere would this be more important than in the playground itself where an adult's actions will be on view to many pupils. In the Sheffield Project, we recommended a hierarchy of sanctions (Boulton, 1994). This could start with a discussion of acceptable and unacceptable behaviour that is linked to a whole-school policy on bullying (see Chapter Three), verbal warnings for first and/or minor offences, involvement of senior managers for subsequent and/or serious offences, contact with parents if the misbehaviour persists or is particularly serious, and eventually exclusion from the playground.

Another structured approach whereby supervisors could respond in a graded way to misbehaviour in the playground, including fighting and bullying, was described by Imich and Jefferies (1989). The system was actually adopted in a large primary school, and its effect on misbehaviour assessed. For minor offences, such as pushing in a line or being off limits, children were faced with a 'time out' situation in which they were told to sit on a chair facing a blank wall and do nothing for five minutes. For more serious offences, such as fighting and bullying, a child was issued with a yellow card, and the headteacher was informed. The child had to have the card signed by the issuing supervisor at the end of each lunchtime play period, but this would only be done if the child had behaved well. On receiving five signatures, the child took the card to the headteacher who signed the child off. Any child that received three yellow cards was automatically issued with a red card. This resulted in the child's parents being informed and the child being excluded from school during lunchtime for one week. Prior to the implementation of this scheme, it was clearly described to the children, along with the rules for the playground which made clear what behaviours were acceptable and unacceptable. Overall, the system was deemed to have had a positive effect on various aspects of the children's playground behaviour, including aggression and bullying.

Playground interventions in the Sheffield Project

Many of the issues discussed in this chapter influenced the design of the Sheffield Project. From the very beginning of the project it was recognised that a focus on the playground would be necessary. However, schools were invited to consider whether or not they would like to select the playground 'option', either on its own or in conjunction with some of the other options (see Chapter One). Out of the sixteen junior schools in the project, thirteen selected the playground option.

It was also apparent from the very beginning of the project that just one all-encompassing playground intervention would not be workable as far as the participating schools were concerned – quite simply there were far too many issues related to reducing playground bullying for this to be possible. Moreover, while we knew that all of the schools shared the common problem of playground bullying (by virtue of their requesting to take part in the project, as well as comments from staff), they were found to differ in terms of such things as the amount of space available in the playground per child, the training and support already offered to lunchtime supervisors, the mechanisms already in place for preventing and responding to bullying, the availability of staff to take responsibility for further action required by the project, and so on. Consequently, within the playground option itself there were several more specific interventions suggested to the schools, and once again, each school could select as many or as few of these as they wanted. Our intention was to address as many of the issues covered in this chapter as possible through these recommended courses of action.

Informal discussions with representatives from participating schools at the beginning of the project also alerted us to the dangers of swamping them with too many 'demands'. One headteacher was aware of the potential benefits associated with tackling playground bullying through the interventions we initially proposed but was also quick to point out that members of his teaching and non-teaching staff already felt over-stretched with their other concerns. He stated that:

> These seem like very good ideas to me and I would like to think I could find members of staff to manage them. The problem is that we all have so much to do as it already is, so if you could make them as simple and straightforward as possible that would really help a lot.

For this reason we tried to make our suggestions for interventions as user-friendly as we could.

The interventions actually offered to the schools included the following:

- raising the status of lunchtime supervisors with pupils;
- building relationships between lunchtime supervisors and pupils;
- building relationships between lunchtime supervisors and teaching staff;
- training course for lunchtime supervisors;
- ways of dealing with bullying when it occurs;
- encouraging positive behaviour in the playground;
- improving the quality of play;
- improving the quality of wet playtimes.

Details of how these interventions may be implemented in schools can be found in Boulton (1994), but here I discuss the rationale behind them, how the schools in the Sheffield Project found them in practice, as well as their overall effect on levels of playground bullying in those schools that adopted our suggestions.

Raising the status of lunchtime supervisors with pupils

As has been noted there are good reasons for raising the status of lunchtime supervisors. At present, many pupils and some teachers do not fully appreciate the valuable contribution that lunchtime supervisors make in school. In some cases, supervisors reported that children sometimes ignored their instructions, were overtly rude to them (see also Sharp, 1994), and gave the impression that even the presence of a supervisor would not deter them from engaging in bullying and other unacceptable behaviour. To help over-come this type of problem, one of the playground options involved a formal introduction of lunchtime supervisors to all pupils. Our suggestion was that it should take place in an assembly to signify its importance. The children were told in clear terms that supervisors have the same level of authority as teachers, and they were made aware of how they should respond to super-visors' requests. We recommended that, if it was agreeable to them, the supervisors could wear name badges, and that children should address them by name. To reinforce the idea that supervisors were just as 'important' as teachers, we suggested that the same system for addressing teachers (i.e. by surname) be adopted.

In one school (P9) that adopted this suggestion, a supervisor thought the name badges had helped. She stated that:

> Yes, the name badges seem to have made a difference. The children, well the difficult ones anyway, seem to see us as real people now, and they do call us by our proper names. Before, it was awful, they used to say 'Oi' or just shout to get our attention. There's this one boy who was always being cheeky to us, but last week he came up to me and was really polite. He said 'My aunty's name is the same as yours.'

Building relationships between lunchtime supervisors and pupils

Many pupils are reluctant to tell an adult if they are being bullied (Whitney and Smith, 1993). We felt that if children could be encouraged to forge closer relationships with lunchtime supervisors then they might be more likely to inform them when they or their peers are bullied in the playground. Certainly, many pupils I have spoken to during my research on playgrounds have expressed the view that they would not tell a supervisor if they were experiencing a problem such as bullying, and in many cases pupils did not even know the name of one, some or all of their lunchtime supervisors. On the other hand some other pupils did show evidence that they were on friendly terms with their lunchtime supervisors, and these children indicated that they were more likely to talk through problems with them than with their class teacher, and, in some cases, than with their parents.

The suggestion for supervisors to wear name badges, discussed above, was also made with this type of problem in mind. We also made two other suggestions that could help to enhance good relationships between pupils and lunchtime supervisors. One involved the matching of a supervisor and a teacher. The teacher and supervisor agreed on times when the supervisor could come into the classroom and spend time with the children. The supervisor listened to the children read, read to them, helped them with their school work, and so on.

The other activity involved a pupil project. The class teacher and supervisor helped the children, who worked in small groups, to plan and carry out a project to investigate a 'day in the life of a lunchtime supervisor'. The actual content of the project was left open to the individuals concerned but we suggested it could take the form of shadowing other supervisors or interviews with them.

One 11-year-old pupil I spoke to about his relationship with the lunchtime supervisors was positive about these initiatives. He said that:

> It was really good when Mrs X came into our class. She helped me with my story about what dinner ladies do and how the children are naughty. I always say hello to her now, except when I'm playing football. She's a nice lady.

Building relationships between lunchtime supervisors and teaching staff

In many of the project schools, as probably elsewhere, there existed poor channels of communication between lunchtime supervisors and class teachers. In any school this would probably be exacerbated by poor or non-existent relationships between the individuals concerned. This type of situation is unlikely to be conducive to reducing levels of playground bullying. On the other hand, good relationships and associated good communication systems between supervisors and teaching staff may facilitate the exchange of information about which pupils have engaged in bullying and why this may have occurred. It will help ensure consistency in the way adults in school respond to unacceptable behaviour such as bullying. It may also encourage supervisors to voice their ideas about ways of improving supervision of the playground.

In order to facilitate good relationships and effective communication systems, we recommended a number of courses of action. One of these involved encouraging a member of staff to arrange a staff meeting focused on why it would be desirable for there to be better links between supervisors and teachers/senior managers. We recommended that this original meeting be followed up by at least one other session where the supervisors give a presentation outlining the major problems they face in their particular school, and what they think could be done to overcome them.

Another suggestion to help foster closer relationships between supervisors

and teachers involved a shadowing exercise. At a staff meeting, or in a way
that a school felt to be more appropriate, teachers and supervisors were asked
to pair up. The teachers were invited to spend a lunchtime shadowing 'their'
supervisor, watching what she (all of the supervisors in the participating
schools were females) did, but *not* intervening to take control of a situation.
The intention was for the teachers to get an awareness of the type of everyday
problems that supervisors face. The supervisors were also invited to spend
time in the classroom (perhaps as part of their attempts to form friendly
relationships with pupils – see above). The shadowing activities were then
followed up by one (or more) meeting(s) where issues raised were discussed.

A third, and relatively simple, way that relationships between supervisors
and teachers were enhanced was through the adoption of a 'staff is everybody' philosophy. The senior managers of the school indicated that the term
'staff' should in future be applied to *all* staff within the school. Thus, if any
communication etc. was to be directed at only one section of the school's
staff, then this should be made explicit, such as 'teaching staff meeting'.

A training course for lunchtime supervisors

Very few of the lunchtime supervisors in the project schools had received any
formal training. As discussed above, there is a clear need for supervisors to
be offered the opportunity to attend training courses designed to enhance
their child behaviour-management skills. The course we offered, designed by
Sonia Sharp and myself, was primarily intended to help supervisors contribute to their school's attempts to reduce levels of playground bullying. It
consisted of two sessions, each of about two and a half hours duration. The
format involved a mixture of mini-lectures, in which basic information was
passed on, and workshop exercises, in which the supervisors discussed a
problem in small groups prior to sharing their ideas with the group as
a whole.

The course began with an introduction to the training programme and the
Sheffield Project by one of the facilitators. We were somewhat discouraged
to find out that some of the supervisors were not even aware that their school
was participating in the project. This prompted several of the supervisors to
express the view that they felt marginalised within their school. For us, this
served to highlight the need for some schools to improve on their channels
of communication within all sections of their staff (see above). It also provided a convenient lead-in to the first activity which was designed to encourage the supervisors to recognise the valuable role they perform in school.
After forming small groups, the supervisors were asked to discuss what they
thought would happen if their school did not have lunchtime supervisors,

and how they as supervisors make a valuable contribution to managing children's behaviour at lunchtime.

The next activity involved the supervisors, again working in small groups, discussing the types of behaviour problems they regularly encounter in the playground. In all cases, bullying was mentioned. We were then able to give a short presentation to the supervisors about bullying in the playground. This was based on research evidence and covered such things as typical levels of bullying in schools, which children are more/less likely to be involved, and some of the likely consequences for both bullies and their victims. A couple of activities were then directed at eliciting the supervisors' conceptions of bullying. We were then in a position to try to dispel some 'myths' about bullying that supervisors, in common with many adults, might hold, such as the view that bullying is character-building, and that bullying is physically hurting someone rather than 'just' teasing.

We then went on to consider some of the problems that supervisors might face when trying to correctly identify bullying in the playground. Using hypothetical playground scenarios, we discussed the possibility that a supervisor might not see the whole of a situation, that a child might be coerced into saying that she/he had not been bullied, and how rough-and-tumble play might be confused with bullying. In each case, the supervisors were presented with information that they might find useful, such as how to distinguish between playful and aggressive fighting, and asked to discuss with their colleagues the best way to respond to each type of situation.

By this stage of the training session, the supervisors agreed that bullying should be viewed as unacceptable, and we were able to present them with a number of options for preventing its occurrence. These included such things as the need to identify and patrol 'bully hot spots' (those out of the way places where bullying is more likely to take place), to be on the look out for lone pupils who may be especially vulnerable, and continually making it clear to pupils what type of behaviour will not be tolerated.

Linked to the theme of preventing bullying was the suggestion that supervisors could encourage good behaviour by pupils. Several suggestions were presented to the supervisors, who were invited to discuss them. They included such things as the adoption of a 'catch them being good' philosophy whereby supervisors look out for, and reward appropriately, good behaviour.

The facilitators of the training course also suggested to the supervisors that despite their best efforts, some cases of bullying would probably still take place. They were then invited to discuss some suggestions for responding to bullying and other unacceptable behaviour. These included such things as trying to be seen by pupils as being calm and in control, refusing to be side-tracked, and not making threats that won't be carried out. In this context, supervisors were also asked to consider some of the benefits associated with having a hierarchy of sanctions. This issue is discussed further in the next section.

Ways of dealing with bullying when it occurs

In a previous section, the issue of finding appropriate ways of responding to bullying and other unacceptable behaviour was discussed. Some of those suggestions were offered in the project, specifically having a hierarchy of sanctions and the 'yellow and red card system' reported by Imich and Jefferies (1989). One lunchtime supervisor (from school P1) reported on the outcome of the introduction of this system:

> I think it has made a difference by stopping bullying and fighting and things like that. The boys seem to like it better than the girls, and I think that's because it reminds them of football. I don't suppose that matters too much since our girls don't usually fight as much as the boys. . . . Now all the children know exactly what to expect if they misbehave.

This supervisor also reported that the system did have its problems, especially at the beginning and with a small number of pupils who felt they gained status from misbehaving:

> At first, one or two of the boys seemed to want to get a yellow card. I remember one boy who often gets into trouble being given a yellow card for disrupting the girls' game. He seemed really pleased and I saw him going round the playground saying 'I've got a yellow card.' His friend, who often copies him, came up to me and said 'Can I have a yellow card?' They seemed to think it was some sort of game. I think it would have been better if the children were told more clearly that it was not good to get a yellow card. Still, they soon got fed up with the time out that went with the card.

Encouraging positive behaviour in the playground

If a child is behaving well, she/he cannot be bullying others; so by encouraging positive behaviour in the playground we can do something to reduce levels of bullying there. A number of simple suggestions were presented to schools towards this end. One involved pupils being asked to make a 'Things I am proud of' book. On a regular basis, each pupil spent some time either writing or drawing the things they did during their time on the playground which they felt proud of. The class teacher gave positive feedback to the children for this activity in the same way as for academic work.

A second activity involved pupil self-monitoring. The children were guided by the teacher in making a record sheet to indicate how they themselves felt about their own behaviour on the playground that day. For the younger pupils, a 'smiley' face system was adopted in which the child simply drew a happy, neutral or unhappy face.

Improving the quality of play

Perhaps one reason why so much bullying takes place in the playground is because children are bored (see also Chapter Seven). I have noticed many cases of children wandering aimlessly round their playgrounds, and we felt that children might benefit by being given some ideas about what to do in the playground. However, as was discussed above, the aim was to do this without adults taking over children's free-play time.

Some schools in the project provided their pupils with items of play equipment, such as balls and skipping ropes. Some teachers devoted some classroom time to teaching pupils how to play specific games on the playground. In some schools, a games library was established where a permanent record of specific games was kept, and which could be visited by all pupils to get ideas for their playground activities.

Improving the quality of wet playtimes

The unanimous view of all of the lunchtime supervisors I have spoken to is that wet lunchtimes, when pupils are forced to stay inside, pose even more problems than when they are allowed to play out. The prospect of wet lunchtimes was treated with such reactions as 'dread' and 'alarm'. Pupils are reported to get frustrated and bored and more likely to fight and bully others. In many schools, it is typical for limited provision, or none at all, to be made for these occasions.

To help with wet playtimes we suggested that schools could set up theme activity rooms such as an active games area in a hall or gym, a passive games area for such things as snakes and ladders, and a quiet reading room. In some schools, older pupils were asked to help supervise some of the younger pupils, perhaps by reading to them or helping them with their work, thus releasing the lunchtime supervisors to patrol the different locations.

Another recommendation was for schools to provide more materials/ equipment for quiet play. For example, modelling materials are relatively inexpensive, cannot be damaged, last for long periods and are attractive to pupils of diverse ages.

The effects of the playground intervention

The fact that so many schools (thirteen out of sixteen junior schools) chose to do something connected with the playground attests to the view that they were aware of how important this particular context is with regard to bullying in school, and that they felt able to implement our suggestions.

Given that there were so many different interventions that schools could select from, that schools could select as many or as few of these as they wished, and that schools varied in terms of the amount of effort they actually put into the interventions they selected (see Chapter Two), it has proved difficult to evaluate how effective each one actually has been in reducing levels of playground bullying relative to the others. Nevertheless, there were two main 'themes' concerning the playground that were selected by schools. One of these was improving the management of lunchtime, notably through such things as the training of lunchtime supervisors, improving their status, more closely monitoring bullying and other categories of misbehaviour on the playground, and devising appropriate ways of responding to them when they occur. The other focused on the playground environment (see Chapter Seven).

Some aspects of both the qualitative and quantitative data from the project do suggest that the former collection of interventions has had some beneficial effects (see also the comments from staff above). This is perhaps most clearly evident in the case of those schools in which the lunchtime supervisors attended our training course. As part of the evaluation of the project, Sonia Sharp interviewed the headteachers from all of the participating schools. When asked about the effect of the lunchtime supervisor training course, one headteacher (from P15) had this to say:

> I think the most successful thing has been those sessions. That has been one of the most subtle and best things that has happened in the school for ages. The difference in the attitudes of the dinner ladies (I have to call them dinner ladies because they call themselves dinner ladies), their confidence, the way they handle the children, the fact that they are aware of what bullying is or isn't. . . . In terms of the school ethos its been the biggest difference over the last year. . . . Brilliant really.

This headteacher also revealed that the supervisors seemed better able to correctly distinguish bullying from playful fighting than they were previously:

> They [the lunchtime supervisors] are aware of what bullying is or isn't. On my way here there were two or three children playing really rough on the grass and on my way over to one of the dinner ladies I noticed

this and said 'Look, a fight. Why aren't you doing anything?' and she said, 'No, look, they are playing rough-and-tumble on the log, then they tig the next person and they play too.' She was telling me to calm down and she was pointing out that there is a difference between the kind of play that is good for them.

In all cases, the supervisors who attended the course expressed their enthusiasm for what they had learnt. For example:

I know now that I do do something valuable in school. As you said, if we weren't here what would happen at playtime? It would be chaos. I now feel I can cope with the children who misbehave better than I could before. Bullying is too important and I won't be side-tracked by the children. They know exactly what to expect if I find they've been picking on each other.

Another way in which the success of the playground interventions was evaluated was by means of monitoring levels of playground bullying at the beginning and end of the project, and at regular intervals as it progressed. Every day for one week (in some cases, a fortnight) each half-term, the children were asked to fill in a short questionnaire. Basically, this asked them to state whether or not they had experienced any of a number of different types of bullying that particular lunchbreak, and if so, where it happened. For each school, for each of the four terms from winter 1991 to winter 1992, the mean proportion of questionnaires that indicated that a pupil had experienced each one of these types of bullying was determined. From these individual school values, the overall mean with which pupils reported they had experienced the different types of bullying at each of the four assessment phases was determined (i.e. across all of those schools where lunchtime supervisors had attended the training course). The latter values are shown in Table 6.1.

There was a clear decrease in the levels of all of the common types of playground bullying over the four assessment points. For several of these different types of bullying, the effect of the interventions on children's reported levels of being bullied was statistically significant using one-factor (time) analyses of variance tests (all F [3,31], see Table 6.1). Moreover, for most of these specific types of bullying there was a steady decrease with time, suggesting that the longer schools persisted in these interventions, and/or maintained the changes, the more positive the effect on bullying. There was however often a particularly marked drop between the second term (spring 1992) and the third term (summer 1992).

TABLE 6.1 CHANGES IN LEVELS OF DIFFERENT TYPES OF PLAYGROUND
BULLYING, IN SCHOOLS WHERE LUNCHTIME SUPERVISORS ATTENDED A
TRAINING COURSE AS PART OF THE SHEFFIELD PROJECT

Type of bullying	Time 1	Time 2	Time 3	Time 4
Pushed, kicked or hit on purpose	19.8	17.1	12.7	12.6
Threatened[a]	8.9	9.5	5.4	4.9
Deliberately excluded[b]	5.6	5.2	1.8	3.4
Target of nasty stories[c]	7.9	6.7	4.4	3.8
Had things stolen	3.5	2.4	2.1	1.4
Racist remarks	3.3	2.3	2.9	1.5
Teased[d]	10.3	7.6	6.0	5.9

[a]Significant differences = Time 1 > Time 4, Time 2 > Time 3 and Time 4
[b]Significant differences = Time 1 > Time 3, Time 2 > Time 3
[c]Significant differences = Time 1 > Time 4
[d]Significant differences = Time 1 > Time 4

In interpreting these results, it is important to keep in mind that bullying tends to decrease with age anyway. Nevertheless, the drop for each of the specific types of bullying shown in Table 6.1 are mostly of the order of 40–50 per cent between the first term (winter 1991) and the fourth term (winter 1992). This is much higher than the 15 per cent annual average drop with age which appears from large-scale surveys (Whitney and Smith, 1993).

Overall, these results from the project are encouraging – they clearly suggest that something can be done to significantly reduce levels of bullying in the playground.

Conclusion

Playtime occupies an important proportion of junior school children's time. There appear to be both important advantages and disadvantages associated with it for many pupils. Bullying, fighting and aggression are among some of the most disturbing behaviours that children may experience at one time or another in the school playground. However, playtime offers an important context in which children can develop social skills and engage in activities that they thoroughly enjoy. Rather than simply banning playtime or severely reducing the amount of time given over to it, adults should look at the various strategies open to them to make playgrounds less violent places. Our aim should be to enable as many children as possible to safely enjoy and benefit from playtime, and to look back on it as providing positive experiences rather than as one of the most distressing aspects of their childhood years. This chapter has considered a number of ways that may enable this aim to be realised.

improving the school ground environment as an anti-bullying intervention

S·E·V·E·N

CATH HIGGINS

Concurrently with other anti-bullying strategies, four of the Sheffield Project primary schools were selected to work on an environment intervention which involved playground redesign and improvements. This project was separately funded by the Calouste Gulbenkian Foundation. It was set up jointly in the Departments of Landscape and Psychology at Sheffield University. The project was directed by Anne Beer and Peter Smith; participatory techniques were developed by Lyndal Sheat (1991a, b). Catherine Higgins, a landscape designer, saw the project through design, implementation and monitoring. Second-year undergraduate landscape design students worked in the schools using participatory design techniques and developed design briefs for each of the schools. Second-year postgraduates produced design and implementation booklets. The schools then implemented aspects of the proposals and this process was monitored. This chapter describes and discusses the processes and results of this project.

School grounds and bullying

Many of us are now aware that the familiar featureless tarmacked school yard is no longer acceptable as part of a child's learning environment. Not only is it a poor educational and play environment but it may also foster bullying behaviour. Much bullying in schools takes place at playtime in the playground (Blatchford, 1989; Ross and Ryan, 1990; Whitney and Smith, 1993). Whitney and Smith's research with twenty-four Sheffield schools showed that the playground was noticeably the most common place for bullying to occur, especially in primary schools. One reason for the high level of bullying in school playgrounds may be ineffective supervision, as discussed in Chapter Six. However, other reasons may relate to the physical environment of the playground. These include boredom, overcrowding, marginalisation, exclusion and lack of opportunities for raising self-esteem.

Boredom is a major factor. With little to stimulate children's interest, dull environments can favour anti-social behaviour. Bored children may, for stimulation or out of frustration, pick fights, tease or bully (Blatchford, 1989).

The overcrowding in many school grounds may also be a factor in bullying behaviour. Large featureless unstructured spaces are supposed to cater for many play activities but in reality are a good resource for few. Children are herded onto a noisy 'free for all' pitch; a frightening, intimidating, confusing place especially for younger children. Conflicts, arguments and injuries inevitably occur as children compete for space and paltry resources, or fly about in frenzied chasing and running games.

Marginalisation is another factor. Older boys tend to dominate the playground with vigorous football games. These can forcibly marginalise other pupils (often girls and younger children) and their activities.

> Girls often find themselves vulnerable to disruption or deliberate intimidation over such things as boundaries or ownership of an activity. The marginalisation of girls to the edges of the playground is both the result and a defensive action.
>
> (Ross and Ryan, 1990)

Because there is often no physical provision or protection for less vigorous or spatially demanding play the message can seem to be: if you are older, physically stronger *and* can play football then the playground belongs to you. This does nothing to encourage a co-operative caring attitude among pupils.

The problem of exclusion is related to the issue of marginalisation. Playgrounds are commonly seen and used by children as proving grounds which establish power relationships (Sluckin, 1981). A playground that is good for active running games (notably football) but poor for many others reinforces certain social relationships. Those who do not excel in skills required for dominant games are noticeably excluded (Besag, 1991) because they have little opportunity to engage in other (solitary) activities. Victims of bullying are frequently those who appear different from their peers. If being 'normal' means the ability to play football or a particular game then those who cannot or do not may be prone to bullying.

Victims' and bullies' self-esteem and competence can be factors in bullying behaviour. Typically victims and some bullies have low self-esteem, and it is possible that this contributes to their being involved in bully/victim problems. The evaluation system in schools engenders a sense of failure in some children. An impoverished playground environment can reinforce the negative effects of academic assessment because it provides few opportunities for children who do not excel in class to achieve through varied outdoor activities.

All these factors can exacerbate the problems of playground supervision. Many playgrounds are hard, if not impossible, to supervise well. Dealing with bullying incidents effectively is crucial to changing behaviour (Chapter Six). On a daily basis supervisors have to deal with the combined effects of boredom, crowding, marginalisation, exclusion and low self-esteem.

There is also the general issue of school ethos – the 'atmosphere' and prevailing beliefs in a school (Chapter Three). This must surely be affected by a barren harsh external environment that often looks more like a prison exercise yard than a place for children. 'School grounds, just like school buildings, are important conveyors of messages and meanings, an external expression of the hidden curriculum of the schools' (Adams, 1990). Inhospitable places do little to encourage a sense of pride and belonging for teachers, pupils, lunchtime supervisors and parents. Bleak school yards do not suggest that school is a caring environment. Bullying, as we have seen, thrives in an 'unsupportive environment'.

These were some of the factors we hoped to influence through improvements to the environments of the four schools.

School ground improvement initiatives, landscape design and participation

During the 1980s there was an upsurge of interest in improving school ground environments. Most initiatives originally focused on and were stimulated by nature conservation interests – creating wildlife gardens, digging ponds and planting trees. In addition, arts projects in schools, often involving a professional artist or community arts group, sought to improve the visual environment with mural painting and sculpture. Some schools improved the quality of play through general improvements such as providing seating or climbing structures. Changes have been frequently supported by organisations such as Learning through Landscapes or local community groups.

Both creative and nature conservation projects have led to an increased awareness of the potential of school grounds in providing an important educational resource. But many improvements still focus on educational aspects alone and are concerned with providing 'features' for teaching. What has often been lacking is a holistic approach where the physical environment is changed to create a complete play and social environment as well as providing teaching resources. We considered a whole-school approach (place and people) to be crucial to making successful changes and influencing bullying.

Many designers are involved in helping to improve school environments. Landscape design is, at its best, the creation of environments which meet the needs of people and nature. Landscape designers are frequently involved in creating solutions to the problems of degraded or poorly functioning environments – in our case the school grounds. But there is often a gap between designers' intentions and ways that environments are actually used. Through inappropriate training, designers frequently do not predict or understand the ways in which people will use their environments (Newman, 1973; Cooper-Marcus and Francis, 1990). The 'designer divorced from user' problem can be ameliorated by ensuring that environment–behaviour research influences the way designers create places. But we can solve this problem through participation of users in design.

Participation in design can mean that the improved school ground environment is exactly what the users (pupils, teachers, lunchtime supervisors) need. In the context of improvements as a bullying intervention the participation *process* is as important as the end result (the improved playground). The mechanisms of participatory design enable discussion, raise awareness of issues and give control and decision making to children, thus enhancing responsibility. Mares and Stephenson (1988) made a list of the social skills benefited by participation. This included: co-operating, discussing, willingness to accept different points of view, persevering, negotiation and compromise, working with other groups from fellow pupils to adults, caring about the needs and desires of other people, empathy. Thus a participatory design process can in turn help with the implementation and setting up of other bullying interventions and policies.

It was with the conviction that poor playgrounds influence bullying, that participatory design had an important role to play, and a belief that it is possible to create diverse rich rewarding environments which promote positive behaviour, that we initiated the project.

The school ground interventions project

The aims of the project

The aims of the school ground interventions project were to:

- provide design processes, participation mechanisms, information, support and resources to enable schools to find out about their school grounds and current use, and then to provide ideas for redesigning and carrying out environmental improvements;
- monitor the effects of improvements and changes in pupils' use and perception of grounds and the degree to which they felt involved in creating changes;
- monitor the implementation of improvements from the view of teaching staff: their perception of the levels of participation of pupils and staff, the practical problems involved and opportunities which the project raised.

A subsidiary aim was to provide a learning exercise for graduate and postgraduate landscape design students to give them the opportunity to work with participatory design techniques.

The participating schools

Four Sheffield primary schools were selected from several who had requested environmental changes as one of their interventions. Their codes are P3, P7, P8 and P15. One school may be described as 'inner city'. The others are located in outlying residential districts of the city.

P7, P8 and P15 had small asphalt yards which surrounded the red brick buildings. These dated from the early part of this century. They all had small areas of trees, shrubs or grass on their boundaries.

P3 was a post-war timber and brick one-storey structure. Its grounds were relatively extensive having playing fields and areas of tree planting as well as three large asphalt playgrounds.

Pupils who took part in the project were aged between 5 and 12 years. Staff, parental and governor involvement varied from school to school.

Project procedures

After consultation meetings with each school represented by one member of teaching staff (the head in three schools, deputy head in the other) a programme of events and meetings with class groups was established. Undergraduate students were to visit schools fortnightly to gather information about each and work with pupils. Postgraduates were to provide designs and implementation booklets for schools to make changes. The process was divided into four main stages:

- gathering information about site and users;
- goal setting;
- creating designs and implementation manuals;
- implementing the designs and monitoring.

We shall look briefly at the process and methods used at each stage to both involve pupils and evolve suitable designs.

Gathering information about site and users

The students and pupils at each school began by gathering as much information as possible about the site and its users. In any design process this is the first step towards creating solutions. The techniques employed had been developed and adapted for schools' use through previous testing by Sheat.

Giant maps

Individual students worked with selected class groups of varying ages. The children were asked to draw a giant map of their school grounds on a base plan which already showed the building(s) and boundaries of the site. The role of the student was to encourage children to include every feature (but not to suggest or prompt any elements) and to note verbal exchanges of pupils that might be useful in subsequent discussion.

The purpose of this exercise was to reveal how pupils and staff perceive their school ground environment, interact with it and with each other in it. The giant map can illustrate what aspects are valued and well used or disliked. The other function of the exercise is to start the process of thinking about the school grounds by stimulating discussion about what's there, who benefits, what sort of games happen? This sharing of ideas paves the way for consideration of how to change the school grounds.

Photo safari

This method involved the use of a (disposable) camera. Small groups of five to eight children were asked to take a student on a guided tour of the playground. Whilst doing so they were to take pictures of features they liked and disliked. Guidance was given on the use of the camera but children decided through group consensus what should be photographed. The pupils took it in turns to use the camera. Discussion throughout the tour plays an important part in revealing pupils' attitudes and was recorded by the student. The processed photographs were made into collages which showed both negative and positive images. These were identified with written quotations from pupils that had been recorded on the safari.

The purpose of the exercise was, as with the 'giant map', to gather information on perceptions and existing use of the environment. It also provided an opportunity for children to work co-operatively and control decision making.

'A day in the life of . . .' activities chart

Groups of children made large charts which recorded activities before and after school and at each break. The students' role was to stimulate discussion and make sure all activities were recorded. Figure 7.1 shows an example of an activities chart.

This exercise aims to encourage the pupils to think about and record their pursuits outside of the classroom. It is a way of identifying favoured activities and how the present environment limits or provides for these. The information is useful when deciding what new elements need to be provided in the playground.

Recording traces

This technique involves looking at the physical environment for traces of activities that have taken place, the degree of frequency and any effects these are having on the existing fabric of the environment. These were categorised under Zeisel's (1984) headings of 'Public Messages', 'By-products of Use', 'Adaptions for Use', 'Displays of Self'. Examples of traces recorded in our project include: litter, gaps in fences and hedges, litterbins moved and used as goal posts, litter bins moved to retrieve balls from roofs, graffiti, trampled vegetation, cigarette ends, worn grass around base of trees. Traces can show how well or poorly the playground meets the needs of children and staff.

Staff interviews

Both teachers and lunchtime supervisors were informally interviewed in open discussion with students who made written notes. They were asked to express their views on the existing playground environment.

Physical survey

The students carried out a physical site survey of the playground at each school. The purpose was to gather physical data which was likely to influence the potential for change, e.g. the identification of positive resources such as existing trees and negative attributes such as exposed windy areas. Due to time limitations pupils were not involved in this process.

Goal setting

Once survey and user information had been gathered it was necessary to evaluate the material. Images and information from the participatory exercises and interviews were made into displays and were then 'presented' by the students to the schools at discussion sessions. This enabled the schools to identify and crystallise a shared picture of the problems and potential of the school grounds and their use. The key limitations and problems of the grounds as well as positive uses that were revealed are discussed under outcomes.

It was now possible to set goals for changing the environment. Goal setting is a process of making decisions about what is desired and what it is possible to create for the new environment. It is achieved through idea generation from exercises which stimulate creativity, imagination and idealism, followed by consensus and decision making based on realistic options. Goal setting exercises may be helpful in raising the self-esteem of pupils and supporting other bullying interventions which involve empathising with victims.

The project used two main participatory techniques. The first exercise involved discussion by groups of pupils using a previously prepared set of 'cue cards'. Each card had an image of an element that might form part of the new playground environment, e.g. Seats, Trees, Hiding Places, Pond. Figure 7.2 shows examples of some 'cue cards'. Each group had to decide by 'voting' on which elements they would like to have in their playground and which should be excluded. The features were then graded from most popular to least popular according to how many of the group(s) voted for or against. The results of this exercise are briefly discussed in outcomes.

The second exercise is very simple and commonly used for many purposes. Pupils were asked to draw a picture of their ideal school playground. They were encouraged by students to include whatever they liked, however fantastic or unrealistic this might be. A simple analysis of popular features was carried out by counting the number of times elements and items featured in children's drawings. The drawings reflected both children's expectations

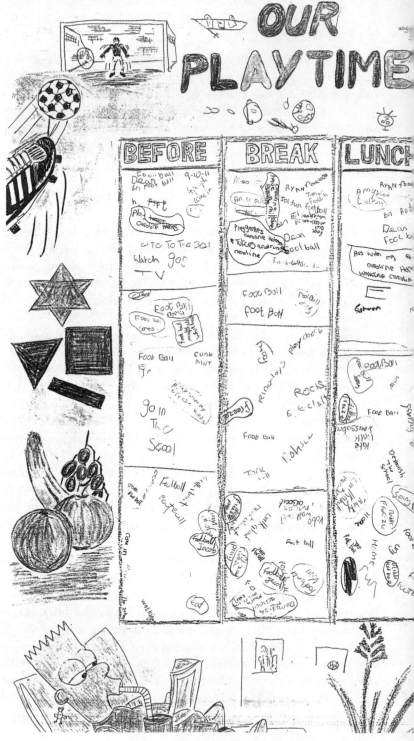

Figure 7.1 An example of 'A day in the life of . . .' activities char

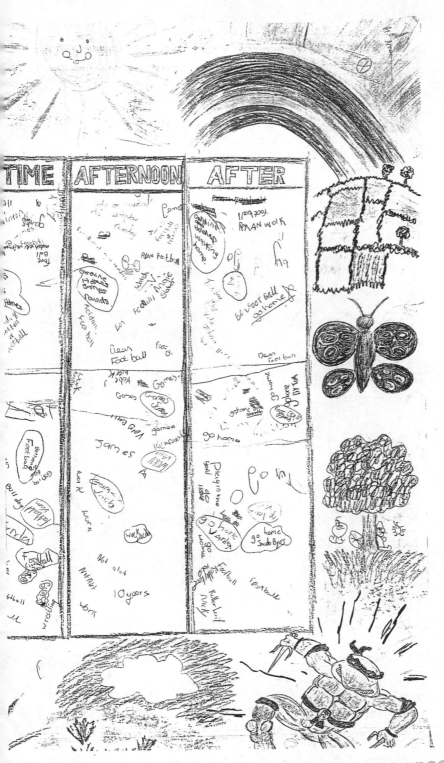

Figure 7.2 Cue cards

and their experience. Although many ideas in the illustrations were obviously impractical they were taken as a serious indication of the types of activities pupils enjoy and are interested in.

At this point in the project, due to time limitations, participation processes involving pupils in decision making ended. Goal setting with staff took the form of an informal discussion session.

The information gathering and goal setting had taken place fortnightly during the autumn term in 1991. In January 1992 students spent the first weeks of the term producing a design brief which incorporated previously identified site-specific goals for each school, e.g. provision of (more) seating or 'quiet' areas and a restatement of the general aims of the project and the limitations or potential that the physical site presented. The draft briefs were discussed with staff and then adopted to form the basis for designs.

Creating designs and implementation manuals

In March 1992 the undergraduate students presented the design briefs and a project summary to postgraduate students. The postgraduates' job was to create designs for the playground based on the brief. At the conceptual development stage, consultation continued with staff (not pupils). Then designs were evolved in detail. The new designs are illustrated in Figures 7.3, 7.4, 7.5. A practical implementation booklet was next produced for each school and presented to them at the end of the spring term. A presentation day was organised to which all school staff and LEA representatives were invited. At this meeting the progress and achievements of the project and implementation booklets were discussed. It was an opportunity for the four schools to meet and exchange experiences and ideas.

The implementation booklets contained the design plan, information on phasing, funding bodies and sources, local suppliers, and detailed drawings of how to construct and plant the playground. The information was presented in a form for use by people with no specialist knowledge of horticulture, nature conservation or construction techniques. The schools were to use these documents to carry out improvements.

Implementing the designs and monitoring

The schools were due to begin implementation in the summer term of 1992. P15 began sooner as resources were available during the Easter vacation. The extent and ways in which improvements were carried out differed for each school. The main elements that were constructed and planted at each school and the ways they were achieved are summarised below under

SCHOOL SKETCH DESIGN

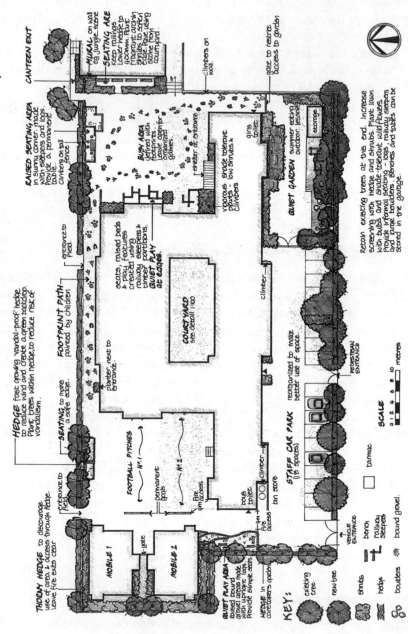

THORN HEDGE to discourage use of area & access through hedge. Leave fire exits clear.

QUIET PLAY AREA Raised bound, shrub bound area made with railway sleepers. Provide simple seats.

HEDGE in caretaker's garden

HEDGE fast growing 'vandal-proof' hedge to reduce wind and create a green backdrop. Plant trees within hedge to reduce risk of vandalism.

SEATING to make a safe edge.

FOOTPRINT PATH painted by children

entrance to field

planter next to entrance

FOOTBALL PITCHES
No 1
No 2

permanent goals

fire exit access

boys toilet

bin store

climber

STAFF CAR PARK (16 spaces) reorganized to make better use of space.

MURAL on wall eg jungle scene

SEATING ARE Keep railings. Lower hedge to 900mm. Plant maximum growth shrubs to soften edge. Pave area using stone from courtyard.

climbers on wall.

gate to restrict access to garden

RAISED SEATING AREA in sunny corner, made with railway sleepers and logs. Provide a permanent table.

Climbers on tall fence

BUSY AREA defined with railings. Leave open for organized games.

seats, raised beds & play features created using railway sleepers & timber partitions. QUIET PLAY at edges.

entrance to field.

COURT YARD see detail 1:100

shelter at entrance

vigorous, shade tolerant plants, low shrubs &

girls toilet

QUIET GARDEN summer eating outdoor lessons.

storage

Retain existing trees at this end. Increase screening with hedge and shrubs. Plant lawn with bulbs and shade-tolerant wildflowers. Provide informal seating - logs, railway sleepers and some boulders. Benches and tables can be stored in the garage.

climber

PEDESTRIAN ENTRANCE

VEHICLE ENTRANCE

SCALE
0 1 2 4 6 8 10 metres

CANTEEN EXIT

KEY:

- existing tree
- new tree
- shrubs
- hedge
- boulders
- bench
- railway sleepers
- tarmac.
- bound gravel.

Figure 7.3 Design for P7

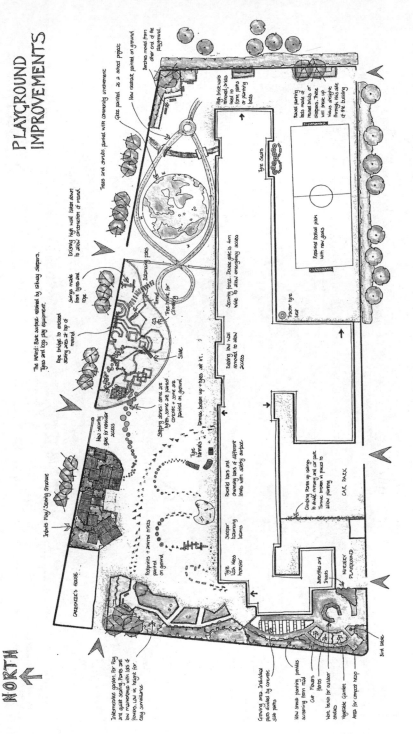

PLAYCROUND
IMPROVEMENTS

SHEFFIELD
UNIVERSITY

NORTH

FEB 92 SCALE

Figure 7.4 Design for P8

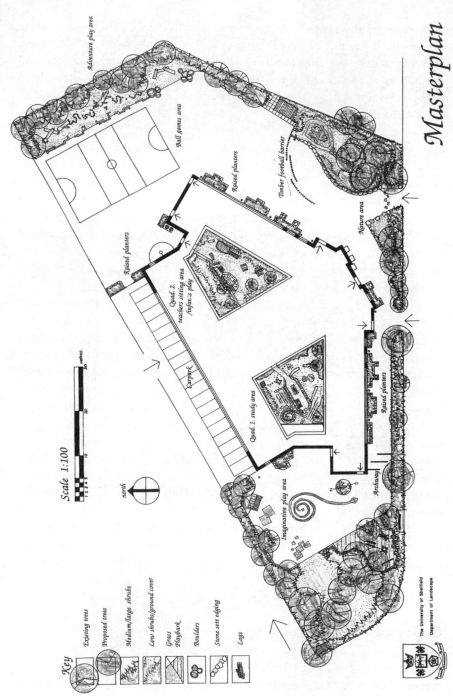

Key

Existing trees

Proposed trees

Medium/large shrubs

Low shrubs/ground cover

Grass

Playbark

Boulders

Stone sett edging

Logs

Scale 1:100

north

Adventure play area

Ball games area

Raised planters

Raised planters

Raised planters

Timber football barrier

Nature area

Quad. 2. teachers sitting area infants play

Quad. 1. study area

Carpark

Imaginative play area

Archway

Raised planters

The University of Sheffield
Department of Landscape

Masterplan

Figure 7.5 Design for P15

'Outcomes of the project'. None of the schools completely changed their whole site. It was not expected that they should be able to do so. They were encouraged to select improvements which they felt were most needed and would have an immediate significant effect. Improvements continued at three of the schools right up to and beyond the end of the monitoring period in late spring 1993.

During implementation of the designs we supported and monitored the changes in a variety of ways. Monitoring was carried out by use of pupil questionnaires and a series of informal interviews with the staff member co-ordinating the environment project. The staff interviews took the form of an extended structured taped discussion covering such issues as participation levels (particularly of pupils), organisation, funding and resources, technical aspects. These were carried out fortnightly initially (summer) and then monthly (autumn–spring). As well as providing us with data for assessing changes, the meetings were used to provide support in the form of advice and information particularly on technical aspects.

Brief questionnaires were filled in by pupils at three time points: before physical improvements were under way (May 1992), once some changes had been implemented (July 1992) and at the end of project after substantial changes had been made (March 1993). Three questions required pupils to select one of five frowning or smiley faces with speech bubble responses which most closely resembled their own answer to the question: ranging from very positive responses (+2) through neutral (0) to very negative (–2). These questions asked about (a) satisfaction with the playground, (b) perception of changes in the playground and (c) feelings of involvement in any changes. Average scores were calculated at each time point. Another question required a brief written answer stating which was their favourite part of the playground; the three most commonly mentioned areas were taken from each time point.

In addition, we also referred to the overall survey results discussed in Chapter Two. We examined the performance of the relevant schools, and in particular whether there had been an appreciable change in bullying 'in the playground'.

Outcomes of the project

First we summarise the general perceptions of pupils and staff of their environments prior to changes as revealed through the participatory information gathering techniques. Salient aspects of the goal setting exercises are then summarised. We then go on to describe the changes at each school separately and examine pupil questionnaire results. These are related to bullying results overall and staff interviews at each school.

The initial physical survey indicated poor quality outdoor environments. Common to most of the schools were large bleak expanses of grey asphalt, a lack of enclosure and seating, windy exposed sites, sparse vegetation particularly shrubs, poorly sited litter and dustbins, car parking which conflicted with play, noise pollution from traffic, and erosion of grassed small areas. The school grounds lacked diversity, spatial structure, colour and stimulation.

Pupils' views of existing school grounds

Many pupils held negative as well as positive images of their playground. Negative perceptions were revealed through shots of graffiti-covered walls, litter and 'boring tarmac' from photo safaris. The 'traces' recorded revealed dissatisfaction with the playgrounds in images and talk of dull, cold, noisy, smelly, ugly, graffitied 'nothing to do' environments. Negative perceptions of use were revealed in 'A day in the life of . . .' charts with recordings of playground activities such as 'not a lot', 'hang about', 'freeze', 'push people'.

The 'football dominates' syndrome occurred at all schools. All exercises revealed this. It was recognised as a problem by both staff and pupils, particularly the way in which it monopolised space. Those who enjoyed the game, however, made it clear that for them it was an important activity each playtime; a striking aspect of many giant maps was the intense precision with which football areas were shown (see Figure 7.6).

A need for privacy or secrecy was frequently illustrated on the photo safaris by the desire to take pictures of areas behind or at the back of buildings or planting. Illicit activities and places that were 'out of bounds' were also popular choices, suggesting restrictive rules were resented – especially at P7 where an adjoining field belonged to the neighbouring school and was out of bounds on most occasions.

On the positive side, the pupils demonstrated inventiveness in utilising 'poor' resources. There was a desire for risk and adventure and a need to manipulate their environment. Every part of the playground was fully utilised and exploited for activities both 'official' (e.g. hopscotch, football) and 'unofficial' (using litter bins to retrieve footballs from roofs, tree roots used for balancing). Activities charts, whilst dominated by football, also showed a wide range of play occurring in a limiting environment. Photo safaris recorded positive perceptions in images of walls for climbing, drinking fountains and sites used for particular games.

The popularity of floor markings such as hopscotch and number snakes was faithfully recorded in giant maps. Features on the maps were often expanded to 'fill' an otherwise empty playground surface. All seats were recorded. Vaguer recording of grass and treed areas was apparent on some maps particularly with younger age groups.

Staff views of existing school grounds

Interviews with teachers revealed some dissatisfaction with their school grounds. They had sympathy for the pupils and their views often exactly matched theirs. The playground was to them equally dull and inhospitable.

Lunchtime supervisors in particular perceived conflict between needs of different age groups and types of play. Crowding on the playground at P7 and P15 was identified as a serious problem. This often led to conflicts over resources and space for games and activities. Concerns for the safety of children at all schools were frequently expressed by teaching and non-teaching staff. Supervisors observed that accidents were common children often fell onto tarmac through collisions or from structures not designed for climbing on. Complaints of getting hurt through falls were also voiced by pupils.

Supervisors described the difficulties of supervising whilst weighed down by children who clung to them for protection from cold, wind and boisterous play. They were concerned about the lack of resources for play and many were particularly worried for those who preferred solitary play.

Goal setting – pupil responses

Goal setting through the cue cards exercise revealed and stimulated amongst pupils remarkably mature responses and an understanding of each others' requirements such as choosing items for younger age groups or suggesting ways to separate football from other play. Features for an improved school ground that received highest votes from all four schools included trees, ponds, climbing equipment, animals, gardens, huts and dens, sports pitches (grass), tables, ropes and tunnels. Unpopular items included mud, car parking and 'tarmac'. Figure 7.7 illustrates a Cue Cards summary sheet produced by students for P8.

The range of ideas suggested in ideal school drawings was vast. Some of the items most illustrated were swimming pools, trees, ponds, football pitches, gardens, flowers, swings, slides and roundabouts. Some drawings resembled funfairs or adventure playgrounds with features such as death slides and helter skelters.

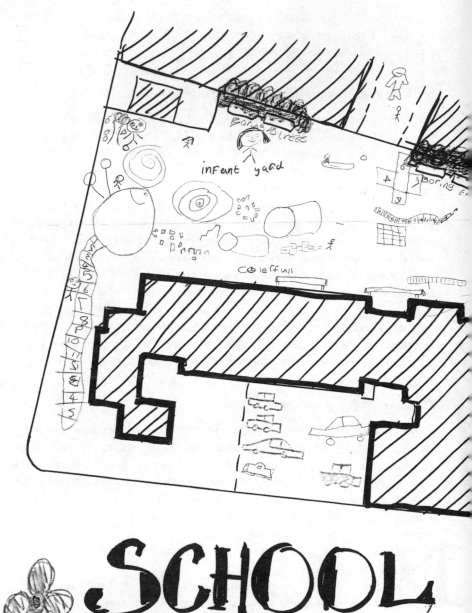

Figure 7.6 A giant map from P8. Note the carefully drawn football pitches and players

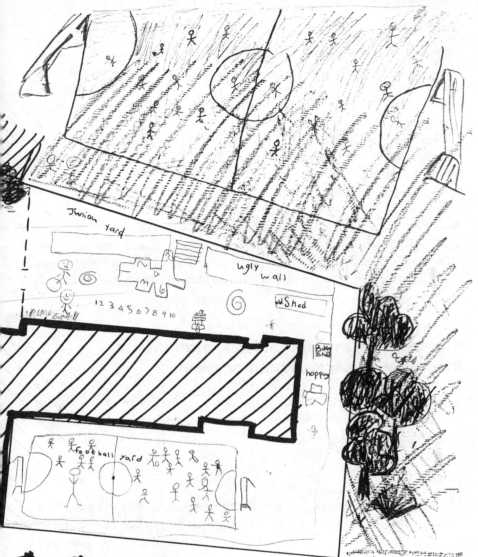

Junior yard

ugly wall

Shed

1 2 3 4 5 6 7 8 9 10

Bike Shed

hoppiy

football yard

MAP

Goal setting – staff responses

Goal setting with teachers emphasised the educational function of school ground improvements, security and safety aspects. Most (though not all) teachers were keen to see changes to the playground environment. Features such as ponds, nature gardens and wild areas were all proposed. There was a strong desire for seating and shelter. Safety issues featured highly in discussion and large play structures such as climbing frames were viewed with suspicion. Supervision aspects were also a concern. Security against vandalism from outside intruders (often older children/teenagers who did not attend the schools) was identified as a necessity.

Discussions with lunchtime supervisors revealed some of the same concerns and wishes as teachers' although with an emphasis on supervisory problems. Seating was the most frequent suggestion for simple improvements. Desires for an easily supervised 'visible' school ground meant there were fears about new tall play structures or dividing up the playground with planting or fences.

Improvements made and interpretation of interview and questionnaire results

The improvements each school implemented are summarised here along with main issues discussed in the regular teacher interviews, and quantified results from the pupil questionnaires.

School P3

P3 had the most extensive grounds of the four participating schools. They chose as their initial project to construct a pond. Every child participated in the digging which took place in June 1992. The caretaker of the school had fenced off and offered to the school part of his garden for this purpose. Parents donated plants and helped with construction. Other construction and planting was carried out by the caretaker. Improvements to the pond area stretched into the autumn term and continued beyond the monitoring period.

The school obtained some large logs, also in June 1992, from trees that had been felled on a nearby public site. These were placed along edges of tarmacked areas to form seating, but were finally grouped after having been 'walked' around the grounds each night by intruders. A netball hoop was installed at the same time. In February 1993 a mural painting was begun on

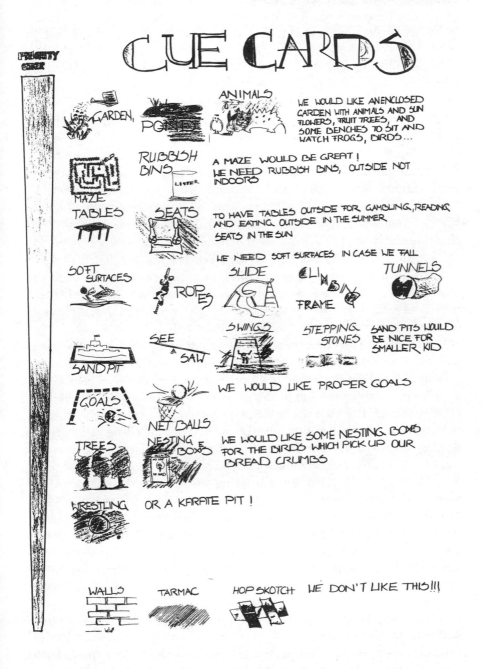

Figure 7.7 Cue cards summary sheet created by students for P8

a blank wall. The painting was a composite design of several winning entries of a school competition. The winning entrants helped paint the mural. Finally tree planting was carried out by children and staff on a designated day in March 1993 with the assistance of National Trust wardens.

According to the staff interviews, high levels of participation of pupils were felt to have been achieved by making it central to each project carried out. Parental involvement extended to purchasing plants and a little help with pond construction. The interviews revealed problems with implementation to be mainly technical and organisational, particularly a lack of experience and information on pond construction and the complexity of some information in the implementation booklet. Technical problems were soon overcome through tireless work and commitment of the teacher involved. Governors and teaching staff were less involved during implementation but kept informed. Supervisors were indirectly informed through witnessing changes and chatting. Changes to the school grounds were observed to become an immediate focus for activities. For example the new logs were instantly used for sitting, hiding behind, jumping, cowboys and Indians. There was a reported increase in problem behaviour (fighting, bullying) in the school grounds half way through the monitoring period. Later, at the end of monitoring, small 'niggling' incidents continued.

Results of the pupil questionnaires are shown in Figure 7.8. Satisfaction with the playground before changes were made was initially positive, showed a slight reduction at the second questionnaire but had shown an increase in popularity overall by the end of the project. Pupils' perception of whether positive changes had occurred in the playground increased markedly from a negative perception to a positive one. Despite every child taking part in pond digging a negative perception of their involvement in implementing changes was recorded initially and at the second time point; but by the end of the project after tree planting and mural painting an overall positive response to their involvement was given.

The grass field was recorded as the most popular site in the school grounds at the first and second time point with the (tarmac) football pitch second favourite on both occasions. At the third questionnaire the football pitch was more popular with the field in second place. The logs gained popularity after installation (third most popular), were replaced by the pond/pond area after its construction but came back to third place by the end of the project. The pond received one vote out of 98 respondents at the third time point.

In the results from the twenty-three schools in the bullying project P3 showed very good results (see Chapter Two). It had the second largest reduction in the frequency of reports of being bullied; specifically looking at bullying in the playground, it had the lowest percentage of pupils who reported being bullied there, and the third highest drop in the number of pupils who reported being bullied in the playground.

School P7

P7 had one of the smallest playgrounds and the largest number of pupils. Improvements began in June 1992 with the construction of woven panel fences to separate car parking and refuse bins from play areas and a proposed 'quiet garden area'. Next, improved access to a canteen entrance was achieved, and two brick walls constructed to contain a viewing area from which children could overlook one playground. A mural was painted on the side of the canteen building in autumn 1992. It was designed and implemented by pupils with the assistance of art students from a local college. Later in autumn railway sleeper planters and seating were constructed by a few committed parents. These were sited around the periphery of each of the two yards. Planting was carried out in the autumn and spring 1993, including shrubs for planters and a new hedge along the front of the school to enclose it from the main road. Pupils were not involved in construction and planting. The quiet garden was not operational by the time our monitoring ended.

During interviews with the headteacher it was reported that a deliberate policy of encouraging parental involvement was being pursued to stimulate pride and responsibility among 'the community'. Most teachers and governors supported changes, but were not generally involved in construction or planting. Problems encountered included conflict between voluntary helpers and theft of plants. The head reported a decrease in playground incidents and fighting but recognised that overcrowding in the playground was still a problem.

Results of the pupil questionnaires are shown in Figure 7.9. These revealed relatively high levels of satisfaction with the playground which increased slightly as the implementation proceeded. By the end of the project satisfaction decreased slightly to the same level at which it had begun. The number of pupils who appreciated that 'nice changes' were being made increased slightly at the second time point but fell slightly again at the third (although still remaining higher than initially). Pupils had a negative perception of their involvement in changes throughout.

The field was one of the most popular areas throughout the project, whether for football or other activities, despite being out of bounds and not belonging to the school. The railway sleeper benches became very popular at the third time point.

The general survey findings for this school were not very positive, with a general trend for a slight increase in bullying (see Chapter Two). There was also an increase in the number of children who said they had been bullied specifically in the playground. A possible confounding factor for this school was a change in pupil intake during the time of the project. A local housing project meant that in the term leading up to the second survey there would have been a number of new pupils entering most classes throughout the school.

School P8

P8 had difficulty starting improvements. They only began in January 1993 with a floor painting depicting a globe, but even this remained incomplete. It was started by students and selected pupils.

The staff interviews revealed staffing difficulties including illness and maternity leave which had contributed to the fact that few changes were achieved. Other problems faced included difficulties of getting voluntary and parental help.

Due to lack of significant changes only the first pupil questionnaire was implemented. Pupils were overall fairly satisfied with their playground. They had a very negative perception of whether 'nice changes' had been made and whether they had been involved. The most popular site, indicated by almost half the pupils as being their favourite place, was the adjacent field (not owned but used occasionally by the school).

In the results of the bullying project there was a small reduction in the number of children who said they had been bullied, both generally (see Chapter Two) and specifically in the playground.

School P15

P15 managed the largest physical changes. Improvements began very promptly in April 1992 with a temporary woven willow 'igloo', a large jungle mural and a snake floor painting. In June 1992 construction began on a nature garden with seats and paths with assistance from nature conservation volunteers. A play hut purchased by the PTA was installed in the same term. The most major change was the construction of an adventure playground amongst existing trees and incorporating a bark safety surface. This was carried out in late summer 1992 by parents and teachers with assistance from the timber company who supplied the materials. Some pupils were involved in the construction of the willow structure (since dismantled), with the mural, and with some planting in the nature garden, but not with the adventure playground or remainder of the nature garden.

Improve-ment made	Term 1 Logs	Term 2 Pond, netball hoop	Term 3 Tree planting, mural

* = Do you like your playground?
○ = Have any nice changes been made to your playground?
□ = Did you help to change the playground?

Three most popular areas	Grass/Field 48% Football pitch 28% Logs 10%	Grass/Field 42% Football pitch 14% Pond/pond area 10%	Football pitch 41% Grass/Field 36% Logs 12%

Figure 7.8 Pupil questionnaire results from P3

The staff interviews indicated that improvements had been due to involvement of one or two very committed staff and several willing parents. There were worries, as at P3, about technical physical problems; but many of these were overcome through seeking advice from voluntary organisations, and, in the case of the adventure playground, help from timber suppliers in detailed design and construction. The improvements were fully utilised by pupils. The headteacher thought the adventure play area had an enormous impact by engrossing large numbers of children fully. It was so popular that a rota system was developed for its use. Some parents appreciated it as a place for their children to 'let off steam' after school. Every new feature became the focus for activities and games. A definite decrease to a very low level of bullying incidents at playtimes was reported. The teacher believed there was less boredom.

Results of the pupil questionnaires are shown in Figure 7.10. The first pupil questionnaires indicated high levels of satisfaction with the playground; the willow igloo and some mural painting had already been carried out with help from students. Satisfaction decreased slightly during implementation and increased slightly again at the final time point. Most pupils also perceived that positive changes were being made. A small majority of children felt they helped with the changes at the first two time points but this fell to an overall slightly negative perception of involvement by the end of monitoring.

The tarmac football pitches were first and second most favourite sites in the school grounds at first and second questionnaires but were almost entirely replaced in popularity by the adventure apparatus area. The latter was the favourite part of the playground for almost half the pupils by the end of the project.

Results of the survey indicated that there was an appreciable reduction in bullying (see Chapter Two); and the number of pupils who reported being bullied specifically in the playground fell by over 13 per cent (the second highest reduction in all schools).

Discussion: problems and opportunities of school ground improvements as an anti-bullying intervention

The project was successful in enabling three of the schools to substantially improve their environment using participatory design methods. It was a valuable learning experience for students, pupils and teachers alike.

Participation was the key to successful interventions. We felt there was success in involvement of pupils during the information gathering and goal

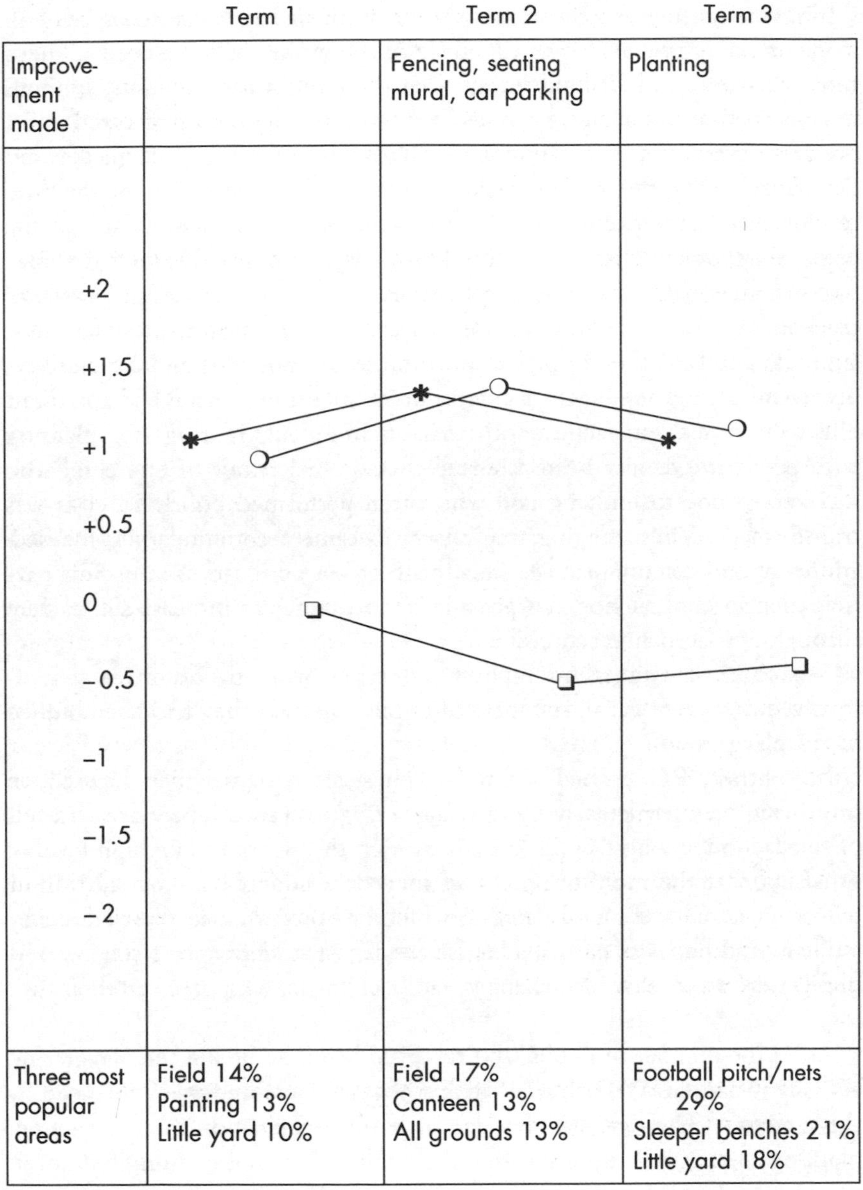
Term 1
Term 2
Term 3
Improvement made
Fencing, seating mural, car parking
Planting
+2
+1.5
+1
+0.5
0
−0.5
−1
−1.5
−2
Three most popular areas
Field 14%
Painting 13%
Little yard 10%
Field 17%
Canteen 13%
All grounds 13%
Football pitch/nets 29%
Sleeper benches 21%
Little yard 18%

*** = Do you like your playground?**
○ = Have any nice changes been made to your playground?
□ = Did you help to change the playground?

Figure 7.9 Pupil questionnaire results from P7

setting part of the project where formal sessions had been arranged with students visiting schools. The timescale of the project and the need to make rapid changes to the grounds meant that the level of participation by pupils in construction and planting was decided by each school. P3 structured in the greatest levels of participation and this demonstrated rewarding results. Satisfaction with the school grounds increased the most out of the four schools as did the perception of 'nice changes' (Figure 7.8). Many of the physical improvements in P3's school grounds did not provide increased play opportunities but rather teaching features – pond, tree planting. Efforts of teachers involved were to encourage interest and environmental awareness amongst pupils. Although play opportunities did not substantially increase, involvement in changing their environment appeared to have had a marked effect on pupils' satisfaction with that environment. During tree planting with pupils the deputy head reported that the behaviour of one child who was very prone to bullying and who often performed poorly in class was transformed. Whilst digging tree pits he became accommodating, focused, confident and communicative. This incident was an illustration of how participation in construction can provide opportunities to increase self-esteem through non-academic achievement.

School P3 had the third highest reduction of all twenty-three schools involved in the project in numbers of pupils who said they had been bullied in the playground.

In contrast, P15 carried out major physical changes which focused on improving play particularly by creating a large adventure play area. Levels of satisfaction amongst pupils remained high throughout. The high level of satisfaction at the monitoring outset may be accounted for by the willow woven structure and mural painting which had recently been carried out by students and pupils as part of a landscape design student spring school. The pupils were aware that nice changes had been made, but perceived their own involvement as limited.

At P7 the number of pupils who reported being bullied in the playground actually increased. We believe that this negative outcome was influenced by three factors. The first was the lack of pupil participation in construction, planting and design – pupils were only involved in mural painting but not in planting and construction of new elements. The second was that many changes were organisational and did not necessarily lead to immediate improved play and social opportunities. For example a proposed 'quiet garden' was fenced off but remained out of bounds throughout monitoring and was therefore potentially a source of frustration for pupils. Thirdly, this school had a very large number of pupils and overcrowding within the small school yards remained a problem.

In all three of these schools changes in favourite parts of the playground demonstrated that any new elements became the immediate foci for play. This was observed by teachers and illustrated in pupil questionnaires, for example by the popularity of the logs which were introduced at P3 (Figure 7.8). The adventure play apparatus at P15 at the third time point dominated as the most popular part of the site for almost half the pupils. The adventure area completely replaced the 'football pitch' as a popular site. This may illustrate that football is popular because it caters for very active play and that if other opportunities for active play are provided predominance of football is reduced. This may however be a short-term effect and the popularity of new elements is undoubtedly influenced by their novelty, for example the pond area in P3. At P7 and P3 grass areas or fields were consistently more popular than tarmac yards. This is presumed to be a positive response to its softness, colour, texture, malleability and diversity in comparison to tarmac.

The participatory techniques that were used to gather information and in 'goal setting' were monitored through discussion with the university students participating, and through study of drawings made by pupils. The techniques were successful both in involving large numbers of pupils, and as a means of finding out about the existing grounds before changes and what pupils and staff wanted as improvements.

Giant maps and photo safaris proved suitable means of engaging all children in thinking about, recording and discussing their environment. The end products (photographs and maps) had the benefit of providing a lasting visual record which could be referred to during goal-setting discussions. Photo safaris in particular elicited very positive and enthusiastic responses from pupils. The degree of control that the process gave pupils was an important factor in this enjoyment. A limiting aspect in the use of giant maps was the difficulty some children (especially younger ones) had with producing plan-view drawings. The problematic tendency for a sub-group or individual to dominate the proceedings was a feature of all exercises. The success of the techniques depended on careful facilitation by the student to ensure democratic decisions and careful recording of information. Good training for facilitators is therefore essential.

The finished maps, photographs and charts were open to wide interpretation and raised difficulties in deciding how strongly they should influence improvements. It would seem that their main benefit was in raising awareness of playground issues and activities. This in turn paved the way for deciding how the school grounds should be changed.

Goal setting was assisted by 'Ideal School' drawings through which pupils could generate ideas for improving the school grounds. Many drawings showed a strong element of fantasy and physically or financially impractical ideas. Lack of discussion with pupils about their drawings was recognised to be a flaw which could have led to frustration amongst pupils if few of their ideas began to materialise. Pupils can rightly view the process as unproductive or sham if no connection between ideas in drawings and final design proposals is apparent. The number of times elements were represented was counted and popularity charts drawn up by some student groups. These were used to influence decisions on changes. Although it did not occur during our project, the drawings can be analysed to discover age and gender differences and similarities.

All of these techniques can be extremely beneficial in dismantling adult preconceptions about pupils' use and perception of their playground and about the types of physical elements that they like. One of the most difficult areas in participatory design is who takes decision making forward to interpretation of ideas into reality. Very often adults make decisions on behalf of children. The project clearly demonstrated that adults do not have to generate ideas (for school ground improvements) for children's consumption. In addition, despite assumptions that children are not good at making democratic decisions, it was clear for example during the cue cards exercises, that groups of older pupils (8, 9 and 10 years) were perfectly capable of discussing each other's needs, suggesting features for pupils other than themselves and reaching agreement. It was this technique and photo safaris that enhanced pupil ability to empathise and take on other viewpoints. This ability is something which is important to the success of some other bullying interventions (for example, the Pikas Method, Chapter Eight).

At P7 and P15 lunchtime supervisor training was also used as an intervention. During monitoring the deputy head at P3 regretted that they had not had supervisor training. Physical improvements carried out without supervisor training can lead to increased tension through behaviour and supervision difficulties. For example, new structures with which supervisors are not familiar and are uncertain of what is appropriate use by pupils may mean there is yet more to shout about or increased confusion in dealing effectively with conflicts which occur in relation to new features. At P7 difficulties emerged as pupils enthusiastically used new railway sleeper seating as 'launching pads' for jumping and were reprimanded for doing so. In cases such as this it would seem appropriate to develop codes of conduct for use of playground elements and features. It is suggested that codes would be most effective if they were developed by or in conjunction with pupils as well as lunchtime supervisors. Ideally supervisor training should occur in parallel with physical changes to the school grounds.

The process of making physical improvements to a school ground is a slow one. This effectively reduced the ability to monitor substantial changes in a

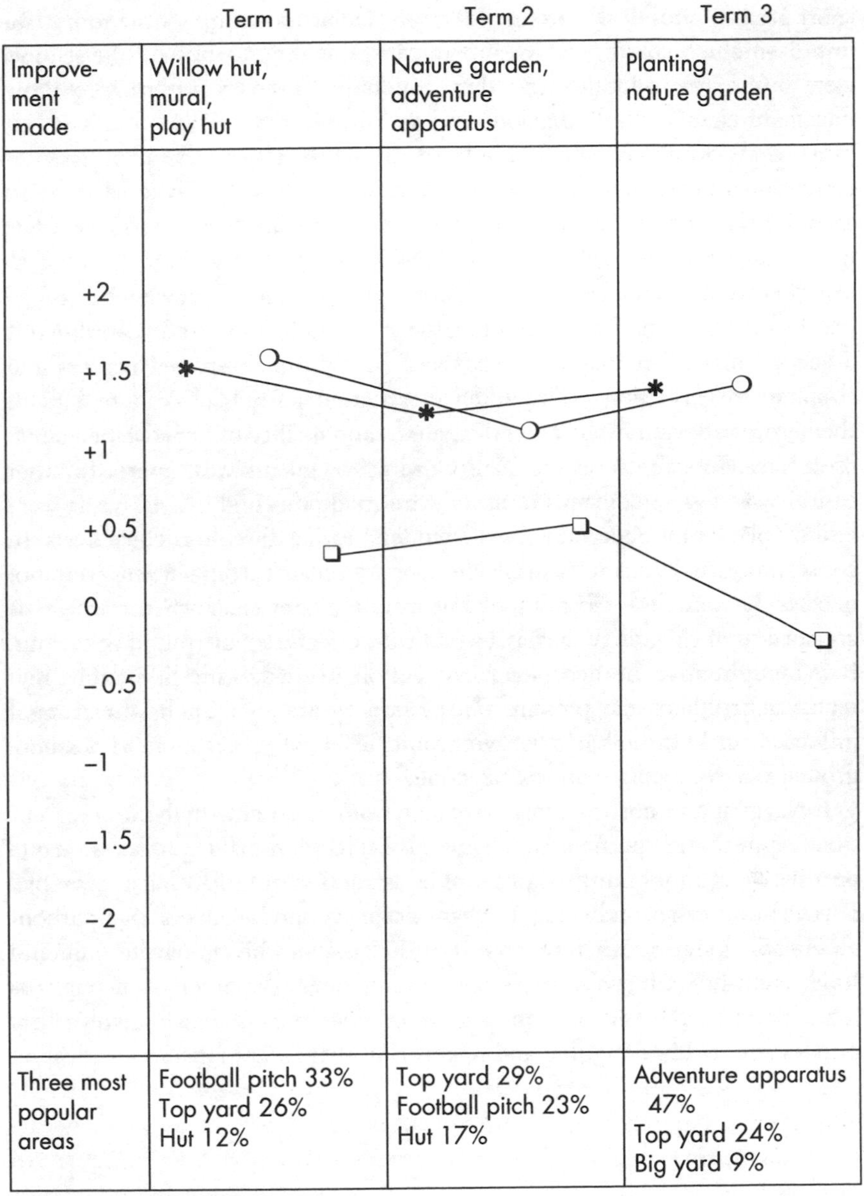
Term 1
Term 2
Term 3
Improvement made
Willow hut, mural, play hut
Nature garden, adventure apparatus
Planting, nature garden
+2
+1.5
+1
+0.5
0
−0.5
−1
−1.5
−2
Three most popular areas
Football pitch 33%
Top yard 26%
Hut 12%
Top yard 29%
Football pitch 23%
Hut 17%
Adventure apparatus 47%
Top yard 24%
Big yard 9%

*** = Do you like your playground?**
○ = Have any nice changes been made to your playground?
□ = Did you help to change the playground?

Figure 7.10 Pupil questionnaire results from P15

short period. During the project P8 in particular took a long time to initiate improvements making it impossible to carry out monitoring. All the schools were studied for a longer time than anticipated (two extra terms) to allow maximum changes to be implemented and monitored.

Physical problems which hindered implementation included lack of technical expertise, human resources and time. These issues were revealed through the regular taped staff interviews. The implementation booklets proved an invaluable resource but some information was hard for staff to interpret and therefore utilise. Success in making improvements relied heavily on the commitment and energy of the individual staff co-ordinator. They in turn relied on a few staff and help from interested parents and voluntary organisations. This often meant that particular skills or lack of them were reflected in the types of changes and quality of improvements that took place. In some cases the quality of improvements was superb. In other cases it was less good: steps or seats were made too high. At P7 walls were built in place of vegetation because builders' rather than horticulturalists' or conservationists' skills were available. Donated plants from gardens were not necessarily suitable for conditions but free. It is not clear whether the type and quality of changes made has a significant effect on playground behaviour. It is thought that the need for participation overrides any limitations that technical problems may present. The *way* things are done can have a stronger influence on both bullying behaviour and levels of satisfaction with school ground environments than *what* is done.

If playground improvements are carried out as an anti-bullying intervention it appears that participation by pupils in decision making, discussion and perhaps most importantly in physical construction and planting is essential. Participation can actually help to change playground behaviour. Simply providing new play and teaching opportunities may not be enough to influence levels of bullying. It is also important that changes are perceived by pupils as beneficial and that satisfaction can be related to how much involvement pupils have had in designing and re-creating their school grounds.

E·I·G·H·T

working directly with pupils involved in bullying situations

PETER K. SMITH
HELEN COWIE
SONIA SHARP

Introduction

One aim for any school seeking to tackle the problem of bullying might be to change the behaviour of the pupils who are involved in the bullying situations. Part of this change may be achieved through preventative work described in other chapters of this book. Other approaches will depend on responding effectively to a bullying situation once it arises. Schools may seek to work with both bullied pupils and those who have bullied them. In particular, they may wish to stop the bullying pupils from continuing with their hurtful behaviour.

The extent to which it is possible permanently to change an individual's behaviour is almost impossible to ascertain. Certainly, intensive behavioural and social learning programmes can result in marked reduction in anti-social behaviour (Herbert, 1987) but these kinds of strategies require specifically focused analysis of the pupil's needs and behaviour followed by formulation and implementation of a treatment programme over a long period of time. They also require intermittent reinforcement to maintain such change. Research into group behaviour (Brown, 1988) shows that group values and attitudes affect behaviour. The Elton Report (DES, 1989) argued that the school 'ethos' influenced strongly the extent to which pupils engage in anti-social behaviour. Therefore, on a general level, schools can do much to establish an atmosphere within the school which discourages bullying behaviour and where peer pressure actively challenges it. On a more intensive and specialised basis, schools can work with the minority of very challenging pupils to bring about particular behaviour change. In this chapter, we aim to consider the middle ground: the short-term responses to bullying behaviour which can improve the situation, resolve the immediate problem and reduce the likelihood of a bullying situation recurring.

In this chapter we discuss three ways of working directly with pupils who have been involved in bullying situations. These are:

- the Method of Shared Concern;
- the No Blame Approach;
- bully courts or school tribunals.

These approaches involve both pupils who bully others and bullied pupils in finding a solution to the problems they are facing. Although each of the three interventions has its own unique qualities, there are common themes which draw them together. First, they are all responsive interventions. They are generally implemented after a bullying incident has occurred. Second, they all seek to empower the pupils themselves and encourage them to retain responsibility for finding a solution to the bullying behaviour. The adults maintain a supportive and facilitative role without imposing solutions. With the exception of bully courts, the interventions focus on resolving the problem rather than apportioning blame. They are not punitive but rather seek solutions. They offer a structure for exploring the problems faced by pupils and emphasise the value of providing direct, clear and honest channels of communication. All of these interventions recognise that pupils can assume an important and helpful role in tackling bullying behaviour.

In terms of implementation, they all require specialised training for both staff and pupils. All operate beyond the classroom as part of the overall organisation of the school. They therefore depend on schools having the commitment to divert resources to enable the intervention to operate.

Evaluation of these interventions has proved difficult on a short-term basis. They are used as and when a bullying situation occurs and consequently researchers have to wait for them to be implemented rather than controlling usage. It may take time to build up sufficient cases to evaluate effectively. There is a tendency for shifts in methods of application to occur as individuals adapt the techniques to suit their own needs. Most evaluation is based on self-report, therefore relying on subjective interpretation of actual processes and outcomes.

Evaluation which has taken place suggests that each approach is effective to a certain extent and under certain conditions. With the possible exception of bully courts, these interventions may form part of a multi-dimensional response to the problem of bullying.

The Method of Shared Concern

The Method of Shared Concern has been pioneered in Sweden by Anatol Pikas (1989); in his earlier writings, Pikas calls it the 'method of common concern'. Pikas argues that in order to design the most appropriate treatment it is essential to differentiate between two forms of bullying. There are occasions when bullying takes place between a single bully and another individual or group of individuals; but, he argues, the most common form that bullying in school takes is that of mobbing – a form of group violence where a gang of bullying pupils attack an individual or group either physically or psychologically over a period of time. Such a gang often includes the leaders, their hangers-on and the regular onlookers who do nothing to protect the victim.

Pikas discusses two methods of dealing with bullying: the direct method, and the Method of Shared Concern. In the direct method, the adult simply tells the child doing the bullying, quite firmly and authoritatively, that this behaviour has to stop. Pikas thinks that this is appropriate for children below 9 years of age; for one-to-one bullying; and for situations where, for whatever reason, the more sophisticated Method of Shared Concern will not work or is not working. However, it is this latter method which is particularly distinctive, and which we have tried out in some detail.

The Method of Shared Concern is suitable for children of 9 years and above, where a group or gang of children have been bullying one or more other pupils. It is an attempt on the part of the adult (referred to by Pikas as 'the therapist') to 'reindividualise' the members of the group. Essentially, the process rests on the premise that the thoughts and feelings of the gang are simpler than those of any of its members. As a group, they are caught up in a collective phenomenon – aggression towards a victim. But within the group there will be a range of individual anxieties and reservations about what is happening. For example:

- there is peer pressure to conform to what the others in the group are doing;
- bullying in a group allows 'diffusion of responsibility' – the blame can be shifted to others;
- a child may fear that if they do not join in bullying, they in turn will become victims.

For such reasons, members of a group may actively participate in bullying or passively collude in it. Rationalisation and justification for the bullying will be found. The victim's unhappiness is likely to be denied or ignored.

The teacher's task is to bring into conscious awareness the feelings of unease or shame which individual group members have about the group's bullying behaviour. Through a series of individual talks with each member of the group, the teacher establishes an area of shared concern about the situation for the victim, i.e. that the bullied child is 'having a bad time in school'. The teacher's task is not to assign blame or to be punitive, but simply to establish agreement that the situation of the bullied pupil is not good. The teacher's understanding of the group's dynamics is combined with initiative and persistence to bring about change in each member of the gang.

Through the first step of establishing an area of shared concern the teacher offers the possibility of an escape from the unpleasantness of taking part in the tormenting of a fellow pupil. How is this done? The method has three stages:

- individual 'chats' with each pupil involved (about five to ten minutes per child) – the 'ringleader' of the children doing the bullying is seen first; and the child who is bullied, last;
- follow-up interviews with each pupil (about three to five minutes per child);
- group meeting of all the children (half an hour).

The time-span between each stage is typically one week.

Each pupil is invited individually to take part in devising a constructive solution to the problem. The teacher considers every suggestion seriously and discusses with each pupil in turn a realistic way of putting it into practice. The first interview must be the most carefully structured. Pikas has devised a script for teachers to follow (for a fuller account, see Pikas, 1987; and Sharp, Cowie and Smith, 1994). He also offers advice on the setting for the interviews and the order in which they are carried out. He places an emphasis on the important messages which these organisational features and non-verbal behaviours send, employing every small detail to ensure the success of the method.

The initial interviews have two phases. In the first phase, each pupil is given time to reflect on the bullied pupil's situation. The teacher opens the interview by asserting that 'unpleasant things' have been happening to the bullied pupil. This is presented as a fact and is not open to negotiation. However, it is not asserted that the pupil being interviewed has been either directly or indirectly involved in this nasty behaviour. The teacher merely wishes to establish that these things have happened, and then to encourage each pupil to recognise that, regardless of the behaviour of the bullied pupil (which may well be seen as provocative by the other pupils), she or he is not as happy in school as she or he could be. Once this 'shared concern' for the bullied pupil has been reached, the interview can progress to the second stage. Here, the teacher and pupil focus on possible solutions to the problems faced by the bullied pupil. Each pupil is encouraged to suggest his or her own ideas for improving the situation. If necessary, the teacher can make suggestions to uncooperative, unimaginative or younger pupils who cannot bring forth suggestions themselves. Once a tenable solution has been agreed, the teacher asks the pupil to try to put it into practice over the following week. A follow-up meeting is arranged.

Finally, the teacher meets the child who is being bullied. Pikas feels it is important to distinguish between ordinary victims (who do not contribute to their being bullied), and provocative victims (who, in part, contribute to their being bullied by their provocative brehaviour). The role of the teacher is to support and encourage the ordinary victim; but to help the provocative victim realise that they have some responsibility for their situation and that they too must change. For some children, this may be the first time that they have had the opportunity to share their misery with another person so this is likely to be an emotional session. Again through discussion an action plan is devised and a contract made. Therapist and victim shake hands on the bargain and agree to meet the following week.

The teacher returns after a week and has shorter interviews to see how things are going. The teacher works towards arranging a group meeting, at which all the pupils will meet face to face to review the situation. This will only take place when the bullied pupil has stated his or her readiness to meet the rest of the group. The success of this meeting depends very much on how well the teacher has prepared for it in advance. There may be reproaches and recriminations on both sides. However, the teacher's prime aim is to promote communication amongst all the participants and to facilitate this through positive responses to all the constructive suggestions which emerge.

Here is an example of the complete process, taken from the records of one of the members of the Sheffield Project team. Geoff, aged 12, had been so cruelly punched and teased by his classmates that he was absent from school more often than he attended. His older sister had also been bullied at the school. As one teacher unhelpfully put it, 'It runs in the family!' Members of staff had tried every strategy they knew to break the pattern but the difficulty was that most pupils seemed to accept that this was 'normal' treatment for Geoff. The deputy head was eager to break this cycle of bullying; she readily agreed that a member of the team should come into school to try an alternative method since, despite frequent appeals to the better nature of Geoff's peer group, nothing seemed to change the situation. The bullying was being done by a group of boys – Clive, Darren, Nigel and Joe. The teachers did not know which one was the ringleader but suspected that it might be Clive.

Here are extracts from the records of the first interview.

> Clive was seen first. He admitted that Geoff was feeling bad so very quickly we established this as 'an area of shared concern'. When he was asked 'What can we do?' he answered that he would like to ask Geoff to sit at his table for lunch once or twice during the next week.
>
> Darren responded differently. It was hard to make eye contact and he denied any involvement in the bullying of Geoff but readily agreed that Geoff was scared to come to school. When asked 'What can we do?' he said (with some prompting) that he would ask 'them' (he, of course, was not one of them!) to stop hitting Geoff.
>
> Nigel found it difficult at first to express any knowledge that Geoff was being bullied but he did admit that 'others' called Geoff 'monkey', and he sniggered in a furtive way as he said it. It took a longer time to establish an area of shared concern since he appeared totally indifferent to Geoff's feelings. However, eventually the contract was that he would say to others 'Stop calling Geoff names' whenever it occurred.
>
> Joe at first denied that Geoff was being bullied and then, when he revised this position, suggested that it was all Geoff's fault since he 'caused trouble' by shouting nasty names at other boys. Since he sat next to Geoff in maths he finally agreed to help him with his work in class.

Once the contract was made, teacher and bully shook hands on the bargain; the teacher agreed to return next week to see how things were going. After each member of the group of bullies had been seen, the teacher talked with the victim. In this case, the teacher did not believe that Geoff was a 'provocative victim' so she focused mainly on being supportive and helping the victim to talk about the experiences which he had had.

> Geoff entered the room last; he was small in stature, very downcast with a dejected posture. It was hard to make eye contact as he kept looking at the floor. He said that Clive used to punch him a lot but that it was much better now since Clive and Darren 'only called him names'. When we explored this further, he told me that they called him 'monkey' and his sister 'mophead'. As he disclosed this information in a very quiet voice his face expressed pain but also relief that someone could listen to his story. His gaze was intent and prolonged. When

I proposed the idea of a group meeting he said cautiously that he would rather wait to see how things worked out. However, he did say that he would be pleased if Clive asked him to sit at his table, though he reserved the right to say 'No'. He was very doubtful that any of the bullies would keep to their side of the bargain. After some more discussion he agreed that if Clive asked him he would sit with him at the lunch table. We shook hands on the agreement and I was struck by the intensity with which he clung to my hand. It was a moving experience which stayed with me long after he had gone.

After another week, the group meeting was arranged.

I went to the class to collect Clive, Darren, Nigel and Joe. Joe flatly refused to come so I said, 'Fine. It's your choice', and left with the others who were eager to come. They had already clustered round me at break as soon as I came in the door of the school. We settled down and talked about what they had done over the past few weeks and how they had helped Geoff. Suddenly the door opened and Joe came in rather aggressively and the atmosphere changed. Everyone then got silly and started laughing at everything. It was difficult to get them to focus on the issue. However, I persisted and tried not to be deflected. Joe stayed very quiet and sullen. The others agreed to repeat the positive things which they had been saying when Geoff came in. I brought out lemonade and crisps and it was as if they had never seen such things before! A great wave of excitement flowed over the group. Joe said that he would keep his crisps for later. I went out to fetch Geoff. His cheeks were glowing and he smiled at me as we walked along the corridor.

When we came in Joe was sitting in my chair. I asked him to pass me another chair and I sat with Geoff on my right and Joe on my left. As we ate and drank we managed to have a discussion. Clive said quite spontaneously to Geoff, 'Why don't you play with us? We'll be your friends.'

We managed to talk a little about tolerance if one or other could not keep his side of the bargain. Geoff quietly said to the others that he felt much happier and they looked pleased at this. I said that I would come in at the beginning of the term to see how things were going and stressed how pleased I was at all that had happened. They were reluctant to go in the end but did quite peacefully. I told the group that I would return in a few weeks to see how they were getting on.

Since then Geoff has attended school and there have been no further reports of bullying.

Evaluation of the Pikas method

Since the Method of Shared Concern goes through a precise sequence of stages, it is essential to be trained before using it. In addition, it is appropriate to form a support group to share experiences and build up a body of expertise.

Pikas has expounded his ideas in a couple of articles (1989), and, in much more detail, in a book in Swedish (Pikas, 1987) for which an English translation is being prepared. He claims great success for his method, though his own published evaluation seems to be based solely on a small number of case studies. Pikas has not been without his critics, foremost amongst whom is Olweus (1988). Olweus challenges Pikas' claim that pupils who bully others feel guilt and argues instead that clinical evidence shows the opposite: pupils who bully others do not show empathy for their victims' feelings. Olweus points out that the method does not include involvement with parents and considers that this is a weakness since parents could co-operate with the teacher to reinforce and sustain the changed attitudes and behaviours. His most stringent criticism is that the method is unethical since it is 'built on manipulation and latent threats' disguised as co-operation between the bullying pupil and the teacher. He says that it would be more honest for the teacher to put his or her cards on the table and simply state that bullying is unacceptable and that there will be dire consequences if it does not stop (rather as in Pikas' 'direct method', in fact).

Our own experience of using the Method of Shared Concern in local schools and of facilitating training workshops for teachers has been a positive one; it appears that it can be a powerful short-term tool for combating bullying, although long-term change may depend on additional action where very persistent bullying is concerned. Twenty-one teachers, representing seven primary schools and seven secondary schools, were trained to use the method. Twelve of the teachers were able to use the method and all have reported that they found it an appropriate and helpful response to bullying. Additional and more focused evaluation has been based on a series of interviews with thirty pupils and six teachers (Simms, 1992; Lucas, 1993). This case-study approach is due to the small number of cases in which it is possible to maintain monitoring over time combined with the wide range of variation between each case in terms of number of pupils involved, school context and the nature of the bullying behaviour. Nevertheless, we have attempted to establish the advantages and disadvantages of the method in the shorter and slightly longer term. The sample size of thirty children and six teachers has been too small to be completely certain to what extent the method changes pupil behaviour. However, the responses of the pupils and their teachers provide insight into ways in which this method can be successful.

Three-quarters of the pupils interviewed felt that in the short term the situation had improved, i.e. the bullying had decreased. They attributed this success to being offered the opportunity to express their feelings and perspectives on the situation individually as well as being encouraged to propose their own solutions rather than having one imposed by an adult. The non-punitive style of the method may also help pupils to concentrate on solving the problem rather than dogmatically defending their character.

It can be difficult for adults who employ a direct interrogational style to discuss with pupils the nature of their bullying behaviour. Ahmad and Smith (1990) compared different methods of investigating bullying behaviour with pupils, and found that only half of those pupils who admitted to bullying in a questionnaire admitted bullying others when interviewed. The Method of Shared Concern circumvents this difficulty by seeking agreement that there is a problem to be solved and by deliberately not apportioning blame or debating the 'truth' of the situation.

All of the teachers interviewed, except one, felt that the method had reduced the frequency and severity of the bullying behaviour. Both teachers and pupils pointed out the importance of the group meeting in providing a forum for long-term maintenance of the behaviour change. Some teachers commented that they had been tempted to miss this stage out as the method had seemed to be successful after the earlier meetings. This failure to continue with the method until its final stage could account for recurrence of bullying behaviour in the long term. A more rigorously controlled study with sufficient numbers of cases would be needed to establish whether or not this was so.

An additional problem identified by the teachers was the tendency in some cases for the bullying pupils to switch their attention to another pupil outside the group. Through a slight adaptation of the group meeting, it may be possible to reduce the likelihood of this happening. Either in this meeting, or perhaps in a subsequent one, the teacher could broaden the discussion to involve bullying generally. Maybe the cue line for this conversation could be as follows:

> OK, we have talked about how we can make sure things stay better for all of you, but what about other pupils who are not here? The rest of the class, year group – all of the other pupils – how can you help them so that they do not experience similar problems?

The small number of cases reflects the difficulty some teachers faced in putting this method into practice. The method requires that the teacher be able to spend time during lessons with the individual pupils, especially for the first interviews. Without a commitment from senior management to enable staff to do this, the method cannot be used. In schools where the method had been incorporated into their anti-bullying policy as one of a range of strategies which might be used if a bullying incident arose, it was implemented more frequently and followed up more effectively. In other schools, teachers had to use the method if and when they could. This was deemed unsatisfactory by the teachers themselves and led to teachers taking short cuts with the method or not using it at all.

The pupils' reliance on the teacher as mediator was evident. Perhaps a future development of this method could be to supplement the approach with the mediation and conflict-resolution training for pupils described in Chapter Five so that they would be able to adopt a problem-solving approach themselves. In one case, the pupils continued to hold group meetings similar to the one facilitated by the teacher during the intervention. Whilst this pupil-initiated support group operated, the bullying within that group did cease. Over time, however, the group feeling dissipated and the bullying began to escalate once again.

Maintenance of the effects of the method over time seems to depend on other measures implemented by the school to improve the situation. These might be specific measures such as manipulation of class membership or involvement of parents, or else other measures within the framework of a whole-school policy (Chapter Three). This is not surprising when longer term and age-focused studies of bullying behaviour are considered. Olweus (1978) and Stephenson and Smith (1989) found that at least two-thirds of pupils who reported bullying others during one school year were still bullying others a year later. Farrington (1993) describes the findings of the Cambridge Study in Delinquent Development which monitored 411 males from the age of 8 until they were 32. He found that 25 per cent of pupils who bullied others at age 14 still bullied others at age 18, and 33 per cent of those who bullied at age 18 bullied others at age 32. For those pupils who persistently bully others, possibly multiple strategies are required.

Lucas (1993) found that the combination of the Pikas method with removal to another class of the 'hard core' bullies (usually only one or two in the group) seemed to lead to long-term positive change. She writes:

> Pikas was right in his attempt to break the 'group psychology'. What the method achieves is an alleviation of the situation for a while, and a way to identify those pupils who are most disruptive so they can be dealt with by other measures. Once the group has been broken and the leaders removed or their behaviour changed, it will not re-form.

The No Blame Approach

Maines and Robinson (1991a, b; 1992) similarly take the view that we cannot ignore the social context of bullying. They argue that bullying arises out of interpersonal interactions in which dominance and status are gained by some at the expense of less prestigious members of a peer group. Membership of the group is to some extent defined by the exclusion of those who are not members. It is only by fostering co-operative values such as empathy, concern for others and unselfishness within the peer group that the bully will relinquish power as a result of peer pressure. Punitive measures are bound to fail since they simply reinforce the values of hierarchy and dominance through power. Punishment may also put the victim at risk of revenge attacks.

The No Blame Approach is quite similar to the Method of Shared Concern, in two main ways. First, Maines and Robinson share with Pikas a belief that most bullying is a group phenomenon – mobbing – which thrives in a particular kind of peer group culture. Second, their method aims to establish an area of shared concern between the bullying group and their victim. However, the No Blame Approach differs in the actual order in which the adult works with the pupils who bully others and the bullied pupil in the following ways.

- Whereas Pikas sees the pupils who bully others individually before he sees the bullied pupil in order to protect the bullied pupil from further intimidation, Maines and Robinson recommend that the adult take the risk of letting bullied pupils speak in their own words of the suffering which they have experienced. Once they have described their feelings about the bullying to the teacher, she or he relays their story to the other pupils. They do this because, in their experience, the impact of the adult speaking on behalf of the bullied pupil is very powerful.
- Pikas interviews each member of the group of bullying pupils individually, but Maines and Robinson speak with the whole group, including active members, hangers-on and those who collude. Some members of this group might remain indifferent to the plight of the bullied pupil but when the majority respond in a kind and helpful way this is a sufficient change to stop the bullying and make the life of the victim tolerable.
- Both Pikas and Maines and Robinson establish a problem-solving approach to the problem but Maines and Robinson place more emphasis on the feelings of each member of the group as a motivator for changed behaviour. They assume that empathy with the bullied pupil's hurt will occur if his or her case is put forcefully by the adult. This counselling approach depends on a basic skill – that of reflecting back to the members

of the group what the outcomes of this bullying behaviour are. Empathy occurs, they argue, when group members are reminded of similar experiences of rejection, intimidation or fear in their own lives. It is this capacity for empathy which enables us to take the perspective of another person and to see things from that person's point of view. The No Blame Approach builds on this fundamental human capacity.

The video and accompanying workbook (Maines and Robinson, 1992) introduce teachers and pupils to a seven-point plan which aims to enhance feelings of concern for the bullied pupil and create the social context in which pupils who bully others, bullied pupils and bystanders can be engaged in a problem-solving approach.

Here is a typical case study (Maines and Robinson, 1991a, p. 17).

> Andrew, a victim, was so distressed at the nasty and persistent name-calling to which he was constantly subjected that he was seriously considering leaving the school. In his words, he 'felt like beating their heads in, like running away; quite unable to cope'. The tutor saw the bullying pupils as a group and explained how unhappy Andrew was. In the course of the discussions, one boy recalled his own feelings when he had been teased in a similar way. A feeling of shared concern for Andrew emerged in at least some members of the group. By the time that she met each boy individually the following week, they had all apologised to him and promised to intervene when they saw others calling him nasty names.
>
> There was no recurrence of the bullying, the boy stayed on at school and is now at university.

Evaluation of the No Blame Approach

The evidence that the No Blame Approach works is derived from case study material. The case study given above is convincing, but only case studies with positive outcomes are presented; are these selectively chosen? Maines and Robinson (1992) present results of an evaluation which suggest that this is not so (see Table 8.1).

The success criterion was that the teachers reported that the intervention had stopped the bullying. This had been confirmed with the students involved after up to six months time lapse. In most cases, parents were involved and reported that they were very pleased with the outcome. Two further and more extensive evaluations are now near completion and have yielded equally positive outcomes.

TABLE 8.1 SUCCESS RATE OF THE NO BLAME APPROACH: AN INITIAL EVALUATION OF THE FIRST PILOT GROUP OF TEACHERS TRAINED IN THE NO BLAME APPROACH, CARRIED OUT BY QUESTIONNAIRE UNDERTAKEN BY THE PSYCHOLOGY SERVICE TASK GROUP AND POSTGRADUATE STUDENTS FROM BRISTOL UNIVERSITY

	Number of teachers	Number of cases	Success rate
Primary	2	8	8/8
Secondary	8	49	47/49

Source: Maines and Robinson, 1992

Although this reported evaluation is encouraging, it would clearly be desirable to have an independent replication with more detail of methodology. Nor do we know *how* the process of change occurs, only that it does. Some inside perspectives from all the people involved would give greater insights. However, the No Blame Approach offers a useful practical method to add to the concerned adult's repertoire of techniques for combating bullying.

School tribunals or 'bully courts'

The school tribunal, or 'bully court', used as a means of dealing with bullying, presents something of an enigma. For a while in 1990/91, it was perhaps the most highly publicised approach. Yet few schools appear to have used it, and it has proved difficult to get evidence about how well it works.

The origins of ideas about school courts or tribunals

The philosophy behind school courts or tribunals goes back a long way. The idea of a school decision-making body, with power largely devolved to the pupils, can be traced to radical democratic reformers such as Homer Lane, who instituted the 'Little Commonwealth' at Flowers Farm, Dorset. Lane worked first in the USA but then came to the UK, and his ideas led to the democratic traditions at Summerhill, founded in 1921 by A.S. Neill, and later to 'the Barns experiment' (Wills, 1945). Although each of these initiatives had its own characteristics, they shared the idea of a regular (usually weekly) meeting of the whole-school community to make and discuss rules, and deal with infringements of rules. Since these schools were residential, there was clearly considerable business for such meetings.

Adults had an equal vote with children (though charismatic personalities such as Homer Lane or A.S. Neill undoubtedly wielded considerable influence in these meetings). They also shared the characteristic that many of the children at these schools had emotional or behavioural problems, and the group processes and sharing of responsibilities involved in the meetings were felt to have therapeutic value. These meetings or tribunals were of course of a general nature; presumably, bullying took up only a small proportion of their business.

Robert Laslett, a teacher who had worked with David Wills, wrote two articles about courts for pupils who bully others (Laslett, 1980, 1982). He described setting up a Children's Court in order to deal *specifically* with problems of bullying at a day school for maladjusted children aged 7 to 12 years. The Court consisted of two justices and a court runner (all pupils), and Laslett as 'Clerk to the Justices'. The Court met for forty minutes, twice a week. A list of possible punishments was agreed by pupils and staff, ranging from the bullying pupil apologising and making-up with the victim, or doing something nice for the victim, to being forbidden to use the grass play area or the go-kart for a certain number of days, to staying in at dinner time and doing sums.

This Court existed for at least ten years. Laslett reported that the sessions were lively, noisy and interesting; and that it was a popular and influential part of the school programme. It did not eliminate bullying, but appeared to help reduce it. The children who bullied others were affected by the criticism of peers and the punishment inflicted by them; and the Court generally strengthened the awareness that bullying would not be tolerated in the school. The children who were justices often gained in self-esteem.

The recent publicity about 'bully courts'

'Bully courts' as such were advocated by the Kidscape organisation in 1990. They issued a one-page sheet of advice which advocated that, as part of school guidelines for behaviour, an arbitration court be set up. This court would comprise four students (two elected by other students, two appointed by teachers) and one teacher. The court would meet perhaps once a week, and would be responsible for solutions or penalties for infractions of the behaviour guidelines (unless these were sufficiently serious to involve the police). The court verdict would be recorded and would be binding. School governors and parents would receive information about the court system.

Kidscape called the courts 'honour courts', but used the term 'bully courts' as the title. (This one sheet of advice was also circulated with the *Sticks and stones* video pack from Central TV, in 1990.) The call for bully courts got considerable media publicity. The *Guardian* for 12 April 1990 had an article headed ' "Bully courts" get teacher backing', while the *Independent* for 15 April 1990 had a quarter-page on 'Bullies may be put on trial in school "courts" '. These articles discussed the general problem of bullying, and mentioned support for the bully court idea from AMMA (Assistant Masters and Mistresses Association).

The *Sunday Times* for 6 May 1990 featured 'Pupils put bullies in the dock' in the Education Forum section. This article stated that 'So far, at least thirty British schools have introduced bully courts. . . . Eight schools – two secondary, six primary – have been monitored by the group [Kidscape]'. Michele Elliott (Director of Kidscape) was quoted as saying that 'At all the schools, bullying has gone down'. However the article only featured a school in north London which was doing preparatory work with role-play and had not yet set up a proper court. The *Guardian* returned to the topic on 22 June 1990, with 'A place to get your own back in the blackboard jungle'. Again the preparatory role-plays at the north London school were detailed, but unfortunately it was stated that 'The thirty schools with the courts understandably won't let anyone near them.'

The concept of the 'bully court' also stirred up strong feelings. On the one hand, delegating power to the children could get them really involved in dealing with the problems of bullying, and develop their sense of responsibility. On the other hand, obvious dangers presented themselves. Would penalties be inappropriate? Would bullies get themselves elected to the court? Was the whole concept too punitive in conception? Would bullies become anti-heroes?

Later evaluations of bully courts

The only published systematic evaluation of a bully court is provided by Brier and Ahmad (1991). Brier was the headteacher at a middle school in a deprived area of Sheffield. She had one term's secondment to look at ways of dealing with bullying in the school, early in 1990. The possibility of using a bully court was drawn to her attention by the local Community Police Inspector. Developing this, she arranged for nine representatives to be elected from the Year Five and Six classes. A visit was made to the local Crown Court, forms were prepared, and preparatory role-plays were carried out. Two cases were heard in the first five weeks of the court; the sanctions imposed were clearing the playground of rubbish for a week, and losing a chance for out-of-school activities. There were no cases in the second five weeks.

The children felt that the court had had a positive effect in school; though there may have been an increase in bullying out of school. Ahmad conducted a questionnaire survey before and after the bully court operations. This showed that there was a moderate fall in reports of being bullied, or bullying others, in the Year Five and Six classes; whereas the Year Four and Year Seven classes showed a slight increase on these measures. The latter classes had not experienced the intervention.

This suggests that the bully court had indeed been helpful. The comparison with the other classes in the same school provide a strong control for any external factors or age-related trends. However, the intervention in the Year Five and Six classes did include some intensive group work with the headteacher as well as the bully courts, so the latter may not be solely responsible. Indeed, the court only met twice! Brier and Ahmad concluded that the *process* of developing the court was perhaps of most use, while pointing out that this had been very time intensive and only possible because of the one-term secondment of the headteacher.

Elliott (1991) describes the use of bully courts, which she states Kidscape had developed independently of Laslett's earlier work. Kidscape monitored the progress of eight out of thirty schools using bully courts in a pilot scheme. Over a three-month period, the number of students reporting they had been bullied dropped from 70 per cent to 6 per cent. This is a dramatic drop, but no further details are available in Elliott's article, nor are they now available from Kidscape, who apparently have not kept the records or even the identities of these schools. Elliott (1991) does, however, emphasise the importance of only using bully courts within the framework of a strong school policy on bullying.

In an attempt to locate other schools which have used bully courts, we have had limited success. None of our twenty-three project schools took up the idea, although several had expressed initial interest, and one secondary school did undertake some initial work. The only additional school that Kidscape could refer us to was in London. Correspondence with the headteacher of this primary school revealed that a children's council was held only for two terms, as after this the school was reorganised, and the 9-year-olds, who had been most involved, left the school. During the two terms, the council met three times. The headteacher did not feel able to comment on any changes produced by the council over this rather short time period, but did feel prepared to try the idea again.

We learnt of one middle school in Oxfordshire which had gone further. A police inspector who was also a parent at this school had attended a Kidscape conference to learn more of bully courts, and a staff working group decided to implement this, as well as other action against bullying. After preparatory work in personal and social education, each class elected one representative to the court, making twelve pupils in all; the court then met in January 1991 to discuss rules and procedures. The headteacher was 'immensely impressed with the insights and common sense which the pupils brought to this meeting'. A booklet was published setting out the Court's rules and procedures, and parents were informed. In a written report (July 1991), the headteacher commented that

> whether or not the Court has been a success, I'm not sure. In the six months since the Court was set up it has never sat. This is not because there has been no bullying in the school, but because we made the decision at the start that only very serious cases would be dealt with by the Court.

In fact, more minor incidents were dealt with by the head or his deputy directly.

We also discovered that a primary school in Edinburgh had implemented a bully court. Correspondence revealed that the headteacher decided to use a bully court after reading about them, in a class with a teacher willing to try it. The headteacher moved shortly afterwards. She reported that she was not now in favour of bully courts, feeling that the jury developed a certain smugness; that (unless controlled by the teacher) decisions could turn into a vendetta; and that parents might dislike the idea, which could backfire. She did say that the class teacher felt it could be managed successfully (but he did not reply to our questionnaire).

Attitudes to bully courts

It appears that school councils, tribunals or bully courts have been rarely used. Why is this? Some information on teachers' attitudes was gathered by Pitfield (1992). She gave a questionnaire on bully courts to nineteen teachers from different schools in the DFE project. A similar questionnaire was also given to forty-seven pupils (aged 10 to 11 years) in a middle school which did not use bully courts; these pupils were told what bully courts were, and shown role-plays on video. The questionnaire asked for agreement or disagreement with pro- or anti- bully court statements.

Teachers generally agreed strongly that 'For bully courts to work, other intervention strategies would have to be used alongside it', and 'It is the preparatory work on the court which is beneficial, the court hearing being irrelevant'. There was considerable variation on some negative items such as 'We disagree with the idea of pupils "judging", and having the power to punish their own peers'; 'Our school does not have a serious enough problem with bullying to warrant bringing in a bully court'; and 'Prospective parents would be alarmed, thinking the school to have a serious problem with bullying'. Some teachers agreed with these statements, others disagreed.

Pupils generally agreed that 'It is good that some children (the jury) have the power to give a punishment to another member of their form (the bully)', but also that 'Bullies would start bullying people *outside* school, where they cannot be taken to court'.

A comparison of identical statements in the teacher and pupil questionnaires showed that pupils, more than teachers, felt that 'It is good that some children have the power to give a punishment to another member of their form' (p<.005), and that 'With a bully court, bullies would not bully so many people because he/she would be scared of going to court' (p<.02); while teachers, more than pupils, felt that 'Bullies would not take any notice of what the court told them to do' (p<.05). In general, teachers' attitudes to bully courts were somewhat ambivalent, while those of pupils were more positive.

Pitfield also gave a short questionnaire to twenty-five pupils and two teachers from the Oxfordshire school and nine pupils and one teacher from the Sheffield school, which had used a bully court, during early 1992. The results suggest that most pupils felt there was less bullying inside school since the court, but possibly more outside (especially at the Sheffield school); some children felt their attitudes or behaviour had changed for the better, so far as bullying was concerned. The teachers felt that there were more reports of bullying since the courts began, but probably because of increased awareness rather than actually a greater problem; they felt the effects on the jury children were beneficial. However, they also stated that a lot of time was involved in setting up the courts.

Factors influencing the use and effectiveness of bully courts

Clearly, there is rather little evidence yet as to whether bully courts are effective. Yet, apart from the headteacher in Edinburgh, evaluations were positive, though often with provisos. Nevertherless, many schools seem reluctant to introduce it. Teachers have mixed views about the idea, whereas pupils may tend to be more positive.

Particular issues for teachers seem to be: issues of time needed to set up bully courts properly; fears that bully courts may be too punitive and/or that they were giving too much power to children; and fear that parents would be alarmed at the idea. It would seem that a precondition for using such courts is an enthusiastic headteacher and class teacher(s) who are willing to take the time to do preparatory work with pupils, explain the idea to parents and governors, and be prepared to really devolve some responsibility to pupils. Many teachers are not prepared to do this.

In so far as bully courts may have some positive effect, this could be due to the preparation-work involved; the deterrent power of the court and its sanctions; peer persuasion; and shared responsibility. Dangers include: shifting of bullying to outside the school and the court's jurisdiction; too punitive an attitude being fostered; a lack of impartiality in forming the jury or in giving verdicts; and possible trauma for shy victims in giving evidence. The psychological effects of bully courts on pupils who bully others, victims and jury members would be very interesting to assess in detail.

The final verdict on the idea of bully courts themselves must be 'the jury is still out'! Frustratingly little evidence is available on this highly publicised method. Meanwhile, since 1990/91 the publicity has faded somewhat. Kidscape give it a very low-key position in their current (1993) *Stop bullying* booklet; they now say that 'we call them Student Councils but the students call them Bully courts and this is the phrase the media has latched onto' (letter from Kidscape, 8 March 1993). The recent Kidscape guidelines are now headed 'Student Councils', giving almost identical suggestions to those headed 'Bully courts' in 1990. Indeed, the term 'Bully court', while direct, may not be the most appropriate. But the idea of a pupil court, or council, or tribunal, to deal with bullying matters, remains an interesting one. It is a pity that as yet, we have no good, well-documented studies of a few schools, or even of one school, in which this method has been used (and in which the council has met reasonably frequently) over more than one or two terms.

Summary

To enable further development of effective responses to bullying behaviour, there is a need for more rigorous monitoring and evaluation over time. A more substantial amount of information about these kinds of approaches is required to facilitate thorough understanding of why and how they work. Nevertheless, it is clear from the limited data available that most of the methods described in this chapter offer teachers and schools who are concerned about bullying some helpful strategies for responding to bullying situations. Each has its own particular merits and possible applications; each has some effect on bullying behaviour in its own right. However, if implemented in isolation, none of these interventions offers more than short-term improvement for pupils who bully others or who are being bullied. Clearly, the full power of these strategies will only be realised if they are implemented as part of a clearly defined intervention process which combines a progressive series of responses with a background of preventative and awareness-raising work. Bullying can be viewed as a complex social phenomenon; as such any change in the behaviour of the pupils involved is only likely to be achieved through a multi-dimensional approach. We may need to combine different approaches to tackle the same problem if we wish to achieve long-term change.

Whatever methods are employed to work directly with pupils involved in bullying, we suggest that schools and teachers should be guided by four principles. Three of these are shared by all the methods reviewed in this chapter:

- focus on solving the problem; in addition the Pikas Method of Shared Concern and the No Blame Approach (but not the Pikas direct method, or bully courts) specifically avoid blaming or punishing;
- encourage the pupils themselves to propose solutions to the problem;
- employ assertive styles of communication rather than aggression or passivity.

The fourth principle has emerged strongly from our own evaluations:

- as well as immediate short-term action, ensure that other steps are taken to deal with the problem on a long-term basis.

N·I·N·E | **bullying and children with special educational needs**

IRENE WHITNEY
PETER K. SMITH
DAVID THOMPSON

Introduction

For children with special educational needs in a mainstream school, problems of bullying and victimisation may be especially important considerations. Often, just being different in a noticeable way can be a risk factor for being a victim. Also, in some cases these children have behavioural difficulties (acting out/aggression or withdrawal) which may make them more likely to get into situations where they act as a bully or victim.

Early on in our investigation of this topic, five special schools in Sheffield were visited, to gain an informal staff perspective on the general issue of the vulnerability of children with special needs to bullying. These visits revealed that the problem of bullying and victimisation may be especially salient for some children who have special needs. For example, the head of one school for children with moderate learning difficulties indicated that children who had been bullied previously in mainstream schools tended to retaliate at first by bullying other children. He commented that the children had been victims of bullying usually because of their learning difficulties or their social and emotional problems.

At a teaching centre for young people described as having school phobia, the head was of the view that although school phobia is viewed by some to be irrational, there are some aspects of schooling where a fear reaction is not at all an irrational response. Such fear-inducing experiences include the bullying, intimidation and ridicule which some of their pupils had experienced. Children who were vulnerable in some way because of learning difficulties, lack of social skills or who had some kind of illness, were regarded as especially at risk for such experiences.

Typical comments from the head of this unit about the children attending included:

> Maureen finds interpersonal relationships difficult. At comprehensive school she did not receive the attention and reassurance she required. The other pupils soon picked on her high degree of sensitivity. This eventually became too much for Maureen and being on the verge of a nervous breakdown she found she couldn't go to school anymore.

> Joan, being epileptic, found comprehensive school too difficult an environment to cope with. Her extreme unhappiness and bullying and violence from her peers resulted in an increase in her fits, truancy and an eventual breakdown.

Some of the young people commented themselves in the following way:

> When I was bullied at school I felt like a reject. One day I took an over-dose, I had violent fits and was rushed to hospital and had my stomach pumped. My school was hell. The boys that bullied me were much older and they used to throw me against the wall, they made me have fits.
>
> (Susan)

> I couldn't stand going back to school because of what the other kids put me through. I was bullied, bruised, called names, kicked under the table, you name it someone had done it to me. I couldn't help being epileptic.
>
> (Julie)

> When I first started comprehensive school, I kept getting bullied. I got used to that a bit. Then after my allergy started coming up on my hands and face, people were calling me names and bullying me worse than before. At nights I was very upset because of what people had called me. I could not face going to school and being bullied.
>
> (Richard)

The head stressed that the unit did not cater for pupils with extreme behaviour of a psychopathic or delinquent nature. They were not children with learning difficulties as such and hence were not statemented, but they were just as vulnerable. Since their vulnerability had not been formally recognised, they had not received the full protection and support that they needed to survive in mainstream schools.

Other research has suggested that children with special needs will be over-represented as victims. O'Moore and Hillery (1989) gave questionnaires on bullying to 783 pupils in four Dublin schools. They found that children in remedial classes were more likely to be victims of bullying; this was especially true of frequent bullying (once a week or more), which was reported by 12 per cent of remedial class children compared to 7 per cent of non-remedial children.

Martlew and Hodson (1991) compared mainstream children with children with special needs within three mainstream schools in Sheffield which had integrated resources. They found, from interviews and observations, that children with special needs were teased significantly more than mainstream children and formed fewer friendships. In addition, mainstream children showed a preference for social interaction with other mainstream peers rather than with children with special needs. Generally, research shows that being alone at playtime or not having many friends is a risk factor for being a victim.

Nabuzoka and Smith (1993) looked at social relationships of children in two schools with integrated resources in Sheffield. Of 179 children inter-viewed, thirty-six had been statemented as having special needs (moderate learning difficulties). Each child was asked to nominate individuals from their class who best fitted eight behavioural descriptions, including 'bully' and 'victim'. Children with moderate learning difficulties were significantly more likely to be selected as victims (33 per cent) than were those without moderate learning difficulties (8 per cent).

Nabuzoka and Smith also looked at the degree of association between other behavioural nominations such as children who were thought to be 'shy', 'seeking help', 'disruptive' and 'starting fights'. Bullies were seen as being disruptive and starting fights. Victims were seen as being shy and need-ing help. This was true for the children both with and without special needs. This implies that the same criteria of vulnerability (implied by shyness and needing help) tend to be used to victimise other children, whether they have special needs or not. On the other hand, these children with special needs were more likely to be selected as victims of bullying than non-statemented children.

An important factor in making statemented children more vulnerable may be lack of protective peer relationships, which are generally found to be less in children with special needs. Indeed, Nabuzoka and Smith found children with special needs to be less popular and more rejected than peers who had no special needs, a finding similar to those by O'Moore and Hillery (1989) and Martlew and Hodson (1991).

Are problems of bullying recognised by teachers? Nabuzoka and Smith found that while there was a high correlation between being a victim and 'shy' as well as 'help-seeking' behaviour in the perceptions of the children's peers, no such relationship was found with teacher ratings. The teachers however, like peers, significantly rated children with special needs as more shy and seeking help than children who had no special needs. The lack of association between being a victim of bullying and these behavioural characteristics by teachers indicates that teachers may not be aware of some factors putting certain children at risk of victimisation.

Altogether, these earlier studies and our own personal investigations suggested that children with special needs may be at greater risk of being bullied, if not of bullying others. There are at least three factors which may enhance their risk of being victimised. First, they may have particular characteristics related to their learning difficulties or have other disabilities which may make them an obvious 'target'; second, children with special needs in integrated settings may be less well integrated socially and lack the protection against bullying which friendship gives; and third, some children with behavioural problems may act out in an aggressive way and become 'provocative victims'.

All these possibilities are indicated by previous studies, but their relative importance is not known. The precise incidence of bullying problems amongst children with special needs compared to mainstream children remains poorly documented. Furthermore, the effectiveness of intervention strategies against bullying, used for mainstream children, needs to be evaluated for children with special needs. It may be the case that children with special needs require help in initiating and maintaining relationships, and in developing coping strategies against teasing and bullying.

We felt that issues regarding children with special needs were not adequately investigated by the main DFE-funded part of the Sheffield Project, described in Chapter Two. The questionnaires used in the survey, although presented in a large-print format, may have been difficult for children with learning or language difficulties. Furthermore, the anonymous format made it impossible to identify whether children with special needs were particularly at risk. We therefore carried out a further study, undertaken at the same period as the larger project described in Chapter Two, to look specifically at bully/victim problems amongst children with special needs, as compared with children of the same age who had no special needs. This investigation was funded by the ESRC. The study involved children from eight of the schools participating in the Sheffield Project, all of which had integrated resources for children who had been statemented. Three were junior/middle schools (codes P9, P2 and P14), and five were secondary schools (codes S7, S3, S1, S6 and S2).

Details of the project

Phase 1

A total of 186 children from the eight schools were interviewed, between late September and early December 1991. Ninety-three of these children had special needs and were either statemented or in the process of being statemented, and ninety-three children had no special needs and are referred to as mainstream children. (The label 'mainstream' is used for convenience and does not imply that children with special needs were not often part of the mainstream.) These children were matched in terms of their age, gender, ethnicity, school and class or year group. Eighty-two pairs were white, ten pairs were Asian and one pair of children were African-Caribbean. Thirty-seven pairs of children, drawn from the three junior/middle schools (twelve girls and twenty-five boys), were aged between 6 and 11 years (mean age 9.3); and fifty-six pairs of children, drawn from the five secondary schools (twenty girls and thirty-six boys), were aged between 11 and 15 years (mean age 13.1).

Each child was interviewed individually, following an interview schedule that included several open-ended questions. The first three questions asked the children how much they enjoyed school, how many good friends they had and if there were any children they didn't like. The remaining twenty-two questions were about being bullied or bullying others. The same definition of bullying that was used in the main survey was read out to children before asking them the bullying-related questions (see Chapter One). The areas which the questions covered included:

- the frequency of being bullied or bullying others, both in school and outside of school during this term;
- the types of bullying behaviour, where it occurred in school and in which class were the pupils who bullied them;
- how often they informed teachers, parents and dinner supervisors that they had been bullied.

Other more qualitative questions consisted of asking how they felt about being bullied; why it happens to them and in the place they have said it occurs; if other children help them; and if they do bully others, why, and how do they feel about this.

For the questions about frequency of being bullied and bullying others the children were given the response options of only once or twice a term, sometimes, about once a week, or several times a week.

Teachers' perceptions of the bullying problems of the children with special needs were also assessed by interviewing the members of staff in each school who knew each of the children best. This tended to be one of the teachers who worked in the resource unit and who had teacher contact with each child. A total of eleven members of staff were interviewed; one from each of the schools P9, P14, S7, S1 and S2 and two from each of the schools P2, S3 and S6.

Teachers were asked standard questions at the start of the interview about the child's special needs in light of their statement, the extent to which the child integrated functionally and socially, and the extent and nature of any support given. They were then asked the same questions as the children, but referring to the child, for example: does he/she enjoy school, does he/she get bullied, etc.; and a few additional questions: whether they thought the child's friends tended to be mainstream children, or other children with special needs; and if the child had been bullied, whether they considered this to be related to the child's special needs.

Phase 2

In the second part of the study, a reduced sample of the children with special needs and their teachers were re-interviewed. The sample size was reduced because of time constraints. These interviews took place in June/July 1992, approximately eight months after the first interviews. Seventy-six out of the original sample of ninety-three children with special needs were interviewed again. Thirty-two children were drawn from the three junior/middle schools and forty-four were drawn from the five secondary schools.

Over this eight-month period, the eight schools (together with fifteen others in the city) had, as part of the DFE-funded intervention project described in Chapter Two, taken various measures to reduce bullying generally. These included (in all schools) developing a whole-school policy on bullying, and (in various schools) focusing on the curriculum (drama, video, literature, Quality Circles), playground (training lunchtime supervisors) and working with victims (assertiveness training). (See other chapters for detailed information about these interventions.)

At time two, children with special needs and their teachers were asked the same questions as already described. Comparisons with the questions from the first set of interviews allowed assessment of the effects of these interventions. Children were also asked a few additional questions: whether or not they thought that bullying in the school had changed in general; what interventions they had been involved in; and how they felt about them. Teachers were also asked additional questions: whether or not they felt that bullying in the school in general had changed; what interventions the school had carried out; whether or not there was a need for interventions specifically for children with special needs; and what provision if any the school made for children at lunchtimes.

General interview procedure

All the interviews took place on a one-to-one basis in a quiet room allocated by the school. In each school all the children and staff were interviewed within three consecutive days. At the start of the interview, each child and teacher was told that the interviews were confidential. The interviewer established a rapport with the children to make them feel at ease by comments such as: 'Are you comfortable sitting there?', 'I'm asking lots of children these questions in your school and other schools, they are really easy, you can say what you want'; and non-verbal reinforcement such as smiling, appropriate eye contact and interpersonal distance. At the end of the interview, the children were encouraged to talk about what were the good things about school and what they liked doing best, so as to end the interview on a positive tone, rather than on negative feelings that may have surrounded the bullying issues. Later, each school received a general report about the findings from the children interviewed, giving them some indication of the extent and nature of their bullying problems, without referring to specific children.

Detailed information about each school

Information about the eight schools is summarised in Table 9.1. This gives details of school size; an advantage/disadvantage (A/D) score (taken from an LEA composite index based mainly on employment status of head of household and adequacy of housing; the range was between -1,071 to +1,415 in the twenty-four schools in the first survey, with negative scores indicating more disadvantage); the percentage of ethnic minority children in the school; the type of integrated resource units; the number of children with special needs interviewed at both times; and the percentage of the time that children with special needs were fully integrated into mainstream.

Results of the project

The quantitative items generated by the questionnaires were statistically analysed using Chi-square, sign tests or Analysis of Variance (ANOVA). Associations and differences were looked for between children with special

TABLE 9.1 INFORMATION ABOUT THE EIGHT SCHOOLS

Schools	P9	P2	P14	S7	S3	S1	S6	S2
Size (no. of pupils)	230	420	430	1118	1447	400	1000	483
(A/D) score	– 207	– 305	– 738	– 423	+1415	+142	N/A	+467
Ethnic minority %	62.5	5	10	15	7	0	7	40
Integrated Resource Units	MLD	HI LD	Mild	HI SEN	VI LD	PD LD	SEN	MLD
Time one: no. of children	9	9	19	11	16	10	11	8
Time two: no. of children	9	8	15	9	8	10	10	7
Percentage time fully integrated in MS	40	50 (HI) 80 (LD)	20	80	60–75 (VI) 100 (LD)	100	90	50

Key:
MLD = children with moderate learning difficulties
Mild = children with mild learning difficulties
SEN = children with varying degrees of special needs
HI = children with hearing impairments
VI = children with visual impairments
PD = children with physical disabilities
LD = children with varying degrees of learning difficulties

needs, mainstream children and teachers. The open-ended, more qualitative sections of the interviews were content analysed.

Are children with special needs at greater risk of being bullied than mainstream children?

Children with special needs were significantly more at risk of being bullied than mainstream children, $x^2(1) = 22.1$, p<.001. Nearly two-thirds of the children with special needs who were interviewed reported being bullied, compared to just over a quarter of the mainstream children (see Table 9.2). The difference was greater for children in secondary schools. Children with special needs were also bullied more frequently than mainstream children, ANOVA F = 11.8, p<.001 (means 1.77 and 0.95). (For the frequency of being bullied we scored the data on a scale of 0 'not been bullied', 1 'bullied once or twice a term', 2 'sometimes', 3 'once or twice a week' and 4 'once or twice a term'.) In junior/middle schools 62 per cent of the children with

TABLE 9.2 THE NUMBERS OF MAINSTREAM CHILDREN (SELF-REPORTS) AND MATCHED CHILDREN WITH SPECIAL NEEDS (SELF AND TEACHERS' REPORTS) WHO HAD BEEN BULLIED AND WHO HAD BULLIED OTHERS AT TIME ONE

Junior/middle schools	Boys	Girls	Both	Boys	Girls	Both
Total N	25	12	37	25	12	37
	Been bullied			*Bullied others*		
Mainstream children (self)	12	5	17	7	2	9
Special needs children (self)	16	9	25	8	5	13
Special needs children (teacher)	8	7	15	8	3	11
Secondary schools						
Total N	36	20	56	36	20	56
Mainstream children (self)	6	5	11	2	5	7
Special needs children (self)	23	12	35	11	4	15
Special needs children (teacher)	19	14	33	11	3	14

Statistically significant results

For those who were bullied:
comparing the self-reports of children with special needs and mainstream children, $x^2(1) = 22.1$, p<.001.
(split by schools: junior $x^2(1) = 3.5$, p<.01; secondary $x^2(1) = 21.3$, p<.001).
comparing reports by children with special needs in junior schools and their teachers, $x^2(1) = 5.4$, p<.05.

For those who bullied others:
comparing the self-reports of children with special needs and mainstream children, $x^2(1) = 4.3$, p<.05.

special needs were bullied sometimes or more frequently, compared to 46 per cent of mainstream children. In secondary schools 59 per cent of the children with special needs were bullied sometimes or more frequently compared to 16 per cent of mainstream children. In secondary schools 30 per cent of the children were bullied once a week or several times a week compared to 11 per cent of mainstream children (see Table 9.3).

Children with special needs were also slightly more likely to be involved in bullying others than mainstream children; just under a third of the children with special needs reported bullying others compared to only about a sixth of the mainstream children (see Table 9.2). This difference was again greater for children in secondary schools. There was no significant difference, however, with regard to the frequency with which the children bullied others (see Table 9.3).

We found that most of the children with special needs who did report bullying others also reported that they were victims of bullying; some of them may fit the category of 'provocative victims', who to some extent provoke bullying by others because of their own actions (Pikas, 1989).

From the interviews it was clear that much of the bullying which the children with special needs experienced (and which sometimes provoked them to bully) was related to their special needs. This is illustrated by the following extracts:

> They used to call me names like cabbage and tell me to cut my hair and brush it and I felt upset but I've got some good friends. My spelling's not too good and when they are handing work out they'll have a quick look at mine, but they don't look at other people's, and my writing because they know I have special needs.
>
> (Jane)

> Michael keeps kicking me and he puts vinegar and salt on my pudding. He keeps calling me names like bob head, light bulb and dickhead.
>
> (Sean)

> They kick me and punch me and they are horrible to me. They smack me and spit on my back. They call me names like eyebrow because they are thick. They also call me spastic.
>
> (John)

> Because of my disability I can't balance and with a heavy tray with my dinner on it I can't balance. So I usually get one of my friends to carry it for me. Others say 'Carry your own tray'. Last year they kept saying 'I'll have you a fight' and they'll say 'You can't fight for toffee' and I'll say 'Why' and they'll say 'Because we've seen you walk'. In class they

TABLE 9.3 THE PERCENTAGES OF MAINSTREAM CHILDREN (SELF-REPORTS) AND MATCHED CHILDREN WITH SPECIAL NEEDS (SELF AND TEACHERS' REPORTS) FOR THE FREQUENCY OF BEING BULLIED AND BULLYING OTHERS AT TIME ONE

Junior/middle	Been bullied				
	I haven't been bullied	Once or twice	Sometimes	Once/twice a week	Several times a week
Mainstream children (self)	54	0	16	16	14
Special needs children (self)	32	5	35	19	8
Special needs (teachers)	60	8	24	8	0
Secondary					
Mainstream children (self)	80	4	5	2	9
Special needs children (self)	38	4	29	9	21
Special needs (teachers)	41	5	43	7	4
	Bullied others				
Junior/middle					
Mainstream children (self)	76	0	11	11	3
Special needs children (self)	65	3	24	3	5
Special needs (teachers)	70	3	16	8	3
Secondary					
Mainstream children (self)	88	2	5	2	4
Special needs children (self)	73	2	18	5	2
Special needs (teachers)	75	0	18	5	2

Statistically significant results

For those who were bullied:
comparing the self-reports of children with special needs and mainstream children, $F = 11.8$, $p < .001$.
comparing reports by children with special needs and their teachers, $F = 15.6$, $p < .001$.

say 'Look Elizabeth's here' and they call me names all the time or they stand up and do impressions of me walking up and down the classroom. They also call my friend names too because she's well built. They call her whale. Linda gets called maggot because she's thin but because of my disability they can't call me maggot, they can call me other names that they know would hurt me so it's worser. So it's not just me, it's not all me.

(Elizabeth)

The likelihood of being bullied seemed to vary with the type of special need, as seen in Table 9.4. Children with moderate learning difficulties were at greater risk of victimisation than children with mild learning difficulties (though not reaching statistical significance on Chi-square); children with visual impairment are least at risk, but the small sample size for children with physical impairment (and the fact that the visually impaired children are all from one school) precludes generalisation here.

Children with special needs were found to have fewer friends than mainstream children. This was statistically significant; ANOVA F = 16.68, p<.001 (means 2.39 and 2.76). (Here we scored the number of friends on the scale 0 'no friends', 1 'one friend', 2 'two or three' and 3 'many friends'.) The teachers thought that children with special needs mainly tended to choose as friends other children with special needs; for about two-thirds of children in junior/middle schools and about half in secondary schools. Teachers also thought that for the majority of children their bullying problems were directly related to their special needs. They thought that this was the case for about 67 per cent of children in junior/middle schools and about 81 per cent

TABLE 9.4 LIKELIHOOD OF BEING BULLIED, OR BULLYING OTHERS, BY MAIN CATEGORIES OF SPECIAL NEEDS

Category	Number	% been bullied	% bullied others
Mild learning difficulties	22	55	27
Moderate learning difficulties	45	78	29
Physical disability	6	50	33
Hearing impaired	6	100	50
Visually impaired	14	29	29

in secondary schools. Teachers commented, for example, that children were bullied because of their disability, because they were deaf, because they had a low IQ, because they lacked social skills and were unable to mix with other children appropriately which made them victims.

This study confirms, in a well-matched sample, the substantially greater risk which children with special needs have of being involved in bully/victim problems, especially of being a victim. It also substantiates the three risk factors, discussed earlier, as enhancing the risk of children with special needs being victims. First, particular characteristics such as clumsiness, dyslexia or other disabilities, may be used as a pretext for bullying as seen from the children's comments and those of the teachers. Second, children with special needs in an integrated setting have fewer friends than mainstream children and are likely to be less well integrated socially; this may result in these children lacking the protection against bullying which friendship can give. Third, children with behavioural problems may act out in an aggressive way and become 'provocative victims'. The majority of the children with special needs in this study who bullied others were also victims of bullying.

Teachers' and pupils' perceptions compared

Teachers' perceptions can be compared with those of the children with special needs themselves (see Tables 9.2 and 9.3). Teachers were fairly accurate about whether a child bullied others and how often. Teachers were, however, inaccurate about two things. First, teachers tended to underestimate whether, and how often, children with special needs were being bullied, particularly for children in junior/middle schools. In junior/middle schools twenty-five children with special needs reported being bullied compared to fifteen as perceived by the teachers; in secondary schools these figures were thirty-five and thirty-three respectively (see Table 9.2). (These differences were significant for junior/middle schools, $x^2(1) = 5.44$, p<.05, but failed to reach significance for secondary schools.) When considering the frequency of being bullied, there was a statistically significant difference, ANOVA F = 15.62, p<.001 (means 1.77 and 1.09). In junior/middle schools 62 per cent of the children with special needs were bullied sometimes or more frequently, compared to 32 per cent as perceived by the teachers. In secondary schools these figures were 59 per cent and 54 per cent respectively. When looking at the more frequent bullying of once a week or several times a week: in junior/middle schools 27 per cent of the children reported bullying at this frequency compared to 8 per cent reported by the teachers; in secondary schools these figures were 30 per cent and 11 per cent respectively (see Table 9.3).

Second, teachers tended to underestimate how many friends children had in school. This was statistically significant; ANOVA F = 6.58, p<.05 (means 2.38 and 2.01). Whereas most children with special needs reported having two or more friends, teachers often reported them having one or no friends.

Were the interventions to reduce bullying effective?

The children's interviews at time two, when compared with their interviews at time one, for the whole sample, revealed significant reductions in the frequency of being bullied, on an ANOVA F = 6.50, p<.05 (means 1.43 and 1.84). In junior/middle schools at time one, 65.7 per cent of the children reported being bullied sometimes or more and 25.1 per cent reported being bullied once a week or more, compared to 59.4 per cent and 9.4 per cent respectively at time two. In secondary schools at time one, 61.4 per cent of the children reported being bullied sometimes or more and 34.1 per cent reported being bullied once a week or more, compared to 54.5 per cent and 15.9 per cent respectively at time two.

The teachers' interviews at time two, when compared with their interviews at time one, revealed reductions in the frequency of being bullied for the secondary schools, but not for the junior/middle schools. This reduction, however, failed to reach statistical significance. In junior/middle schools at time one, 31.3 per cent of the children were reported as being bullied sometimes or more and 9.4 per cent as being bullied once a week or more, compared to 37.5 per cent and 9.4 per cent respectively at time two. In secondary schools at time one, 56.8 per cent of the children were reported as being bullied sometimes or more and 11.3 per cent as being bullied once a week or more, compared to 36.3 per cent and 11.3 per cent respectively at time two.

Similar results were found for bullying others: the children's reports showed a significant reduction in the frequency of bullying others at time two compared with time one, for the whole sample; on an ANOVA, F = 24.32, p<.001 (means 0.21 and 0.63). There were no significant reductions in bullying others for the teachers' reports.

These changes over time for being bullied and bullying others did not vary significantly across the eight schools; most of the changes were present in all the schools (see Table 9.5). (The figures shown in Table 9.5 are mean scores on the scale previously described for the frequency of bullying.)

The reductions in bullying measures are encouraging. However, they might be due to age changes through the year and/or settling in with peers in the year group. We examined the likelihood of age changes being responsible, by looking at age differences cross-sectionally in our total sample of

TABLE 9.5 MEAN SCORES OF THE FREQUENCY OF BEING BULLIED AND BULLYING OTHERS, FROM THE PUPILS WITH SPECIAL NEEDS' AND TEACHERS' PERSPECTIVES IN THE EIGHT SCHOOLS, BETWEEN TIME ONE AND TIME TWO

School		Been bullied		Bullying others	
		Time 1	Time 2	Time 1	Time 2
P9:	pupil	1.89	1.22	1.11	0.22
	teacher	0.67	0.89	1.00	0.67
P2:	pupil	2.25	1.86	0.75	0.25
	teacher	1.50	1.88	0.25	0.50
P14:	pupil	1.20	1.20	0.60	0.27
	teacher	0.53	0.47	0.53	0.27
S7:	pupil	1.78	1.56	0.44	0.22
	teacher	0.67	0.33	0.22	0.44
S3:	pupil	1.25	1.13	0.38	0.25
	teacher	0.75	0.38	0.50	0.38
S1:	pupil	2.70	1.70	0.90	0.30
	teacher	1.90	1.20	1.20	1.10
S6:	pupil	1.60	1.40	0.30	0.00
	teacher	1.70	1.40	0.20	0.30
S2:	pupil	1.86	1.43	0.57	0.14
	teacher	1.71	2.00	0.86	1.43
Total pupil		1.84	1.43	0.63	0.21
Total teacher		1.14	1.02	0.60	0.64

children with special needs. The age range varied from 8 to 15 years. The average change in being bullied and in bullying others over this age range was actually a very small increase, compared to our significant decrease, over the eight-month intervention period. Thus the changes we found appeared not to be due to age effects and most likely to be due to the interventions carried out, as there were no other systematic changes affecting all eight schools at this time.

By the second interview, children reported that they had more friends at school. This was statistically significant; ANOVA $F = 4.34$, $p < .05$ (means 2.4 and 2.6). There was no significant difference for the teachers' reports on the children's friends. Children in junior/middle schools who were bullied were more likely to have told someone about it, usually a lunchtime supervisor or someone at home, 81 per cent having told someone at time one compared to 90 per cent at time two (not statistically significant). This was also true for teachers' reports of the numbers who were telling someone; in junior/middle schools 50 per cent of the children at time one were thought to have told someone compared to 62.5 per cent at time two; in secondary schools these figures were 81 per cent and 90.5 per cent, respectively (again, not statistically significant).

To get a further perspective on changes in bullying, teachers and children were asked whether bullying had changed generally in school since they were last interviewed and to give their reasons why, if they thought it had changed. A majority of the children and teachers thought that bullying had got a bit better; some were not sure, and only eleven children thought it had got a bit worse (see Table 9.6). Here are some examples of the reasons children gave for bullying in their school having got a bit or a lot better:

> The teachers tell me off now for bullying, children are a bit more friendly now.

> Kids tell teachers more now, teachers are doing more things about it now.

> There are more rules about it now. I think the teachers are clamping down on it a bit now.

> I see less bullying now, before I saw people with nose bleeds who had had their heads kicked against a wall or kids crying but I hardly see that now because the teachers have got stricter and do more about it, now the bullies do what the teachers say a bit more.

Children's and teachers' comments on the interventions

Interviews with the children revealed that, while some children did not realise or remember specific interventions, some did. For example, at school P9 a child commented that they had talked about bullying in class and had been told it was a bad thing to bully others. At school P2 a child remembered seeing a video about bullying and said: 'It was good because it let them [the bullies] see I'm not stupid, and helps them understand about deafness.' At school S7 a child commented that he had done some drama work on bullying and it had made him know what it was like to be picked on. Several

TABLE 9.6 PUPILS WITH SPECIAL NEEDS AND TEACHER RATINGS OF WHETHER BULLYING HAS GOT BETTER IN SCHOOL IN GENERAL, AT TIME TWO (76 PUPILS, 11 TEACHERS)

School	A lot better	A bit better	No change/ don't know	A bit worse	A lot worse
P9	0	4,T	4	1	0
P2	1	5	1,T,T	1	0
P14	0	10,T	2	3	0
S7	0	4,T	2	3	0
S3	0	5	3,T,T	0	0
S1	0	5,T	4	1	0
S6	2	3	3,T,T	2	0
S2	3	4,T	0	0	0
Total	6	40, 5T	19, 6T	11	0

children at school S3 commented positively on watching videos, doing drama and work in English on bullying. At school S1 children again commented about the video work. At school S6 many children had had assertiveness training and many thought it had helped. Their comments about the different assertiveness techniques included:

> I just use the one where you ignore the bullies and I tell them to please get off. I tried the breathing and it made me feel better.

> They usually pick on me, but if they want to borrow money for their bus fares they can be nice and then I have to do the broken record, so I told them I wasn't lending them any money. I tried the fogging [agreeing with nasty comments] and I try ignoring kids and I sometimes do the breathing if I get angry and I calm down.

Several children said that the assertiveness techniques had made them more confident and one child said that they had made her happier because now when she got called names she just ignored them. Interviews with teachers about the interventions revealed both positive and negative comments about the effectiveness of the interventions. These comments also covered the issue of whether there was a need for interventions specifically for children with special needs.

School P9

Attempts to provide playground activities had not been successful because of a lack of supervision. There were not adequate staff to cover both yards and the dining room. Other interventions included *The Heartstone Odyssey*. Sandra commented, however, that children with special needs did not participate in *The Heartstone Odyssey* because they were in a composite class for this period. She also said that Quality Circle work would prove difficult with children with learning difficulties because:

> you are dealing with children who are two or three years behind in terms of their learning difficulties, and you are actually dealing with top nursery children in terms of mental ability and they are very egocentric and those sorts of concepts are very difficult to get across.

When asked about the need for specific interventions with children with special needs she replied: 'Yes I think they may need to be simplified.'

School P2

Interventions included the Armadillo Theatre Group; counselling children with special needs as a group about acceptable behaviour; and the Neti Neti video which raises awareness about deafness. Angela also gave mainstream children tapes to show how it sounds to be deaf and commented that she felt this work had had positive results. She felt that the children with hearing impairments at this school were not picked on just because they were deaf. Sally commented, however, that her group of children who had moderate learning difficulties had not been involved in any specific interventions. Angela's comments about the need for interventions specifically for children with special needs were:

> Yes, I think there is a need for interventions to educate children to relate to children with special needs. The children here are quite good at communicating with the deaf children but on the other hand they hadn't realised what it was like to be deaf so the deaf awareness video was good for that.

Sally's comments were:

> Yes, because a lot of children with special needs do struggle with communication and social interaction and getting on with other children; and a lot of time is spent trying to help them relate to each other and to think about the things they say to each other and how that hurts them.

School P14

The provision of playground equipment as an intervention had proved unsuccessful because of a lack of supervision and because the playground was too small. Jane felt that there was no need for interventions specifically for children with special needs since this would make them different in some way.

School S7

A lot of assembly work had been done throughout the year about bullying. They had taken articles out of the paper, about two suicides, and used these to highlight the horrible consequences that bullying can lead to. They had developed a Whole-School Policy which involved pupils and parents; video work; working with bullies (Pikas); and bullying discussions in PSE lessons. When asked if there was a need for interventions specifically for children with special needs, Sharon commented:

> No, the children with special needs are involved in all mainstream interventions, for example assemblies and tutorials discussing bullying. I don't see a need for specific ones but perhaps the partially hearing children may have problems.

School S3

Interventions included a Whole-School Policy, in preparation; PSE lessons about bullying; the Armadillo Theatre Group; assertiveness training; and the *Sticks and stones* video. When asked if there was a need for interventions specifically for children with special needs Fay commented:

> Yes, in PSE work in upper school they have been shown a video of a badly handicapped child. It may be a good idea to get something similar for the younger children. People tend to hide away from disability and are embarrassed by it. So I think if the children are seeing that, they may have some empathy with the situation.

Maxine commented: 'No, but awareness of disability is OK. I'd call it that rather than something aimed at bullying.'

School S1

The Whole-School Policy was in process of development and the formulation had involved pupils and parents. Pat commented that they had had very positive feedback from parents. Other interventions included the *Sticks and stones* video. Pat's comments on the follow-up work with this were positive:

> We spent two or three weeks, one or two lessons a week on follow-up work and homework. I think it had a positive effect. The work I did with my group was to ask them to go home and ask their parents if they had been victims of bullying at school. It was quite interesting because you could see where the kids were coming from because if their parents had been bullied, their parents tended to tell their children to stick up for themselves, if they had done so themselves. If the parents were unable to stick up for themselves they tended to intervene on the child's behalf like informing school.

Her comments about the need for interventions specifically for children with special needs were:

> Yes possibly but then you make them different, you are sectioning them off. Maybe they could be adapted so that all kids do the same but that some points are brought out more clearly.

School S6

Interventions included the *Sticks and stones* video and working with bullies (Pikas); but Carol commented that the main intervention work with children with special needs was the assertiveness training. She was very positive about the effects of this and commented:

> They all got something out of it. They all enjoyed it at the time and wanted to continue. I think they felt good about themselves in the situations so it probably gave them a little bit more confidence out and about.

When asked if the children had used any of the techniques she said:

> Some of them did report that they had tried some of the techniques, for example when someone was trying to get some money off one of the children the other day they kept saying 'No'. One was ignoring the name calling and I think someone else was trying to relax about it. They felt that some of the things worked quite well for about three of the children but for the others I'm not sure if they just weren't commenting along with the others. It was easy to carry out because the kids felt it was beneficial and they were very keen to take part and were very co-operative. I think it was all useful. Any things that get them talking are good. I think we should continue doing this. The children coped

OK with the breathing exercises and later, when they were walking around role-playing, they were doing the breathing themselves and quite often they were trying the rainbow breathing. They could remember that.

When asked if there was a need for specific interventions for children with special needs Jan commented: 'Yes, in a sense they need to be appropriate for the child's ability, preferably in small group situations.' Carol commented:

> Yes, in the sense that I think you have to apply what you are doing to the group that you've got. The children I had for the assertiveness training all had difficulties in terms of relating to each other and coping in mainstream situations and it was a very secure environment for them. They enjoyed being able to talk in a way that they hadn't before. The problem is that with children with special needs they all understand things at different levels. The difficult thing is getting them to use the techniques when they need them.

School S2

A Whole-School Policy was being worked out by staff, in consultation with students and parents, and there was a draft policy in place. Mark knew of no other interventions but commented that: 'Myself, I deal with individual behavioural problems including bullying with kids in the resource. It's more of a counselling role really, but I do this thoroughly and consistently.' When asked if there was a need for interventions specifically for children with special needs his comments were:

> Not necessarily specific interventions but appropriate interventions for children. For example, the assertiveness intervention is appropriate for some children but not for others. This would be appropriate for those kids in school who you would class as vulnerable and that could be kids from mainstream or children with special needs.

Can the provision of a special room at lunchtime be an effective intervention to reduce bullying for children with special needs?

Three secondary schools in our sample had a room where children with special needs could go at lunchtimes, to provide a more sheltered environment.

Since much bullying goes on in the playground, and this is true of children both with and without special needs, we asked teachers and children to comment on the usefulness of this provision.

School S1 provided a purpose-built room for children with physical disabilities to use at lunchtimes. These children were allowed to take one friend with them into this room, a child with or without special needs. Children who had special needs that were not classed as physically disabling were not allowed to use this room unless as a friend of a disabled child. Pat's comments about this room were:

> We do have a room for children at lunchtimes but it is only for children with disabilities. There are four children in school at the moment and they can bring in one friend. We don't allow children with other special needs in. It is for the disabled children, for practical reasons such as the toilet and shower. They get tired easily and there is less chance of them being knocked over.

Did she think it was a good idea to have this room? 'I do and I don't. Really they need the practical things but we are treating them differently to mainstream children.'

Some of the children's comments about this room were:

> It's a place where disabled people can come in without getting knocked down outside and they can play with their friends without people pushing you and shoving and calling names. I was thinking of moving schools, so I'd get away from them [the bullies], but I decided to stay because of the resource room. At breaktime I can get away from it by going into the resource room. If it were to stop for permanent and everyone was to be my friend, then things like the resource room – I could go out and play because I'm not exactly – can't walk but I can, I can run and everything. If everyone started hitting me there is no-one to turn to out there. That's why I go in the resource room all the time now.
>
> (Elizabeth)

> I go there sometimes, because I don't get pushed and knocked around like you do outside or get bullied or picked on.
>
> (Jane)

> I need it. It caters for disabled people.
>
> (Mark)

School S6 provided a lunchtime room for all children with special needs and permitted them to bring along one mainstream friend. Jan's comments on this provision were:

Nearly all the unit children use it sometimes but we do encourage them to play outside. They often play outside but near to the room. I think it is as important to offer this facility for children with learning difficulties and behavioural problems since children who are socially inadequate sometimes cannot cope with being out there every day. I think there should be this provision because if they feel relaxed and happy then this has got to be better. Some children need a shelter, a safe haven. I give up my free time to resource the room. There is no special provision allocated to us.

Carol's comments were:

Yes the room is for all children with special needs, children with physical handicaps and children with learning difficulties. If anything children who have difficulty in relating to other kids need it more than some children who are physically handicapped. When we have to turf them all out because there isn't a teacher here to supervise, they tend to play not more than fifty yards from the window. It's like the security of the room. It may be a hindrance to integration but at the same time it's a lot to expect for some children to cope in a totally unstructured hour and twenty minutes.

Some children's comments were:

There are people I know won't pick on me in that room. We've all got special needs and it's mainly us that get picked on and they understand more because they have it as well.

(Judy)

You sometimes get bullied in the playground but you don't get bullied in that room.

(Sally)

School S2 provided a room which was supervised by a CCA, but was open to all children at lunchtimes, children with or without special needs. Mark's comments about this room were:

There is provision but it's for all children, 'the lunchtime club'. We have insisted that some of the children go there when there has been crisis times because it limits their environment. It limits the possibilities for them to get into difficult situations outside in the playground or about the school.

Unfortunately this lunchtime cover reduced the dining room provision and this has caused further problems as Mark comments:

> The problem is however because the CCA is there she cannot be in one of the dining rooms and the children with special needs are left to struggle. It has been a matter of making that choice. We would like some extra dinnertime supervision of some sort. We've had incidents that wouldn't have happened if we had sufficient resources. The kids that are going into the dining room without support are struggling and they will have the same meal every day. Sometimes it's an inappropriate meal, and this means they are having an unbalanced diet.

The other five schools in our sample did not provide a lunchtime room for children. Some of the teachers from these schools, however, commented that they felt there was a need for such a provision whilst others felt that such a provision would be detrimental to the aims of integration.

Children with non-statemented special needs who are getting little support

An additional problem highlighted by our work was that there is a tendency for other children's special needs to go unrecognised in mainstream schools. Comments from members of staff indicated that seven out of the eight schools in our sample had children whose educational needs had not been recognised formally or statemented. The proportion of these children was estimated to range from 2 per cent to 30 per cent. In two of these schools these children were receiving no support and in the other six schools the support was only minimal. The reasons for this situation appeared to be a lack of resources to provide the support they needed and the fact that these children had not been identified as children who should have a statement of special need. Whether or not these children were statemented was dependent on differing school philosophies and the severity of the child's needs. As one teacher commented: 'It's a haphazard system, the support we can give the children is minimal and is often provided in our free time.'

Implications of the findings

Children with special needs are at greater risk for bullying problems

Children with special needs are clearly at particular risk for victimisation; they may also be over-represented as bullies and bully-victims. Teachers may realise a child is being bullied, but underestimate the frequency with which it is happening. A child who is being bullied is often unable to concentrate on their lessons as they may be preoccupied with the bullying. For children with special needs, those with learning difficulties for instance, this adds another burden to an already difficult task. Being able to recognise a problem of bullying for a particular child can therefore help the teacher to have a clearer picture as to the factors contributing to the overall learning difficulties of the child.

The effects of the interventions

School interventions against bullying can be successful, and our findings have shown that there were significant reductions in reports of children with special needs being bullied and bullying others, and an increase in friends, over the eight-month period. Most of the changes were present in all eight schools. Furthermore, comparisons with the size effects expected from normal age changes, using cross-sectional data from this study, strongly suggest that the changes are not age-related and can reasonably be ascribed to the school interventions. Particularly useful for children with special needs may be targeted videos, assertiveness training and having a special lunchtime room.

However, the detailed interviews with both children with special needs and teachers indicated that some interventions may not always impact optimally on problems of children with special needs. Sometimes these children were not in the lessons where curriculum activities took place; for example at one school children with special needs did not take part in *The Heartstone Odyssey* because they were in a composite class for that period. Children with hearing impairments may not have fully understood the video work or have been able to join in class discussions; this would be true for children with visual impairments, as one teacher commented about a child called Helen:

> she had difficulty in joining in the discussion after the video because of her speech and it was more difficult for her to follow. When I do this work I do it in smaller groups so the children with special needs can be given more support and hence can follow it better.

Children with physical disabilities were left out of the drama work in some cases because of mobility problems.

The Neti-Neti video had very positive effects at school P2 and some members of staff felt there was a need for such specific special needs awareness videos; as one teacher commented about how she felt about showing a video to the children based around a severely physically handicapped child: 'People tend to hide away from disability and are embarrassed by it. So I think if the children are shown this video they may have some empathy with the situation.'

Work involving difficult concepts, such as the Quality Circles work, needs to be simplified greatly to be effective for children with learning difficulties, and presented in small group situations. Teaching assertiveness and other social skills is a way of overcoming the problem for both the victim and the bully. The former can be taught things like how to say 'No', how to get help and also not to be afraid to do what they want to do. The child bullying others can also be taught how to cope with their frustrations and to appreciate the needs of others in the same way they would like their needs to be appreciated. This intervention was very successful at school S6 and the teacher said that she felt it was something which they should continue doing and that some of the children with special needs needed long-term help like this. She also commented that without more time and resources they wouldn't be able to continue. We have also seen how a lack of resources can lead to the failure of playground interventions.

Support at lunchtimes

In general most of the staff interviewed felt there should be some provision for vulnerable children at lunchtimes. Most felt this should be available to all children rather than predominantly for children with special needs. Children's comments about this provision do highlight the fact that they see it as a safe haven from bullying. However, there seems to be some bias in making this provision for children with physical disabilities but a failure to recognise children with learning difficulties as being equally vulnerable at lunchtimes. This raises an important issue since we have found a tendency for children with the more severe learning difficulties to be bullied the most. Schools, however, perceive a lack of resources which can have consequences other than bullying, as is highlighted at school S2 where a lack of adequate lunchtime supervision can lead to children with special needs having an inadequate diet. Staff giving up their own free time to fulfil these needs also leads to greater stress on teachers.

Pressures on schools in supporting vulnerable children

In general, these findings seem to reflect the overall pressures on schools and staffs when attempting to support children who are vulnerable. This includes those with the label of a statement of special needs, investigated in this study, who clearly are at considerably greater risk of being bullied. It also includes those children who are not in the bottom 2 per cent of ability, attainment or behavioural stability but whom the DFE would say schools should be able to teach effectively under the current funding arrangements. These non-statemented vulnerable children may also be at risk from bullying, and schools are expected to deal with them from their own resources.

The general view of Parliament at the time of the 1988 Act was that the main way of improving quality of education in schools was to increase the possibilities for competition between schools, by developing standardised assessment methods on a standardised curriculum and encouraging parental choice (Education Act, 1988). This clearly is a way of putting direct pressure on schools to increase the effectiveness of their education of most children, but it is very difficult to see how that mechanism could lead to improvements in education for children with special needs, both those with a statement and those on the borderlines of needing a statement but who do not have one. They are few in number compared with the other children, so the mechanism above will operate very much less effectively to improve services; they often need educational services of a different type from the bulk of mainstream children, which can easily be seen by schools as diluting their drive to improve general standards for most children; and good educational services for children with special needs have little appeal in the public relations battle between schools, when most parents do not consider their own children to have special needs and may even be slightly suspicious of a school which found it necessary to include references to such services in its prospectus.

Clearly the DFE is aware of these problems, and at present is approaching them through non-financial means such as asking governing bodies to appoint a 'special needs' governor who can keep the needs of the children visible in the school management, and setting up various performance indices (such as truancy rates) to stand alongside the attainments of the children in school when new parents are making their judgements. However, such palliatives are not likely to be effective as long as the financial support for children with special needs is lacking. Schools will need positive financial incentives, tied to special needs provision in the school, before the pressures on school staffs and children of the kind detailed above (and elsewhere – see for example, Wade and Moore, 1993) will ease.

Conclusions

Our findings have considerable relevance for teachers with responsibilities for children with special needs in integrated settings. These children are likely to be at much greater risk of involvement in bully/victim problems with peers. School-based interventions can be expected to reduce this bullying. But in order to target specific intervention programmes at particular children, teachers need to be able to identify which children are at particular risk of victimisation and of bullying others. Vulnerable children should be adequately provided for at playtimes and lunchtime. For schools with integrated resources, care needs to be taken that the children with special needs are included in the curriculum-based interventions, which need to be appropriate for the child's ability and preferably carried out in small group situations. Schools must ensure that children with special needs are as fully involved in these as other pupils.

appendix
grading criteria
for whole-
school policy
development and
implementation

Consultation phase (score between 0 and 27)

Awareness raising (score between 0 and 5): schools were recorded as having or not having held activities, events or meetings which would raise awareness about bullying amongst teaching staff, non-teaching staff, parents, pupils and governors. These activities, events or meetings were mainly information giving and need not have included any form of consultation. They were discrete from policy communication and generally occurred before the final policy was completed.

Consultation at initial stage (score between 0 and 15): these are events, meetings or activities which aimed to provide an opportunity for teaching staff, non-teaching staff, parents, pupils and governors to contribute their ideas about the content of the policy. They took place prior to or alongside the draft policy being formulated. The criteria for grading varies according to the group being consulted and the school could score up to three points for consultation with each group. Given that most schools have a regular series of staff meetings with teaching staff, there had to be be more than four staff meetings or consultation events for the school to gain three points for consultation with its teachers. For consultation with non-teaching staff, parents, pupils and governors there needed to be more than one opportunity for consultation to take place to score three points. No consultation scored zero; a first or incomplete attempt at consultation would score one (i.e. one teaching staff meeting, on agenda at PTA); a reasonable but not extensive effort (i.e. two or three teaching staff meetings, one governors/parents meeting) scored two.

Comments invited on draft (score between 0 and 5): schools were recorded as having/not having provided an opportunity for teaching staff, non-teaching staff, parents, pupils and governors to comment on the draft policy before it was finalised.

Multi-disciplinary working party (score 0 or 1): schools were recorded as having or not having established a multi-disciplinary working party to work on the policy which consisted of two or more of the following groups: senior management, teaching staff, non-teaching staff, parents, pupils and governors.

Final draft completed (score 0 or 1): schools were recorded as having or not having completed the final policy.

Content of policy (score between 0 and 22)

For each of the eleven core features of the policy content each school could score up to two points. The features included: definition of bullying; information for teaching staff, non-teaching staff, parents, pupils about responses to bullying; preventative strategies; details of communication, monitoring and review of policy. The school scored zero if it failed to include a specific feature; it scored one if it was included but not elaborated; it scored two if it was included and was covered in some detail, e.g. it is made clear not only that teachers should respond to bullying but specifically how they should do it.

The school's policy could also score up to two points for the clarity of language used in it. If the policy was difficult to read and obtuse, then it scored zero. If the policy was written in reasonably clear terms and would at least be understood by adults, it scored one. If a policy was written in very clear language and would be easily understood by the pupil population as well as the adult population, then it scored two.

The policy content was scored in the term that the draft policy began circulation for consultation. Thereafter, schools scored two points for each term the policy document existed. If there were changes to the policy as a result of further consultation, thus rendering the final version different from the draft version, the policy was re-scored at the appropriate time. Minor lexical adjustments were not considered as warranting re-scoring of the policy.

Communication (score between 0 and 10)

Schools could score between zero and two points for communication of the policy to teaching staff, non-teaching staff, parents, pupils and governors. To score zero, the school would not have communicated with the relevant party about the policy at all; to score one the school had informed the relevant party that the policy existed or would have sent a copy to the relevant party. To score two the school must have provided each person with a copy of the policy and have made some attempt to draw attention to the policy or discuss the policy with that group of people, e.g. by holding a specific event, meeting or activity.

Implementation (score between 0 and 6)

Schools could score up to two points if they showed evidence of supporting the implementation of the policy by re-communicating it to more than one of the following groups: teaching staff, non-teaching staff, parents, pupils and governors; by using recording systems and response systems as referred to in the policy; and by utilising curriculum time to work preventatively with pupils.

Time (score between 0 and 8)

Schools could score two points for each term since the draft policy had been constructed. The draft was chosen rather than the finished policy because our interview data showed that in fact schools did not always wait until the policy had been 'finalised' to begin to implement it.

references

Adams, E. (Learning Through Landscapes Team) (1990) *A report on the design management and development of school grounds*. Winchester: Learning Through Landscapes Trust.

Ahmad, Y. and Smith, P.K. (1990) Behavioural measures: bullying in schools. *Newsletter of Association for Child Psychology and Psychiatry*, 12, 26–27.

Ahmad, Y. and Smith, P.K. (1994) Bullying in schools and the issue of sex differences. In J. Archer (ed.), *Male violence*. London: Routledge.

Ahmad, Y., Whitney, I. and Smith, P.K. (1991) A survey service for schools on bully/victim problems. In P.K. Smith and D.A. Thompson (eds), *Practical approaches to bullying*. London: David Fulton.

Alberti, R. and Emmens, M. (1975) *Stand up, speak out, talk back – the key to assertive behaviour*. San Louis Obispo, CA: Impact.

Aldis, O. (1975) *Play fighting*. New York: Academic Press.

Andrews, C. and Hinton, S. (1991) *Enhancing the quality of play in school playgrounds: A pilot project*. London: National Children's Play and Recreation Unit.

Applebee, A.N. (1978) *The child's concept of story*. Chicago: Chicago University Press.

Arora, C.M.J. and Thompson, D.A. (1987) Defining bullying for a secondary school. *Education and Child Psychology*, 4, 110–120.

Arora, T. (1989) Bullying – action and intervention. *Pastoral Care in Education*, 7, 44–47.

Arora, T. (1991) The use of victim support groups. In P.K. Smith and D. Thompson (eds), *Practical approaches to bullying*. London: David Fulton.

Bandura, A. (1977) *Social learning theory*. Englewood Cliffs, NJ: Prentice Hall.

Battle, J. (1981) *Culture-free self-esteem inventory*. Seattle, Washington: Special Child Publications.

Bennett, N. and Dunne, E. (1992) *Managing classroom groups*. Hemel Hempstead: Simon and Schuster.

Besag, V. (1989) *Bullies and victims in schools*. Milton Keynes: Open University Press.

Besag, V. (1991) The playground. In M. Elliott (ed.), *Bullying: A practical guide to coping for schools*. Harlow: Longman.

Besag, V. (1992) '*We don't have bullies here!*' V. Besag, 57 Manor House Road, Jesmond, Newcastle-upon-Tyne NE2 2LY.

Birmingham City Council Education Department (1991) *Practice to share: The management of children's behavioural needs*. Birmingham: National Primary Centre.

Bjorkqvist, K., Lagerspetz, K.M.J. and Kaukainen, A. (1992) Do girls manipulate and boys fight? Developmental trends in regard to direct and indirect aggression. *Aggressive Behavior*, 18, 117–127.

Blatchford, P. (1989) *Playtime in the primary school: Problems and improvements*. Windsor: NFER-Nelson.

Blatchford, P., Creeser, R. and Mooney, A. (1990) Playground games and playtime: The children's view. *Educational Research*, 32, 163–174.

Boal, A. (1979) *Theatre of the oppressed*. London: Pluto Press.

Board of Education (1927) *Handbook of suggestions for teachers*. London: HMSO.

Bolton, G. (1989) Drama. In D.J. Hargreaves (ed.), *Children and the arts*. Milton Keynes: Open University Press.

Boulton, M.J. (1991a) A comparison of structural and contextual features of middle school children's playful and aggressive fighting. *Ethology and Sociobiology*, 12, 119–145.

Boulton, M.J. (1991b) Partner preferences in middle school children's playful fighting and chasing: A test of some competing functional hypotheses. *Ethology and Sociobiology*, 12, 177–193.

Boulton, M.J. (1992) Participation in playground activities at middle school. *Educational Research*, 34, 167–182.

Boulton, M.J. (1993a) Proximate causes of aggressive fighting in middle school children. *British Journal of Educational Psychology*, 63, 231–244.

Boulton, M.J. (1993b) A comparison of adult's and children's abilities to distinguish between aggressive and playful fighting in middle school pupils: Implications for playground supervision and behaviour management. *Educational Studies*, 19, 193–203.

Boulton, M.J. (1993c) Children's abilities to distinguish between playful and aggressive fighting: A developmental perspective. *British Journal of Developmental Psychology*, 11, 249–263.

Boulton, M.J. (1994) Preventing and responding to bullying in the junior/middle school playground. In S. Sharp and P.K. Smith (eds), *Tackling bullying in your school: A practical handbook for teachers*. London: Routledge.

Boulton, M.J. (submitted for publication) Patterns of bully/victim problems in mixed race and gender groups of children.

Boulton, M.J. and Smith, P.K. (1994). Bully/victim problems in middle school children: Stability, self-perceived competence, peer perceptions, and peer acceptance. *British Journal of Developmental Psychology*, 12, in press.

Boulton, M.J. and Underwood, K. (1992) Bully/victim problems among middle school children. *British Journal of Educational Psychology*, 62, 73–87.

Bowers, L., Smith, P.K. and Binney, V. (1992) Cohesion and power in the families of children involved in bully/victim problems at school. *Journal of Family Therapy*, 14, 371–387.

Bowers, L., Smith, P.K. and Binney, V. (1994) Perceived family relationships of bullies, victims, and bully/victims in middle childhood. *Journal of Social and Personal Relationships*, 11, 215–232.

Brier, J. and Ahmad, Y. (1991) Developing a school court as a means of addressing bullying in schools. In P.K. Smith and D.A. Thompson (eds), *Practical approaches to bullying*. London: David Fulton.

Britton, B.K. and Pellegrini, A.D. (1990) *Narrative thought and narrative language*. Hillsdale, NJ: Lawrence Erlbaum Associates.

Britton, J. (1977) The role of fantasy. In M. Meek, G. Barton and A. Warlow (eds), *The cool web*. London: Bodley Head.

Brown R. (1988) *Group processes*. London: Blackwell.

Brown, A. and Palinscar, A. (1989) Guided, cooperative learning and individual knowledge acquisition. In L.Resnick (ed.), *Knowing, learning and instruction*. Hillsdale, NJ: Lawrence Erlbaum Associates.

Bruner, J. S. (1986) *Actual minds, possible worlds*. Boston: Harvard University Press.

Bryant, B.K. (1992) Conflict resolution strategies in relation to children's peer relations. *Journal of Applied Developmental Psychology*, 13, 35–50.

Burk, F.L. (1897) Teasing and bullying. *Pedagogical Seminary*, 4, 336–371.

Burnage Report (1989) *Murder in the playground*. London: Longsight Press.

Carr, R.A. (1988) The city-wide peer counselling program. *Children and Youth Services Review*, 10, 217–232.

Carty, L. (1989) Social support, peer counselling and the community counsellor. *Canadian Journal of Counselling*, 23, 92–102.

Casdagli, P. and Gobey, F. (1990) *Only playing, Miss*. Stoke-on-Trent: Trentham Books.

Cawley, G. (1992) Working with bullies and victims. In H. Cowie (ed.), *Working directly with bullies and victims*. Conference Pack, Bretton Hall, W. Bretton, Wakefield, W. Yorks WF4 4LG.

Central Television (1990) *Sticks and stones*. Community Unit, Central Television, Broad Street, Birmingham.

Childs, K. (1993) A follow-up study of the long-term effects of assertiveness training for victims of bullying. Unpublished BA dissertation, University of Sheffield.

Clemmer, J. (1992) *Firing on all cylinders: the quality management system for high-powered corporate performance*. London: Judy Piatkus.

Cohn, T. (1988) Sambo – a study in name calling. In E. Kelly and T. Cohn, *Racism in schools – new research evidence*. Stoke-on-Trent: Trentham Books.

Connor, K. (1989) Aggression: Is it in the eye of the beholder? *Play and Culture*, 2, 213–217.

Cooper Marcus, C. and Francis, C. (eds) (1990) *People places, design guidelines for urban open space*. New York: Van Rheinhold Nostrand.

Costabile, A., Smith, P.K., Matheson, L., Aston, J., Hunter, T. and Boulton, M. (1991) Cross-national comparison of how children distinguish serious and playful fighting. *Developmental Psychology*, 27, 881–887.

Cowie, H. (1994) Ways of involving children in decision-making. In P. Blatchford and S. Sharp (eds), *Breaktime and the school: Understanding and changing playground behaviour*. London: Routledge.

Cowie, H. and Pecherek, A. (1994). *Counselling: Approaches and issues in education.* London: David Fulton.

Cowie, H. and Rudduck, J. (1988) *Learning together, working together.* BP Education, PO Box 30, Blacknest Road, Blacknest, Alton, Hants GU34 4BR.

Cowie, H. and Rudduck, J. (1990) *Cooperative learning: Traditions and transitions.* BP Education, PO Box 30, Blacknest Road, Blacknest, Alton, Hants GU34 4BR.

Cowie, H. and Sharp, S. (1992) Students themselves tackle the problem of bullying. *Pastoral Care in Education*, 10, 31–37

Cowie, H. and Sharp, S. (1994) Tackling bullying in your school. London: Routledge.

Cowie, H., Smith, P.K., Boulton, M.J. and Laver, R. (1994). *Co-operation in the multiethnic classroom.* London: David Fulton.

DeCecco, J., and Richards, A. (1974) *Growing pains: Uses of school conflict.* New York: Aberdeen Press.

Denzin, N.K. (1977) *Childhood socialization: Studies in the development of language, social behavior and identity.* San Francisco, CA: Jossey-Bass.

Department of Education and Science (1988) *Working together for the protection of children from child abuse: Procedures within the education service*, Circular No. 4/88. London: HMSO.

Department of Education and Science (1989) *Discipline in schools: Report of the committee chaired by Lord Elton.* London: HMSO.

de Rosenroll, D.A. (1986) A peer counselling centre for school-based peer counselling: An experiment in progress. *Journal of Child Care*, 2, 1–8.

de Rosenroll, D.A. (1989) A practitioner's guide to peer counselling: Research issues and dilemmas. *Canadian Journal of Counselling*, 23, 75–91.

Dickson, A. (1982) *A woman in your own right.* London: Quartet.

Dodge, K.A. (1980) Social cognition and children's aggressive behavior. *Child Development*, 51, 162–170.

Dodge, K.A., Murphy, R.M. and Buchsbaum, K. (1984) The assessment of intention-cue detection skills in children: Implications for developmental pathology. *Child Development*, 55, 163–173.

Donaldson, M. (1978) *Children's minds.* London: Fontana.

Dunne, E. and Bennett, N. (1990) *Talking and learning in groups.* London: Macmillan.

Dygdon, J.A., Conger, A.J. and Keane, S.P. (1987) Children's perceptions of the behavioral correlates of social acceptance, rejection, and neglect in their peers. *Journal of Clinical Child Psychology*, 16, 2–8.

Education Reform Act (1988) London: HMSO.

Egan, K. and Nadaner, D. (1988) *Imagination and education.* Milton Keynes: Open University Press.

Elliott, M. (1991) Bully 'courts'. In M. Elliott (ed.), *Bullying: A practical guide to coping for schools.* Harlow: Longman.

Elliott, M. (ed.) (1991) *Bullying: A practical guide to coping for schools.* Harlow: Longman.

Evans, J. (1990) The teacher role in playground supervision. *Play and Culture*, 3, 219–234.

Farrington, D.P. (1993) Understanding and preventing bullying. In M. Tonry and N. Morris (eds), *Crime and justice: An annual review of research*, vol. 17. Chicago: University of Chicago Press.

Fisher, R. and Ury, W. (1990) *Getting to yes, negotiating agreement without giving in.* London: Hutchinson.

Foster, P. and Thompson, D. (1991) Bullying: Towards a non–violent sanctions policy. In P.K. Smith and D. Thompson (eds), *Practical approaches to bullying.* London: David Fulton.

Foster, P., Arora, C.M.J. and Thompson, D. (1990) A whole-school approach to bullying. *Pastoral Care in Education*, 8, 13–17.

Fry, D.P. (1987) Differences between playfighting and serious fights among Zapotec children. *Ethology and Sociobiology*, 8, 285–306.

Galloway, D., Ball, T., Bloomfield, D. and Seyd, R. (1982) *Schools and disruptive pupils.* London: Longman.

Gilham, B. (1984) School organization and the control of disruptive incidents. In N. Frude and H. Gault (eds), *Disruptive behaviour in schools.* Chichester: John Wiley.

Gillborn, D. (1992) Citizenship, 'race' and the hidden curriculum. *International Studies in Sociology of Education*, 2, 57–73.

Gilmartin, B.G. (1987) Peer group antecedents of severe love-shyness in males. *Journal of Personality*, 55, 467–489.

Gobey, F. (1991) A practical approach through drama and workshops. In P. K. Smith and D. A. Thompson (eds), *Practical approaches to bullying.* London: David Fulton.

Gougeon, C. (1989) Guidelines for special issues training sessions in secondary schools peer counselling programs. *Canadian Journal of Counselling*, 23, 120–126.

Grunsell, R. (1980). *Absent from school: The story of a truancy centre.* London: Writers and Readers.

Guggenbhul, A. (1991) Tales and fiction. *School Psychology International*, 12, 7–16.

Hannan, G. (1992) *Inset notes: pro-active measures against bullying.* Shropshire: Simon and Schuster.

Hardy, B. (1977) Narrative as a primary act of mind. In M. Meek, G. Barton and A. Warlow (eds), *The cool web.* London: Bodley Head.

Hargie, O., Saunders, C. and Dickson, D. (1991) *Social skills in interpersonal communication.* London: Routledge.

Heathcote, D. (1980) *Drama in context.* Sheffield: National Association for Teaching English.

Heinemann, P.P. (1973) *Mobbning – gruppvåld blant barn och vuxna.* Stockholm: Natur och Kultur.

Henrikson, E.M. (1991) A peer helping program for the middle school. *Canadian Journal of Counselling*, 25, 12–18.

Herbert, G. (1989) A whole-curriculum approach to bullying. In D.P. Tattum and D.A. Lane (eds), *Bullying in schools.* Stoke-on-Trent: Trentham Books.

Herbert, M. (1987) *Conduct disorders of childhood and adolescence.* London: John Wiley and Sons.

Horton, A.M. (1991) The Heartstone Odyssey: exploring the heart of bullying. In P.K. Smith and D.Thompson (eds), *Practical approaches to bullying.* London: David Fulton.

Housden, C. (1991) The use of theatre workshop and role play in PSE in a secondary school. In P.K. Smith and D.A. Thompson (eds), *Practical approaches to bullying.* London: David Fulton.

Huey, W.C. and Rank, R.C. (1984) Effects of counselor and peer-led group assertiveness training on black adolescent aggression. *Journal of Counselling Psychology*, 31, 95–98.

Humphreys, A.D. and Smith, P.K. (1987) Rough-and-tumble, friendship and dominance in schoolchildren: Evidence for continuity and change with age. *Child Development*, 58, 201–212.

Imich, A. and Jefferies, K. (1989) Management of lunchtime behaviour. *Support for Learning*, 4, 46–52.

James, J., Charlton, T., Leo, E. and Indoe, D. (1991) A peer to listen. *Support for Learning*, 6, 165–169.

Jennings, S. (1986) *Creative drama in groupwork*. Bicester: Winslow Press.

Johnson, D.W. and Johnson, R.T. (1989) *Cooperation and competition*. Edina, MN: Interaction Book Company.

Johnson, D.W. and Johnson, R.T. (1991) *Teaching children to be peacemakers*. Edina, MN: Interaction Book Company.

Johnstone, M., Munn, P. and Edwards, L. (1991) *Action against bullying: A support pack for schools*. Edinburgh: SCRE.

Keise, C. (1992) *Sugar and spice? Bullying in single sex schools*. Stoke-on-Trent: Trentham Books.

Kelly, E. (1990) Use and abuse of racial language in secondary schools. In P.D. Pumphrey and G.K. Verma (eds), *Race relations and urban education*. Lewes: Falmer Press.

Kelly, E. and Cohn, T. (1988) *Racism in schools: New research evidence*. Stoke-on-Trent: Trentham Books.

Kidscape (1990) *Bully courts*. Kidscape, 152 Buckingham Palace Road, London SW1W 9TR.

Kidscape (1993) *Stop bullying*. Kidscape, 152 Buckingham Palace Road, London SW1W 9TR

Kingston Friends Workshop Group (1987) *Ways and means: An approach to problem solving*. Friends House, Euston Road, London NW1 2BJ.

Kirkland, K.D., Thelen, M.H. and Miller, D.J. (1982) Group assertion training with adolescents. *Child and Family Behaviour Therapy*, 4, 1–12.

Knox, J. (1992) Bullying in schools – communicating with the victim. *Support for Learning*, 7, 159–162.

Kreidler, W.J. (1984) *Creative conflict resolution*. Glenview, IL: Goodyear.

Kumar, A. (1985) *The Heartstone Odyssey*. Allied Mouse Ltd, Longden Court, Spring Gardens, Buxton SK17 6BZ.

La Fontaine, J. (1991) *Bullying: The child's view*. London: Calouste Gulbenkian Foundation.

Lagerspetz, K.M.J., Bjorkqvist, K., Berts, M. and King, E. (1982) Group aggression among school children in three schools. *Scandinavian Journal of Psychology*, 23, 45–52.

Lane, D. (1989) Violent histories: Bullying and criminality. In D.P. Tattum and D.A. Lane (eds), *Bullying in schools*. Stoke-on-Trent: Trentham Books.

Lange, A. and Jakubowski, P. (1976) *Responsible assertive behaviour*. Illinois: Research Press.

Laslett, R. (1980) Bullies: A children's court in a day school for maladjusted children. *Journal of Special Education*, 4, 391–397.

Laslett, R. (1982) A children's court for bullies. *Special Education*, 9, 9–11.

Latane, B. and Darley, J.M. (1970) *The unresponsive bystander: Why doesn't he help?* Englewood Cliffs, NJ: Prentice Hall.

Latane, B. and Nida, S. (1981) Ten years of research on group size and helping. *Psychological Bulletin*, 89, 308–324.

Ledford, G.E. Jr., Lawler, E.E. III and Mohrman, S.A. (1988) The quality circle and its variations. In J.P. Campbell and R.J. Campbell (eds), *Productivity in organisations*. San Francisco: Jossey–Bass.

Leimdorfer, T. (1992) *Once upon a conflict*. Education Advisory Committee, Friends House, Euston Road, London NW1 2BJ.

Light, P. (1980) *The development of social sensitivity*. Cambridge: Cambridge University Press.

Lowenstein, L.F. (1978a) Who is the bully? *Bulletin of the British Psychological Society*, 31, 147–149.

Lowenstein, L.F. (1978b) The bullied and non-bullied child. *Bulletin of the British Psychological Society*, 31, 316–318.

Lucas, P. (1993) A long-term follow-up study of the Pikas method of common concern. Unpublished BA dissertation, University of Sheffield.

Maines, B. and Robinson, G. (1991a) *Stamp out bullying*, video and book. Lame Duck Publishing, 10 South Terrace, Redlands, Bristol B56 6TG.

Maines, B. and Robinson, G. (1991b) Don't beat the bullies! *Educational Psychology in Practice*, 7, 168–172.

Maines, B. and Robinson, G. (1992) *Michael's story: The 'no-blame approach'*. Lame Duck Publishing, 10 South Terrace, Redlands, Bristol B56 6TG.

Mares, C. and Stephenson, R. (1988) *Inside outside*. Brighton: Keep Britain Tidy Group Schools Research Project.

Martlew, M. and Hodson, J. (1991) Children with mild learning difficulties in an integrated and in a special school: Comparisons of behaviour, teasing and teachers' attitudes. *British Journal of Educational Psychology*, 61, 355–372.

McCaffery, T. and Lyons, E. (1993) Teaching children to be good friends – developmental groupwork with vulnerable children. *Educational and Child Psychology*, 10, 3.

Meddis, W. (1992) The work and intentions of the Armadillo Theatre in Education Company. In H. Cowie (ed.), *Working directly with bullies and victims*. Conference Pack, Bretton Hall, W. Bretton, Wakefield, W. Yorks WF4 4LG.

Mellor, A. (1990) Bullying in Scottish secondary schools. *Spotlights* 23, Edinburgh: SCRE.

Mellor, A. (1991) Helping victims. In M. Elliott (ed.), *Bullying: A practical guide to coping for schools*. Harlow: Longman.

Mellor, A. (1993) *Bullying and how to fight it: A guide for families*. Edinburgh: SCRE.

Mellor Smith, H. (1992) The effect of quality circles on bullying behaviour in schools. Unpublished BA dissertation, University of Sheffield.

Mooney, A., Creeser, R. and Blatchford, P. (1991) Children's views on teasing and fighting in junior schools. *Educational Research*, 33, 103–112.

Moran, S., Smith, P.K., Thompson, D.A. and Whitney, I. (1993) Ethnic differences in experiences of bullying: Asian and White children. *British Journal of Educational Psychology*, 63, 431–440.

Moreno, J. L. (1964) *Psychodrama*. New York: Beacon House.

Mortimore, P. (1980) Misbehaviour in schools. In G. Upton and A. Gobell (eds),

Behavioural problems in the comprehensive school. Cardiff: University College.

Munn, P. (1993) *School action against bullying: Involving parents and non-teaching staff*. Edinburgh: SCRE.

Murphy, H.A., Hutchison, J.M. and Bailey, J.S. (1983) Behavioral school psychology goes outdoors: The effect of organized games on playground aggression. *Journal of Applied Behavioral Analysis*, 16, 29–35.

Musgrave, R. (1988) Groups for the sexually abused child. In W. Silveira, G. Trafford and R. Musgrave (eds), *Children need groups*. Aberdeen: Aberdeen University Press.

Nabuzoka, D. and Smith, P.K. (1993). Sociometric status and social behaviour of children with and without learning difficulties. *Journal of Child Psychology and Psychiatry*, 34, 1435–1448.

Nasby, W., Hayden, B. and de Paulo, B.M. (1979) Attributional bias among aggressive boys to interpret unambiguous social stimuli as displays of hostility. *Journal of Abnormal Psychology*, 89, 459–468.

National Curriculum Council (1993) Statutory Instrument 1993/2231 (Designation of Staff). London: HMSO.

Neti Neti (1990) *Only playing, Miss* (video and playscript). Neti Neti, 44 Gladmuir Road, London N19 3JU.

Newman, O. (1973) *Defensible space, people and design in the violent city*. London: Architectural Press.

Olweus, D. (1978) *Aggression in the schools: Bullies and whipping boys*. Washington, DC: Hemisphere.

Olweus, D. (1980) Familial and temperamental determinants of aggressive behavior in adolescent boys: A causal analysis. *Child Development*, 16, 644–660.

Olweus, D. (1987) Bully/victim problems among schoolchildren in Scandinavia. In J.P. Myklebust and R. Ommundsen (eds), *Psykologprofesjonen mot ar 2000*. Oslo: Universitetsforlaget.

Olweus, D. (1988) *Critical views on the Pikas method*. Unpublished paper.

Olweus, D. (1991) Bully/victim problems among schoolchildren: Basic facts and effects of a school-based intervention program. In D. Pepler and K. Rubin (eds), *The development and treatment of childhood aggression*. Hillsdale, NJ: Erlbaum.

Olweus, D. (1993a) Victimisation by peers: antecedents and long-term outcomes. In K.H. Rubin and J.B. Asendorf (eds), *Social withdrawal, inhibition, and shyness in childhood*. Hillsdale, NJ: Lawrence Erlbaum.

Olweus, D. (1993b) *Bullying in schools: What we know and what we can do*. Oxford: Blackwell.

Olweus, D. (1993c) Bullying among schoolchildren: intervention and prevention. In R. DeV. Peters, R.J. Mahon and V.L. Quinsey (eds), *Aggression and violence throughout the lifespan*. Newbury Park, CA: Sage.

O'Moore, A.M. and Hillery, B. (1989) Bullying in Dublin schools. *Irish Journal of Psychology*, 10, 426–441

O'Rourke, M. (1980) Patrol or participate in the playground? *Education*, 1, 29–30.

Patterson, G.R., DeBaryshe, B.D. and Ramsay, E. (1989) A developmental perspective on antisocial behavior. *American Psychologist*, 44, 329–355.

Pellegrini, A.D. (1987) Rough-and-tumble play: Developmental and educational significance. *Educational Psychologist*, 22, 23–43.

Pellegrini, A.D. (1989) What is a category? The case of rough-and-tumble play. *Ethology and Sociobiology*, 10, 331–341.

Pellegrini, A.D. and Davis, P.D. (1993) Relations between children's playground and classroom behaviour. *British Journal of Educational Psychology*, 63, 88–95.

Pentz, M.A. (1980) Assertion training and trainer effects on unassertive and aggressive adolescents. *Journal of Counselling Psychology*, 27, 76–83.

Pepler, D., Craig, W., Zeigler, S. and Charach, A. (1993) A school-based anti-bullying intervention: preliminary evaluation. In D. Tattum (ed.), *Understanding and managing bullying*. Oxford: Heinemann Educational.

Perry, D.G., Kusel, S.J. and Perry, L.C. (1988) Victims of peer aggression. *Developmental Psychology*, 24, 801–814.

Pikas, A. (1987) *Sa bekampar vi mobbning i skolan*. Uppsala: AMA Dataservice Forlag.

Pikas, A. (1989) A pure concept of mobbing gives the best results for treatment. *School Psychology International*, 10, 95–104. (A similar article appears in E. Roland and E. Munthe (eds), *Bullying: An international perspective*. London: David Fulton, 1989.)

Pitfield, M. A. (1992) An investigation into interest in, and effectiveness of bully courts. Unpublished BA dissertation, University of Sheffield.

Pitts, J. (1993) Developing school and community links to reduce bullying. In D. Tattum (ed.), *Understanding and managing bullying*. Oxford: Heinemann Educational.

Protherough, R. (1983) *Developing response to fiction*. Milton Keynes: Open University Press.

Rakos, R. (1991) *Assertive behaviour: Theory, research and training*. London: Routledge.

Rigby, K. and Slee, P.T. (1991) Bullying among Australian school children: Reported behaviour and attitudes towards victims. *Journal of Social Psychology*, 131, 615–627.

Rigby, K. and Slee, P.T. (1993) Children's attitudes towards victims. In D. Tattum (ed.), *Understanding and managing bullying*. Oxford: Heinemann Educational.

Robinson, S.E., Morrow, S., Kigin, T. and Lindeman, M. (1991) Peer counsellors in a high school setting: Evaluation and training impact on students. *School Counsellor*, 39, 35–40.

Roland, E. (1989) Bullying: The Scandinavian research tradition. In D.P. Tattum and D.A. Lane (eds), *Bullying in schools*. Stoke-on-Trent: Trentham Books.

Roland, E. (1993) Bullying: A developing tradition of research and management. In D. Tattum (ed.), *Understanding and managing bullying*. Oxford: Heinemann Educational.

Roland, E. and Munthe, E. (eds) (1989) *Bullying: An international perspective*. London: David Fulton.

Ross, C. and Ryan, A. (1990) *'Can I stay in today miss?' Improving the school playground*. Stoke-on-Trent: Trentham Books.

Salmon, P. (1992) The peer group. In J.C. Coleman (ed.), *The school years*. London: Routledge.

Salmon, P. and Claire, H. (1984) *Classroom collaboration*. London: Routledge and Kegan Paul.

Salter, A. (1949) *Conditioned reflex therapy*. New York: Capricorn Books.

Sarah, E., Scott, M. and Spender, D. (1980) The education of feminists: The case for single sex schools. In E. Sarah and D. Spender (eds), *Learning to lose*. London: Women's Press.

Schofield, R.G. (1986) Quality circles: Introducing change in educational systems. *Social Work in Education*.

Schostak, J. (1982) Black side of school. *Times Educational Supplement*, 25 June, 23.

Schwartz, D. (1993) Antecedents of aggression and peer victimisation: A prospective study. Paper presented at the Society for Research in Child Development conference, New Orleans, March 1993.

Shah, S. (1992) The effects of the Heartstone Odyssey story after its implementation in three primary schools, with particular regard to bullying incidents. Unpublished BA dissertation, University of Sheffield.

Sharp, S. (1994) Training schemes for lunchtime supervisors in the UK: An overview. In P. Blatchford and S. Sharp (eds), *Breaktime and the school: Understanding and changing playground behaviour*. London: Routledge.

Sharp, S., Cowie, H. and Smith, P.K. (1994). Responding to bullying behaviour. In S. Sharp and P.K. Smith (eds), *Tackling bullying in your school: A practical handbook for teachers*. London: Routledge.

Sharp, S., Sellars, A. and Cowie, H. (in press) Time to listen: Setting up a peer counselling service to help tackle the problem of bullying in schools. *Pastoral Care in Education*.

Sharp, S. and Thompson, D. (1992) Sources of stress: A contrast between pupil perspectives and pastoral teachers' perspectives. *School Psychology International*, 13, 229–242.

Sheat, L. (1991a) *How to improve our school grounds?* School Grounds Design Pack, Department of Landscape, Sheffield University.

Sheat, L. (1991b) *Why improve our school grounds?* School Grounds Design Pack, Department of Landscape, Sheffield University.

Simms, J. (1992) An examination of the effectiveness and success value of Anatol Pikas's working with bullies intervention strategy for combatting bullying situations in school. Unpublished BA dissertation, University of Sheffield.

Skinner, A. (1992) *Bullying: An annotated bibliography of literature and resources*. Youth Work Press, 17–23 Albion Street, Leicester LE1 6GD.

Sluckin, A.M. (1981) *Growing up in the playground: The social development of children*. London: Routledge and Kegan Paul.

Smith, G. (1991) *Safer schools – safer cities*. Unpublished report, Wolverhampton Education Department.

Smith, P.K. (1991) Hostile aggression as social skills deficit or evolutionary strategy? *Behavioral and Brain Sciences*, 14, 315–316.

Smith, P.K. and Boulton, M.J. (1990) Rough-and-tumble play, aggression and dominance: Perception and behavior in children's encounters. *Human Development*, 33, 271–282.

Smith, P.K. and Lewis, K. (1985) Rough-and-tumble play, fighting and chasing in nursery school children. *Ethology and Sociobiology*, 6, 175–181.

Smith, P.K. and Thompson, D.A. (eds) (1991a) *Practical approaches to bullying*. London: David Fulton.

Smith, P.K. and Thompson, D.A. (1991b) Dealing with bully/victim problems in the UK. In P.K. Smith and D.A. Thompson (eds), *Practical approaches to bullying*. London: David Fulton.

Smith, P.K., Bowers, L. and Binney, V. (1993) Perceived family relationships of bullies, victims, and bully/victims in middle childhood. In S. Duck (ed.), *Understanding relationship processes, Vol. 2: Learning about relationships*. Newbury Park: Sage.

Smith, P.K., Cowie, H. and Berdondini, L. (1994) Cooperation and bullying. In P. Kutnick and C. Rogers (eds), *Groups in schools*. London: Cassell.

Stephenson, P. and Smith, D. (1989) Bullying in the junior school. In D.P. Tattum and D.A. Lane (eds), *Bullying in schools*. Stoke-on-Trent: Trentham Books.

Tattum, D.P. (1982) *Disruptive pupils in schools and units*. Chichester: John Wiley.

Tattum, D.P. (ed.) (1993) *Understanding and managing bullying*. London: Heinemann.

Tattum, D.P. and Herbert, G. (1990) *Bullying – a positive response*. Faculty of Education, South Glamorgan Institute of Higher Education, Cyncoed Road, Cardiff CF2 6XD.

Tattum, D.P. and Herbert, G. (1993) *Countering bullying*. Stoke-on-Trent: Trentham Books.

Tattum, D.P. and Lane, D.A. (1989) *Bullying in schools*. Stoke-on-Trent: Trentham Books.

Tattum, D.P., Tattum, E. and Herbert, G. (1993) *Cycle of violence*. Cardiff: Drake Educational Associates.

Thompson, R.A. (1986) Developing a peer group facilitation program on the secondary school level: an investment with multiple returns. *Small Group Behaviour*, 17, 105–112.

Thompson, D.A. and Arora, T. (1991) Why do children bully? An evaluation of the long-term effectiveness of a whole-school policy to minimise bullying. *Pastoral Care in Education*, 9, 8–12.

Thompson, D.A. and Smith, P.K. (1991) Effective action against bullying – the key problems. In P.K. Smith and D.A. Thompson (eds), *Practical approaches to bullying*. London: David Fulton.

Thornton, M. (1993) *An evaluation of a peer counselling service*. Unpublished report, University of Sheffield.

Titman, W. (1989) Adult responses to children's fears. In D.P. Tattum and D.A. Lane (eds), *Bullying in schools*. Stoke-on-Trent: Trentham Books.

Tonge, D. (1992) Assessing the effects of assertiveness training on victims of bullying in three Sheffield schools. Unpublished BA dissertation, University of Sheffield.

Troyna, B. and Hatcher, R. (1992) *Racism in children's lives: A study of mainly white primary schools*. London: Routledge.

Tucker, N. (1982) *The child and the book*. Cambridge: Cambridge University Press.

Turkel, S.B. and Eth, S. (1990) Psychopathological response to stress: Adjustment disorder and post-traumatic stress disorder in children and adolescents. In L. Eugene Arnold (ed.), *Childhood stress*. New York: John Wiley.

Vygotsky, L.S. (1978) *Mind in society*. Boston: Harvard University Press.

Wade, B. and Moore, M. (1993) *Experiencing special education*. Buckingham: Open University Press.

Wagner, B. (1979) *Dorothy Heathcote, drama as a learning medium*. London: Hutchinson.

Walker, J. (1989) *Violence and conflict resolution in schools*. Quaker Council for European Affairs, 50 Square Ambiorix, 1040 Brussels, Belgium.

Whitney, I. and Smith, P.K. (1993) A survey of the nature and extent of bully/victim problems in junior/middle and secondary schools. *Educational Research*, 35, 3–25.

Wills, W.D. (1945) *The Barns experiment*. London: Allen and Unwin.

Wolpe, A.M. (1988) *Within school walls: The role of discipline, sexuality and the curriculum*. London: Routledge.

Yates, C. and Smith, P.K. (1989) Bullying in two English comprehensive schools. In E. Roland and E. Munthe (eds), *Bullying: An international perspective*. London: David Fulton.

Zeisel, J. (1984) *Inquiry by design, tools for environment behaviour research*. Cambridge: Cambridge University Press

Zuker. E. (1983) *Mastering assertiveness skills*. New York: AMACOM.

name index

Carty, L. 115
Casdagli, P. 97, 98
Cawley, G. 112
Charach, A. 55, 61, 64
Charlton, T. 115
Childs, K. xii, 123, 126, 127
Claire, H. 87
Clemmer, J. 74
Cohn, T. 6, 104
Conger, A. J. 137
Connor, K. 140
Cooper-Marcus, C. 163
Costabile, A. 139, 143
Cowie, H. 18, 25, 26, 27, 84, 87, 90, 91, 108, 116, 119, 125, 193, 196
Craig, W. 55, 61, 64
Creeser, R. 133, 134, 145

Darley, J. M. 88
Davis, D. P. 146
DeBaryshe, B. D. 8
De Cecco, J. 113
Denzin, N. K. 137
Department for Education xi, 2, 3, 19, 21, 31, 72, 116, 216, 218, 239
De Paulo, B. M. 143
De Rosenroll, D. A. 115, 116
Dickson, A. 125
Dickson, D. 123
Dodge, K. A. 143, 144
Donaldson, M. 87
Dunne, E. 87
Dygdon, J. A. 137

Economic and Social Research Council xi, 2, 15, 19, 216
Education Acts (1988), (1992) 64, 109, 239
Edwards, L. 4, 21, 57
Egan, K. 99
Elliott, M. 4, 5, 6, 7, 26, 207, 208
Elton Report (1989) 3, 58, 193
Emmens, M. 122
Eth, S. 7
Evans, J. 146

Farrington, D. P. 4, 8, 202
Fell, G. 28

Fisher, R. 111
Foster, P. 21, 60, 82, 146, 147
Francis, C. 163
Fry, D. P. 139, 141

Galloway, D. 58
Gazzard, M. xii, 18
Gilham, B. 58
Gillborn, D. 104
Gilmartin, M. J. 7
Gobey, F. 24, 97, 98, 99
Gougeon, C. 117
Greenwood, C. R. 115
Grunsell, R. 58
Guardian, The 206, 207
Guggenbhul, A. 103

Hannan, G. 129
Hardy, B. 103
Hargie, O. 123
Hatcher, R. 68, 104
Hayden, B. 143
Heartstone Foundation 25, 106
Heathcote, D. 97
Heinemann, P. P. 3
Henriksen, E. M. 115
Herbert, G. 3, 4, 18, 23, 145
Herbert, M. 193
Higgins, C. 19, 160
Hillery, B. 215
Hinton, S. 135, 136
Hodson, J. 215
Home Office 60
Hops, I. T. 115
Horton, A. M. 25, 105
Housden, C. 98
Huey, W. C. 130
Humphreys, A. D. 139
Hunter, T. 139
Hutchinson, J. M. 138

Imich, A. 134, 135, 147, 154
Independent, The 207
Indoe, D. 115

Jakuboski, P. 122
James, J. 115
Jefferies, K. 134, 135, 147, 154

subject index

absenteeism 7, 58, 64
adolescents 115
age 15, 43, 55; equivalent comparisons 10
aggression 5, 8, 28, 57, 89, 111
anti-bullying networks 23; climate 89
assertiveness skills 8, 26, 66, 229; evaluation of training 125–8, 229; in girls 123; training 26, 29, 108, 121–30, 218, 229, 231–2, 238
authority 142

behavioural difficulties 213; *see also* children with special needs
boredom 161
breaktime 43, 47; *see also* playgrounds
bully courts 26–8, 194, 205–11; attitudes towards 209–10; effectiveness of 207–11
bullying in schools, 1–2; Asians as victims of 6, 104; assessment of 11–14, 201; attitudes towards 17, 43, 59, 63, 69, 74, 76, 101, 144–5; in the classroom 88–9; consequences of 3, 7–9; definition of 2, 12–13, 61, 66, 97; dis-

tinction between aggressive behaviour and 28, 133; effects of 63–4; frequency of 14–15, 33, 43, 47, 49, 51, 61, 63–4, 76; gangs and 88, 195; generational links within 8; incidence of 6, 9–10, 15, 17; long-term effects of 7–8; monitoring trends in 32–7, 70; nature of 6–7, 9, 11–14, 58–9, 69; origins of 8–9; persistent 36; previous research 1–11, 57, 61; racist forms of 6, 16, 104; raising awareness about 62, 101; reporting 5, 16, 44, 49, 51, 63, 69, 144, 228; responses to 121, 146–8, 154; role of adults in 44, 47; school grounds and 160–2; studies of 2–4; surveys on 10, 14–18, 88; types of 6, 13, 16–17; what we know about 4–6
bully line (case study) 118–20
bystander behaviour 43, 47, 88, 144–5

Childline 3
children's experiences with bullying 1, 58, 68; interviews with 11, 19; literature 25; perceptions of their families 9; relationships with staff 57; reports of